# THE SERMON

## ITS HOMILETICAL
## CONSTRUCTION

BY

**R. C. H. LENSKI**

1368

Introduction by

Ralph G. Turnbull

BAKER BOOK HOUSE
Grand Rapids, Michigan

Reprinted 1968 by
Baker Book House Company
from the original printing
made in 1927 by
The Lutheran Book Concern

PHOTOLITHOPRINTED BY CUSHING - MALLOY, INC.
ANN ARBOR, MICHIGAN, UNITED STATES OF AMERICA
1968

# Notable Books on Preaching

Among the helps for the minister and the theological student are the many volumes on preaching and homiletics. On our shelves are the single volumes written by individual men. There are well known series of lectures, such as the Yale or Lyman Beecher given at Yale Divinity School, New Haven, and the Warrack given to the four University Theological colleges in Scotland. Not many today possess full sets of these famous lectures. Earlier works are unobtainable as they are out of print and some cease to appeal. Nevertheless, the preacher who has access to this thesaurus of preaching and homiletics finds much to suggest and stimulate. Because of this, the time is opportune to select and reissue some of the books which have stood the test of time and have proved of abiding value.

It is proposed to issue a selection over the next few years. Not all will be alike. The homiletical techniques will be observed in them, but the emphases will vary. The wisdom and experience of those who have labored in other days may prove of lasting value in many a difficult hour. The particular books have been chosen in the belief that each will minister to the preacher in different moods of the soul. Representative of those which will be selected are:

*The Public Worship of God*, by J. R. P. Sclater
                                        (Worship)

*In Christ's Stead*, by A. J. Gossip

                                        (Ambassador)

*The Building of the Church*, by C. E. Jefferson
                              (Church)
*The Preacher and his Models*, by J. Stalker
                              (Isa. & Paul)
*Puritan Preaching in England*, by J. Brown
                              (Puritan)
*God's Word through Preaching*, by J. Hall
                              (Bible)
*The Romance of Preaching*, by C. S. Horne
                              (History)
*The Cure of Souls*, by J. Watson
                              (Pastoral)
*The Glory of the Ministry*, by A. T. Robertson
                              (Exegetical)
*Good Ministers of Jesus Christ*, by W. F. McDowell
                              (Devotional)

"Preaching can never lose its place so long as the mystery and wonder of the human spirit remain" is the judgment of Charles Sylvester Horne, *The Romance of Preaching*. Believing in the supremacy of preaching as God-appointed for the Church, the minister must equip himself for an incredible task of service. One of the causes of failure in the ministry lies in the lack of definite reading and study. These books will serve to spur on the preacher to greater deeds. We need not copy any man, but we can learn from all who have blazed the trail before us. "Who keeps one end in view, Makes all things serve" (R. Browning).

In issuing these volumes it is our hope and prayer that they will help to keep the ideals fresh and the standards from sagging while the vision remains clear. We must "plod on and keep the passion fresh."

RALPH G. TURNBULL

The First Presbyterian Church
of Seattle, Washington

# Introduction

Richard C. H. Lenski (1864-1936)
*The Sermon: Its Homiletical Construction*

Lenski is known for his ability as a teacher. Born in Germany, he studied and served pastorates in the American Lutheran Church in Maryland and in Ohio. He became Professor of Languages and Theology at Capital University, Columbus, Ohio (1911-1920); Professor of Dogmatic and New Testament Exegesis in the Seminary (1921-1928); and Dean of the Seminary (1919-1935).

After teaching hours he filled his days with study and writing in his library. He was Editor of *Lutherische Kirchenzeitung* and the author of a complete *Commentary of the New Testament* and of much other exegetical and homiletical material. His books reveal an acute mind and a skill in exegesis which was his special contribution to Biblical knowledge.

This volume on *The Sermon* came out of sixteen years of teaching Homiletics. The scientific principles are discussed in a popular way. The illustrations are Biblical and serve as exercises in the art of sermon preparation. Pitfalls are pointed out and the ideals are stressed for the pastor. Sermon construction is taught in the light of the then psychological norms that made preaching effective.

Here is a useful tool for the student and the preacher. The beginner will find it most serviceable and almost a "do it yourself" book. The pastor will find it a stimulating refresher course. Everything of Lenski is based upon Biblical exegesis and his insights and interpretations are shared on every page. From text to theme, by analysis and synthesis, the sermon is produced and exposition is developed. The professor's enthusiasm for his subject points the way in spirit and method to Biblical preaching.

RALPH G. TURNBULL

# CONTENTS

# PART ONE

# THE TEXT

## FIRST CHAPTER

## THE TEXT

Christian preachers, the world over, place a portion of Scripture at the head of the sermon, and call this "the text." The custom dates back to Origen, who was the first to base a formal and orderly address on some longer or shorter portion selected from the Scriptures. The advantage of preaching in this fashion has been universally recognized, with the result that at present only a few men with odd minds venture to preach even as much as a single sermon without employing a text.

### *What is a Text?*

The answer to this question depends on what the preacher expects of his text.

If he expects the text to furnish him only *a subject* for his sermon, he will, of course, define the text accordingly. It will then be the Biblical nail from which he suspends the string of his sermon thoughts. Expecting so little from the text, he will get little more out of it.

Some preachers are after a text that furnishes *a key thought,* and not merely a subject, for their sermon. They are especially pleased to find a text in which this key thought is expressed in *a striking phrase or sentence,* around which they can group their reflections. So they ring the changes on that phrase or sentence, repeating it again and again as the sermon proceeds. These, too, expect too little of a text.

We may arrive at what a text really is, and should be, by studying the etymology of the word. "Text" is derived from *textus*, genitive *textūs*, a web. The verb is *texo, texui, texere*, to weave. Etymologically a text is that section of Scripture which is woven into the sermon. Dropping the figure, a text is that section of Scripture upon which the sermon is built.

There is a connotation in this idea of a text. The portion of Scripture that is fit to be used as a text must be one that forms *a unit* in itself. It may be a single verse or a sentence. Generally it will be a paragraph, or the main portion of a paragraph. Again it may comprise more than a paragraph. Always, however, it must be a unit in thought and a unit rich and weighty enough for the purpose of a sermon.

With this conception of a text, we have little difficulty in answering the question,

## Should there be a Text?

The sermon which rightly uses a text is always superior to the sermon which uses no text.

Of course, there is no divine commandment for using texts. Abstractly speaking, the Gospel can be preached with or without a sermon text.

When Jesus preached at Nazareth, Luke 4, 16 etc., He used a text. Peter's sermon on the day of Pentecost was based on a text from Joel. These are good precedents for using texts.

At Athens, and at Antioch in Pisidia, Paul had no text. Jesus had none for the Sermon on the Mount. One might say, these are equally good precedents for dispensing with texts. In the early Church, too, no texts were used.

However, Justin Martyr's account of the services in the early Church states that when the writings of the apostles had been read by the lector, the address that followed instructed and admonished the people to take to heart what they had heard read. Thus a text was virtually used.

As far as the preaching of Jesus to the multitudes is concerned, and the two addresses of Paul at Athens and at Antioch, these were of a general missionary character, apart from a set service, and thus in their very nature different from our regular Sunday sermons in established forms of Christian worship.

Our question is fully answered when we consider

### The Reasons for Preaching on Texts.

1. The preacher is to preach the Word of God, that is, something definite out of the Word of God. It is obvious at once that the simplest and most direct way to meet this requirement is to take a text, a portion of the Word of God, and expound that.

It is true, the mere employment of a text does not guarantee that the sermon will be Biblical. Very unbiblical sermons are preached this very day from the choicest Scripture texts. In the heyday of Rationalism a preacher once preached a Christmas sermon on Luke 2, 1-14 and used the theme, "The Advantage of Stall-Feeding Cattle."

When the preacher thus abuses his text, or turns his back upon it, the text itself already judges the preacher and his sermon. And there are always some hearers who are aware of that judgment. Often enough their verdict is, "The preacher had a good text, but he did not preach on it!" If he abuses his text, the hearers will likely raise the question, whether the preacher really said what the text means.

2. The preacher is to preach on some Biblical theme. Every proper text offers one or more good themes. There is no better way to arrive at such a theme than to draw it from a definite text. A simple way is to summarize what the text says. Another way is to present a central thought of the text, in a formulation which opens up the entire text.

But let us suppose I have a theme for which I cannot find a suitable text. Either there is no text for my theme — then I ought to drop it entirely as really not proper for the pulpit, — or I do not know my Bible sufficiently to find the proper text readily. I have been too indolent in thorough Bible study.

It is an excellent homiletical rule, always to begin with the text, not with thoughts evolved by myself or picked up at random. If, however, some theme suggests itself for which a really fitting text cannot be found, drop the theme entirely — nothing of special value will be lost thereby. Learn to attach more value to intensive text study and its results in Biblical themes than to your own or other men's ideas.

3. The text is to be the real source from which the substance of the sermon is drawn. Once this is fully settled, there will be no question about employing a text and using it in the right way after it is selected.

Whatever else we may use in the sermon, other passages of Scripture, elucidating thoughts, illustrations, applicatory ideas pertinent to our circumstances and times, everything must be amalgamated with the central contents of the text. The thoughts furnished by the text are always chief and supreme. Whatever leads away from these thoughts is unsuitable material.

4. The text limits the sermon. It gives the sermon point. The preacher is kept in line, he cannot deviate from the true course. The text before him is his monitor.

A well chosen text presents one grand Biblical idea, the textual elaboration of which constitutes the sermon. That is why we have texts.

5. A real text prevents the sermon from degenerating into a lecture. There is a place for lectures, namely the platform; sermons alone belong in the pulpit. Church members rightly decline to hear one or two lectures a week by the same man, yet they flock to hear a continuous line of sermons by him.

A sermon unfolds the heart of a text. A lecture unfolds a man's own thoughts and conclusions. The number of good lectures any one man is able to produce, even on Biblical subjects, is limited. Many preachers have produced good sermons for half a century. They were able to do so because they preached on texts.

The freedom of thought and of form offered by the lecture is delusive. It is freedom indeed, of a kind that uses up a man's resources so fast that he never can replenish his fund rapidly enough to keep on indefinitely. A man with all outdoors before him may indeed run freely in all directions, but he will soon run out of wind.

Texts confine a man to definite limits. But that is really a blessing, although it may be a blessing in disguise to some. The text marks out a limited course for the man to run, and puts a goal at the end of that course. Every text has a new course and a new goal. The preacher never becomes exhausted.

Perhaps you have heard of the young preacher who ruefully came to the conclusion that he must give up preaching. He had used about all the subjects he could handle and did not care to repeat himself endlessly. An older man advised him to preach on texts, and to cease delivering half-hour lectures on subjects.

6. Thus texts open up an inexhaustible fountain for sermons. They prevent a man from "preaching himself out."

No man can possibly preach on all the texts in the Bible, though he took a new text every time he preached. You cannot pick all the flowers that grow.

Most texts can be preached on repeatedly with great profit. They are so full of life and power that one effort always leaves a great abundance of material for future use. This is due to the fact that the Scriptures are divine. No human book is like them. The last commentaries have not yet been written on even the smaller books of the Bible.

### Only Real Texts Satisfy.

1. If one or two sentences are plucked from the Bible and made to adorn a religious address, we have a mere motto, not a text at all. To use mottoes of this kind means not only to lose the advantages of a text, it means something worse. It amounts to a degradation of the Word of God. That Word in all, even its minutest parts, is not intended for ornament, but as food for the soul.

A discourse, for which at best only a motto can be found in Scripture, by that very fact proves its own unfitness for the pulpit.

2. Scrap texts are sham texts, not real texts at all.

When Abraham Lincoln was assassinated, some preacher perpetrated what he thought was a sermon on the words in John 8, 52, "Abraham is dead." The thing was not even catchy.

3. Allegorizing turns a text into a sham. It passes by the real meaning of the text, and imposes on the sacred words some fancy of the preacher.

Sometimes this thing becomes ludicrous. At a high school commencement a preacher of national prominence used as his text the words in John 11, 44, "Loose him, and let him go." Jesus ordered the men to remove the linen wrappings from Lazarus who had been brought to life after being dead four days. This preacher used the sacred words allegorically for his own cheap idea, that when our young people reach a certain age their parents must give up their parental control and allow them to shape their own lives.

It is always out of place to allegorize a text. A preacher once chose Ex. 17, 8-12 as a text on missions. Joshua smote the Amalekites while Moses held up his hands. When Moses grew tired, Aaron and Hur supported his arms, until the victory was complete. The preacher imposed on this holding up of the arms of Moses his own cheap fancy that thus we ought to hold up the hands of our missionaries by our prayers, interest, and contributions. But killing off the Amalekites is by no means like rescuing men from heathen darkness.

Christ's miracles are often allegorized. He heals a leper with a word or touch. Now Christ heals no lepers to-day in such a way. So we are treated to a sermon on the leprosy of sin. Christ heals a blind man with a word. He does nothing like that to-day. So we hear a sermon on the cure of spiritual blindness. The true sense of the texts is ignored, and instead we get something not in the text at all. In preaching on a miracle the preacher ought to focus our attention on Christ and how in that miracle He attests His divinity, shows His omnipotence, offers His love and help, etc.

Martha and Mary at Bethany have been allegorized. Martha is forced to represent the Catholic Church, busy with works; Mary, the Protestant Church, contemplating His Word. Here the allegory itself is false. When the supper was made for Jesus in Bethany Mary not only served beside Martha and the other women, but rendered to the Master a service so high that Jesus said, wherever the Gospel would be preached her deed would be remembered. When Martha was cumbered with much serving she was making a mistake. For when Jesus speaks women should not rattle dishes but should sit with Mary and let Jesus serve them with heavenly food.

Jesus stilling the tempest is often allegorized. The tossing sea is the hostile world, the boat with Jesus and the Twelve is the Church, etc. But the allegory is fancy, not fact. Jesus is master over all the forces of nature — that is the burden of the text.

The effect of allegorizing is always bad. It leaves the impression that the preacher is able to preach almost anything on any text. People lose their appreciation of the native sense of the Word, and get to wondering what fancy can be inserted into this and that passage of Scripture. Scoffers are quick to fall upon this weakness of preachers, and use it for under-mining the sense of Scripture generally.

If I need a mission text, I have scores of them in the Bible, all treating the subject literally. If I need a text for young graduates, the Bible has an abundance of such texts. This is true of every legitimate need of the preacher. Allegories are superfluities of naughti-ness, turning the impregnable rocks and cliffs of divine truth into mere wreaths and flowers of human fancy.

### Use Only One Text.

A text constitutes a unit, one full and rich enough in itself to serve as the basis of a sermon. Naturally we need no second and no third text to combine with the first.

We are free to use in the sermon, for the full elucidation of the text, any other Scripture passages we may require. Sometimes a text presents only one side of the truth, let us say the positive side, or perhaps only the negative side. The side not specifically pre-sented in the text itself must be set forth in the sermon. But this does not compel us to add a second text. The sermon freely adds the side that is needed and intro-duces the necessary Scripture passages.

If my text speaks of faith, I am free to contrast faith with unbelief in the sermon. Likewise, if my text speaks of salvation, life, light, pardon, peace, etc., I need not hunt for additional texts, but may freely contrast these positive truths with the corresponding negatives. Negatives are in no way different. Yet negative texts seem to cause preachers uneasiness. Some of them even preach sermons that are entirely negative, under the mistaken idea that this is "sticking to the text." I stick to my text when I fully elucidate it, and that means, when I illumine it with all the Scripture I need for the purpose.

The trouble, however, is that at times a preacher chooses an inadequate text for his purpose. Then he sees no way out except by adding a second and perhaps even a third text. He probably will base the first part of his sermon on the first text, and the other part or parts on the added texts. Such a procedure is a sign of helplessness. He does not know his Bible sufficiently, or he could readily find a text that covers all the ground he intends to cover in the sermon.

On rare exceptions the use of more than one text may be justified. The author once preached a series of sermons on certain evils that were rife in the community and were invading his congregation. One of these was drunkenness. For that sermon he used as his text about a dozen of the strongest passages treating of this sin, and after he had read them he concluded by saying, he would stop with these, since he lacked time to read all the many passages which condemned this sin. The purpose of this proceeding was not to supply by means of additional texts any lack in the first one, but to impress the congregation from the start with the overwhelming testimony of Scripture against this great sin. Of course, he might also have heaped up these testimonies in the sermon itself. It was more a question of personal preference than anything else.

When I employ an Old Testament text I need not read a corresponding text from the New Testament.

When I use a gospel text, I need not supply a corresponding epistle text and vice versa. The sermon offers all the room necessary for bringing in, not merely one, but as many passages as are needed, from other grand sections of the Bible.

## SECOND CHAPTER

# CHOOSING THE TEXT.

## I. Free Texts for Sunday Sermons.

Where the ancient and the modern Pericope Systems are not known or used, the preacher of necessity must choose all his texts himself. Texts so chosen are often called "free texts." The word "free" implies that the texts are not prescribed by church authorities or by a fixed ecclesiastical custom.

The necessity of choosing a free text for every sermon imposes no small burden. To be faced week in week out with the question, What shall I preach on next Sunday morning, and again next Sunday evening? wastes much energy of the mind which might be put to better use. Young preachers, with no comprehensive knowledge of the Bible and the Christian life, are not competent to make a wise choice for the many sermons required. Choosing texts in this way is not a desirable task for any one.

Perhaps the worst feature attending the constant selection of free texts is the subjective element that necessarily enters into such a choice. The preacher will be inclined to select only such texts as he personally prefers. For one thing, he will likely take texts that seem easy to preach on, and texts that seem difficult will be discarded. He will choose along the lines of his own personal thinking, and will reject what lies beyond that range. Most men are not broad enough for this task. The congregations they serve must suffer in consequence.

Hence a number of homiletical works present chapters on choosing texts. They warn the preacher against making his Bible a woodpile of texts, to which he may go again and again just to pick out a chunk that has not too many knots in it. There is good reason for the warning. Fears may also be entertained that it will not be sufficiently heeded. Helpful suggestions are offered to the preacher for selecting texts. His own devotional reading; hearing what other men preach on, or reading their sermons; providential happenings, may lead him to a text. At best these suggestions are weak. A wise choice and a prompt choice can often not be made, however one may try to profit by the suggestions. Often, in the press of work and in the mental distraction incident to a minister's life, the time is consumed and no text definitely selected. The preacher finally chooses what he happens on, and the sermon suffers. The very feeling that he has not chosen well dampens his enthusiasm as he starts to work on his sermon. What a blessing it would be if he could be freed, at least from the greater part of this chasing after free texts!

The system of leaving to the preacher the choice of text for every sermon has brought about the selection of very short texts, very often the choice of a single verse only. Thus scraps of Scripture are preached on, tiny bits here and there are treated, while a more extensive study of the contents of the Bible is neglected. The use of short texts becomes a habit, a kind of homiletical tradition. There is grave danger that the preacher will curtail his study of the Word by making the Bible merely a storeroom of disjointed texts for sermonizing. He is hunting some verse as a text; a paragraph, or a combination of paragraphs no longer appeal to him. If such a rich portion were prescribed as a text for him, he would not know how to handle the wealth. The man who thinks only in sermon dimes would be upset if suddenly he had to think in sermon thousands.

The man who depends on free texts for his sermons is tempted only too often to choose his text, not from the great spiritual wealth of the Bible, bringing forth treasures old and new, but from the transient happenings of the day. Some political, economical, social, criminal, or other occurrence will furnish some topic for his Sunday address, and he will hunt around for a catchy word of Scripture to which he may attach his "sermon." Preaching of this type, drawn from the pages of the daily press, tends to become sensational enough to be quoted again in the press. Thus the great Biblical themes are crowded out by great and small secular themes. A mere veneer of religious sentiment is added to some kind of scrap text. Personal ambition for prominence does the rest.

There is a legitimate field for free texts, but only men of exceptional Biblical knowledge and of the soundest spirituality can use them year in year out and keep their preaching on the spiritual plane their holy calling demands. The great majority of preachers, as well as their congregations, would be greatly benefited by the use of pericope systems in the place of free texts for the main service.

## II. Free Texts for Special Occasions.

The real field for free texts is that of special occasions. There will always be many of these, funerals in particular, and festive celebrations, such as dedications, jubilees, etc. The old name for this entire group is "Casual Sermons." They occur only now and then, and each presents a particular and individual so-called case.

It is the case that determines the choice of the text. The better the text fits the case, the better the choice of text. And almost invariably, the better also will be the sermon. The reverse is also true. If a text is found that fits the case exactly the sermon is three-fourths completed. A faulty casual text usually makes the sermon a labored effort.

There are three general ways in which a text may fit the case.

1. Similarity between the text and the case.
2. Text and case may be like the species and an individual in that species.
3. Historical difference, with inward agreement.

For the first type of fitness the following may serve as an example. An old godly church member is to be buried at Christmas time. A good text would be Luke 2, 29-32. As Simeon was ready to depart in peace, so this our aged brother has departed, blessed as was Simeon with a vision of the Christchild.

For an example of the second kind of fitness take the death of a little child, and the text Is. 40, 11. The theme may be, Your Little Lamb in Jesus' Arm and Bosom. What the text says of the lambs in general is applied to the dead child individually.

For the third kind of fitness this may serve as
an example. A congregation celebrates the anniversary of its church dedication. The text is Acts 20, 32,
spoken by St. Paul in saying farewell to the elders
of Ephesus. Historically there is complete dissimi-
larity, but the words of the apostle express exactly
what the preacher desires to lay upon the hearts of
the congregation in their anniversary service. He
would commend them to the Word of God's grace
which hitherto they have heard preached in their
church; he would see them built up spiritually by the
power of this Word; and he points them to the inheritance promised by that Word.

Ill chosen texts are the bane of casual sermons.
We here indicate some of the faults that are to be
avoided.

1. The text may be *too general and broad,* so
that hundreds of cases could be ranged under it.

A faithful old member, who had been the leader
of the church for years, and had held the office of
treasurer for half a century, finally passed to his
reward. The preacher used John 3, 16, and never
touched upon one of the outstanding features of this
attractive case. John 3, 16 is broad enough for ten
thousand cases.

Yet a broad text may be in place, even John 3, 16.
This text summarizes the way of salvation as being
by faith alone. A young woman turned on her death-
bed from Romanism to the true Gospel faith. John
3, 16 made a fine text for her funeral, bringing out
the faith in which she died. Broad texts are in place
when there is specific reason for them.

2. The text may *fail to hit* the case.

A hotel man in a certain village committed suicide, and a preacher from the county seat buried him. His text was the first half of Luke 12, 37. What connection the case and the text could possibly have, who will tell? A text that is beside the mark is always a homiletical misfortune, and may be a homiletical tragedy.

3. A text is sometimes chosen because of an *attractive expression* in its wording, without due reference to the real meaning of the text as such. This at best produces a lean sermon.

In the Easter text, Mark 16, 1-8, the rock that was rolled away from the sepulcher took the preacher's fancy. Forthwith he allegorized that rock and also multiplied it: He preached on "Resurrection Rocks," and became almost comical when he made the first rock that ought to be rolled away the sin of rising late on Sunday morning — for Jesus rose "early" on Easter Sunday morning! This is what happens when men look for catchy expressions in texts. The audience is given funny little pebbles instead of the costly diamonds and rubies of saving truth.

4. The list of *far-fetched* texts which preachers have used is a long one. The invariable effect is a labored sermon. The preacher tries so hard to pull his text into line with the case or occasion, and he succeeds but half.

Holding up the arms of Moses while Joshua smote the Amalekites, Ex. 17, 8-12, is a far-fetched text for a mission sermon, to say nothing about the faulty allegory. — 1 Tim. 4, 16 is far-fetched as a text for a brotherhood meeting. It is addressed to Timothy as a pastor, not to the men as members of the Church. — 1 Cor. 3, 9a is far-fetched when a Christian congregation is addressed as "laborers together with God." These laborers in St. Paul's word are the apostles and pastors. The congregation is "God's husbandry and God's building," as the second half of the verse shows. Many more flagrant cases might be catalogued.

5. Texts that are *opposites* to the case or occasion always tend to jar the feelings of the hearers and to produce a decidedly unpleasant effect.

When a man who never went to church was buried the preacher chose as his text Ps. 122, 1, "I was glad when they said unto me, Let us go into the house of the Lord."

6. Only men with trivial minds will take a *trivial* text. Acts 9, 37, "She was sick, and died," is no text for a woman's funeral.

In choosing texts for casual sermons the following hints may prove helpful:

1. Give preference to texts that are *rich in doctrinal and ethical contents,* or that afford full opportunity for presenting the essentials of salvation and of Christian life. With the Bible full of the choicest kind of texts of this type, one wonders why so often they are passed by while some meager word of Scripture is chosen.

2. The text should be *not too short*, and, of course, also *not too long*. It should be a rounded whole. Its central thought may suffice for the sermon, but one may add in the text the immediate setting for

any words that state the central thought, even if the complete setting is not worked into body of the sermon.

3.   For any casual case, say a funeral, a dedication, a jubilee, etc., first study the case carefully and determine *the evangelical features* which it presents.   Take the outstanding ones only.   There may be only one that dominates; there may be two or three that go together.   Let these features impress the mind fully, and then select a text that matches.

A faithful pastor died after ten years of the most patient suffering.   Neither the text nor the sermon at the funeral touched upon this outstanding feature. — We have already mentioned the faithful Christian who served his congregation as its treasurer for half a century, yet neither text nor sermon hinted at this feature.

A faithful pastor who had lived and died as a confessor of his Lord, and in whose life up to the last there were several well known evidences of his confessional loyalty, received Matth. 10, 32-33 as a funeral text, with the theme, "Confess the Lord, Your Savior, Before Men."   Take the burden of that confession upon you; let the glory of that confession cheer you; and at last receive the reward of that confession from the lips of the Lord Himself.   That text and that sermon fit the case.

Sometimes the determining features are not in the person directly concerned, but in the relatives, or in the congregation, or in the community.   When a child is buried, there may be nothing specific for the sermon in regard to the child, but very much that applies to the parents, in the way they take the death, and in what their souls may need at that time.

4. The text should be selected with a view to *the spiritual capacity of the audience*. Do not serve strong meat where the milk of the Word is in place. Shoot too high, and though you shoot ever so well, not a heart may be touched.

The preacher who is well versed in his Bible and has studied deeply in theology must always bear in mind that many things quite commonplace to his mind are probably quite beyond the minds of those that face him from the pews. Choose the text from the pew side, not from the library and study side. This applies especially at funerals where people appear who do not even read their Bibles and who may not even know the way of salvation.

For a case of this kind Acts 4, 12 was chosen, "Salvation in Christ Jesus." The sermon had these thoughts: 1) Jesus Christ bought it for us; 2) He offers it to us; 3) He uses the preaching of the Gospel to make it ours; 4) He gives us ample time to accept it; 5) He comes at times and urges us in the most touching and effective way; 6) He lets us reject it if we will; 7) He will demand an account of us in the end; 8) Blessed are we if we accept it now, rejoice in it during life, die in it at last. The day after the funeral the husband of the deceased arranged with the pastor to join the church. The simple text and sermon had proved effective.

5. Always prefer *lucid* texts for casual sermons, especially for mixed audiences. Discard dark and difficult texts. This applies also to the materials used in the sermon. Many historical incidents of the Old Testament are wholly unknown to the bulk of our audiences. To use them then is useless. At times

we must not even take for granted that all our hearers know who St. Luke is or St. Paul. Words like "justify" and "sanctify" must be fully elucidated in the simplest manner. "Grace" may be a novelty to those who know only about "being good," and "faith" may leave no clear impression unless explained.

It is the missionary interest that thus calls for simplicity and lucidity in texts and in sermons. A preacher of national fame discoursed at length on protoplasm before a large gathering. What could the soul of a simple washer-woman get out of that?

6. Be sure you have *God's words,* and not the devil's or some godless man's utterance! Acts 5, 38b-39 is only Gamaliel's counsel of indecision, never a word of God Himself. Job is a hard book from which to cull texts, for the body of the book contains the words of Job and his miserable comforters. Even Job 19, 25-27 is not true because Job said it, but because the Scriptures in many other places corroborate it. The same is true of Job 14, 1-2. — Mary's word at Cana, "Whatsoever He saith unto you, do it," John 2, 5, makes a fine text for an ordination, an installation, or a wedding address, but only after the preacher shows that Mary's word expresses the Lord's own will. — The word of the centurion under the cross, "Truly this was the Son of God!" is true indeed, but only because the Bible itself attests it as true, not just because the centurion uttered it.

7. When *historical texts* are chosen, the story must be fully told in the sermon. There are many such texts, especially in the Old Testament, that must be set aside for the simple reason that it would take

up too much space in the sermon to make the incident clear. The sermon is not the vehicle for giving instruction on ancient Biblical history.

### III. Pericope Texts.

The term "pericope" is derived from the Greek περί + κόπτειν = to cut around. A pericope is a section cut out of some piece of writing. While the etymology of the word might make it suit any text, ecclesiastical usage restricts the word to the texts that are arranged in a series which covers every Sunday and every church festival in what is called the church year. The different pericope systems all cover the church year, beginning with The First Sunday in Advent and extending to The Twenty-Seventh Sunday after Trinity.

The Old Testament was read systematically in the old Jewish synagogues which sprang up after the captivity. The Pentateuch was divided into sections called *Parashas*, and the prophets were divided into sections called *Haphtharas*. One of each was read on each Sabbath, and this was done in a fixed order.

In the early Christian Church the Old Testament Scriptures were likewise read, including the Apocrypha. Soon the latter were dropped. When the New Testament canon began to be formed the books of this canon were read in place of the Old Testament. At first a few excellent uninspired books entered the collection, but as the canon crystallized these, too, were dropped.

In a very natural way certain appropriate sections were regularly read at the great Christian festivals and thus became fixed for these festivals. Cycles were formed around the festivals by including the Sundays

close to them.   Thus a system of lections, namely
sections to be read on each Sunday and each festival,
were arranged.   The oldest is the *Lectionarium Galli-
canum* dating back to the fourth century.   The lection-
ary that has come down to our time was arranged in
the second half of the fourth century.   Its author was
Jerome Stridonensis.   Its old Latin name was *comes*,
"Companion."   Other lectionaries came into use, but
gradually disappeared.

In the eighth century Charles the Great induced
Paul Warnefried, deacon in Aquileja, to write a postil
on the old lections.   It bore the name *Homilarium
Caroli*, and contained a sermon on each text of the old
*Comes*.   As far as we know, this was the first postil —
a term derived from the Latin *post illa* (sc. *verba*) =
"after those words."   A Postil thus consists of what
the pastor preaches as a sermon "after the words of
the text."   It was this collection of sermons which
preserved the set of texts they expounded.   A few
changes and additions in the selections were made
during the Reformation.   The bulk of the old texts is
in use to this day.

It will be observed that they were intended at
first as texts to be read at the altar or lectern in the
liturgical part of the service.   Eventually they served
a double use; they came to be also the regular preaching texts for the pulpit.   In fact, these texts were
prescribed in great sections of the church and continued so for long periods.   There were two texts for
each Sunday and each festival, one taken from the four
gospels, and a second taken from the epistles.   At
present, in America, these old pericope texts, together
with the prayers (collects) and other liturgical ele-

ments that were added to them, are used as lections or Scripture readings in the churches that have fixed liturgies. They are also used as regular pulpit texts for the main service, although not exclusively, since other systems of preaching texts are used extensively in Germany and in the Lutheran churches of this country.

One feature of these systems of pericopes should be noted. Practically all are composed of texts of a fair size, few are quite short (and then for a special reason), and some of them are of considerable length, for instance the entire chapter 1 Cor. 13 forming one text. The texts of any one pericope system for the church year cover a goodly portion of the part of the New Testament from which they are taken (gospels — epistles). The entire line of the ancient gospels and epistles are printed in the hymnals of the churches that use them.

There are a number of marked *advantages* in preaching on the pericopes.

1. There is a fixed order of texts for the entire church year. The preacher is no longer under the necessity of trying to find a text for the next Sunday morning. His text is ready for him. It is invariably well chosen. Unripe beginners and one-sided men are prevented from making a possibly poor choice of text and subject.

2. The entire line of texts for the year is arranged so as to cover all the important doctrinal and ethical contents of the New (and Old) Testament. There is a fine balance and a fine proportion when one surveys the entire system.

3. Not all the texts are easy, some of them are actually difficult to master. This is a good thing. The preacher is driven to thorough study. He might prefer to dodge the more difficult texts, if he were himself making choice from Sunday to Sunday. With the text selected for him, he will not hesitate, but begin his work early, with profit for himself and for his congregation.

4. The line of texts used for one year will sooner or later be used again, usually a number of times in the preacher's life. Such repetitions compel the preacher to dig deeper. He will master each text more fully. His second, third, and fourth effort on the same text, with an interval of a few years, will enable him to produce finer sermons than the first effort could possibly bring forth. The congregation is profited accordingly.

5. For these pericopes the best of helps, both exegetical and homiletical, can be, and have to a large extent been, prepared. Of course, there are Bible commentaries, and they are very necessary and helpful. But if the preacher depended entirely on commentaries, he would be compelled to have several, to say the least. He would have to devote sufficient time to this study. Even then, on many a text, he would find gaps, unsettled points, unreconciled differences of interpretation, etc. The special works on a pericope system simplify all this. Every point and every question in each text is treated. The entire text is worked out for homiletical purposes, with a view to building sermons on it. Preacher, as well as people, profit by this kind of efficient help.

6. After able men have preached on a set of these texts a goodly number of times, they are ready to offer the cream of their efforts in a volume of sermons on such a line of texts. They leave a precious legacy to posterity. In all the mass of sermon literature extant there are no more excellent volumes than those on the old gospel and epistle pericopes. Naturally. No texts were ever studied like these, and none received such repeated try-outs in the pulpit. The first study of any text rarely produces a sermon that is fully ripe, and this holds true even of men theologically highly trained and spiritually strongly developed.

A pericope system, even with some faults in selection, is in every way superior to the free selections a preacher is able to make from Sunday to Sunday.

7. When one begins to preach on a line of pericopes he will, of course, try to follow it through without a break. Yet, if necessity should arise, the preacher is free to drop the text of the line he is using, and to choose a free text that will fully meet the need he happens to face.

In recent years the two old lines (gospels and epistles) have been increased in number. The most prominent new lines of texts are the Eisenach Selections, so-called from their origin, the Eisenach Conference in Germany. There are three different Eisenach lines, a gospel, an epistle, and an Old Testament line, each covering the church year. Other excellent lines are named after their authors, such as the lines by Thomasius and by Nitzsch; still other lines are named from the territory in which they were used.

In all there are some 25 lines of pericope texts, not counting the Norwegian and Swedish pericopes.

Those sections of the Church which have had the pericopes for centuries would never dream of giving them up, for the reason that these text systems produce the highest type of sermons.

A criticism of the old pericopes as we have them at present is in place. Originally there were three texts in each line (gospel and epistle) for each week, namely a text for Sunday, one for Wednesday, and one for Friday. With the texts for the week days omitted, the Sunday texts taken by themselves are not well connected. Among the texts for week days, some of the choicest portions of the New Testament were dropped, for instance the parable of the Prodigal Son. Moreover Christ's Entry into Jerusalem is used twice as a Sunday text, for The First Sunday in Advent and for Palm Sunday. So we must say the old gospels and epistles are not perfect lines, and could be improved. Because they are so ancient they are retained nevertheless, and in spite of these imperfections they have an enduring value.

The new pericope lines, of course, are selected to furnish only Sunday and festival texts. They thus form perfect chains, like chapters in a continued narrative. This is one of their especial attractions. They use none of the texts that are in the two old lines, but they do use the choicest texts otherwise available, and there is no repetition of a text. The many new lines, however, are not all composed of different texts — a thing impossible. Thus the Eisenach, the Thomasius, the Nitzsch gospel lines often have the same text for the same Sunday or for different Sundays.

Preaching on pericope systems will increase. It may even invade the churches where free texts are now the vogue. The general observance of Christmas, Lent, and Easter tend in that direction. If more of the church year comes to be recognized, the tendency will most likely grow.

## THIRD CHAPTER

# THE RELATION BETWEEN THE TEXT AND THE SERMON.

The preacher's conception of the relation between the text and the sermon to a great extent governs his entire idea of a text, its advantages, functions, ways to choose, etc. Misconceptions regarding the relation referred to are sure to pervert the preacher's entire view of the text, and will, of course, act detrimentally also on the sermon. Soundness of view in regard to the connection between the text and the sermon helps to clear up many other questions pertaining to the text, and will certainly also clarify one's idea of what a sermon ought to be.

There are two general misconceptions that should be cleared away. The relation between the text and the sermon should not be *too loose,* nor should it be *too close.*

If the sermon is in any way independent of the text, the relation is decidedly faulty. If the text degenerates into a mere pretext it is better to preach entirely without it. A sermon uncontrolled by its text makes a pretense of the text, and in the pulpit there should be no pretense. All kinds of pulpit addresses are offered on political, social, literary, scientific, on national and municipal subjects, and what not. To use Bible texts for such subjects is an abuse of the divine words. Such a thing can be done in one way only, namely by making the relation between the text and the sermon too loose.

On the other hand, if the preacher in his sermon fears to step beyond the threshold of his text, he does not correlate text and sermon aright. A mere commentary of the text is not a real sermon. Even if the exegesis is sound and thorough, a sermon that goes no farther is a failure. The tie between text and sermon is too close. While a sermon that does not venture beyond its text is by far preferable to a sermon that relinquishes its text, both types are gravely at fault. They are homiletical extremes that should be gently but firmly abolished.

In the sermon the preacher should look through the text at his congregation. The more he succeeds in that the truer will be the combination of his text and his sermon. The moment he drops his text and looks only at his congregation, he commits a serious fault. The moment he fails to see his congregation through the glass of his text, he is likewise at fault.

The ideal relation lies exactly mid-way between too loose and too close. The scales that bear on the one side the text, on the other the sermon, should balance, at least nearly. The one with the text in it should not fly up; nor the one with the sermon in it.

To get the right relation between the text and sermon,

### 1. *Stick to the text!*

That means, Be faithful to it. By reading a text in the pulpit the preacher virtually promises that he will preach on that text. The pulpit is the last place in the world in which to break, or fail to redeem, a promise, even though that promise be only implied. It is vastly better to omit the text and the promise it involves, than to be faithless to the text and its promise.

The limit in this respect is to read the text with all due solemnity, and then to say in the sermon, Our text speaks of (say) justification by faith, but this morning we will speak of (say) human service. But this very thing has been done.

In the days of the Reformation it was a matter of course for the preacher to stick to his text. Luther and others in those days knew of no other way to preach. They were certainly brainy men, and Luther especially drew crowds with his type of preaching. His sermons are models in this respect.

One of the fruits of the old vulgar Rationalism is that its exponents grew expert in preaching anything from any text. Modern rationalism still cultivates this treacherous art to a considerable degree. Each text is seemingly rubber, and nobody can guess beforehand in which direction the preacher will stretch it.

But some preachers of a truly evangelical type have also given way to this fault, even those trained to use set pericopes. There may be something they wish to impress upon their people, and under this inner urge they lose sight of the text, and expostulate on the things they have on their mind, regardless of the restrictions of the text. Why not take a text that is full of the subject with which your heart is surcharged? Admonitions that are backed by the divine words of the text penetrate more deeply than when delivered without such backing. Tangential preaching is always a mistake. Running at a tangent from a text either makes the preacher lose himself, so that he finally closes, perhaps awkwardly, far away from the text; or it necessitates a labored and apologetic return, which makes one feel sorry for the man.

Sticking to the text does not prevent the preacher from using related Scripture passages, as well as other pertinent material. There is always more of this than he can possibly use. For all proper Scripture themes there is wealth enough to embarrass even an expert preacher. Why then should any man cart in unrelated material, or build up thought structures far removed from his text.

### 2. *Exhaust the text!*

That means, in the first place, that the main thought of the text is to be the main thought of the sermon, and not some side thought, some fragment, some tatter of the text. Put the question squarely to the text, and do not stop till it answers you what it really stands for. Get at the heart of it. Discover what is distinctive in it, peculiar and different from other and similar texts.

In getting at the main thought do not be satisfied with broad generalities. The story of the Canaanitish woman is, of course, a text on faith. Look more closely. It is a text on persevering faith, a faith that goes on trusting even when the Lord Himself seems to thrust it away. There are other stories of faith, but very few with this distinctive feature.

Secondly, all the essential points of the text should find their corresponding place in the sermon. Take your text apart. Lay each piece out before you. See how each part is related to the center. There is the draught of fishes, an ocular demonstration of the power of the Word for the apostles who were to preach that

Word. Here are the essential features encircling the central idea: 1) fishing vainly all night; 2) rowing out in mid-day, the worst possible time; 3) in mid-lake, the poorest possible place; 4) in the face of a crowd that might jeer and laugh; 5) at the word of Jesus who had learned carpentry and not fishing; 6) do all this in the face of long years of experience and the expertness thus attained. With these important features all properly laid out the sermon should easily take care of them all.

Thirdly, nothing of real importance in the text should be omitted in the sermon. You cannot leave out the elder brother when your text is the entire parable of the Prodigal Son. The old pericopes offer Luke 15, 1-10 as a text, which means that you must include in the sermon both Jesus and the woman, both the sheep and the coin. If you intend to use Jesus and the sheep alone, omit from your text the companion parable.

Exhausting the text does not mean a complete emptying — a thing never possible. One will return to a text, perhaps repeatedly, and always new wealth will appear. The sermons will be different. For the chief thought may be approached now from this, now from that side, and the additional thoughts arranged accordingly. The general substance, of course, remains the same, just as the Gospel itself is and continues to be just one thing. But the presentations will vary. As time passes the preacher grows spiritually. When he looks at a sermon preached a few years ago he is often surprised at its poverty, and he eagerly tries the same text again for a much better sermon. All good homiletical helps offer at least several outlines on each text, and when the preacher uses these helps he will end by building still another good outline — his own this time.

Take the great Easter text, Luke 24, 1-12. My theme this year may be The Great Easter Gospel of our Lord's Resurrection from the Dead, as this is preached to us 1) by the useless spices, 2) the empty tomb, 3) the shining angels, 4) the startled women, 5) the doubting disciples, 6) to fill our hearts with the great Easter faith. Another year I may preach on the same text, The Open Sepulchre — it tells us, 1) death is gone, 2) life is come, 3) and faith should rejoice.

Sticking to the text, and exhausting the text, are two sides of the same thing. There is, however, a necessary complement to both.

### 3.   Adapt the text!

Only a student in the Seminary prepares a sermon, and then repeats that identical sermon here and there where he may be asked to fill in. When a pastor gets into his work each sermon is a distinct thing, intended for a definite audience, a particular Sunday, and a specific set of local circumstances. The pastor moves amid his people, and in a hundred conscious and unconscious ways receives impressions from them. All these local contacts influence his heart when he takes up his text and begins the preparation of his sermon. His eyes seek in the text what may profit his own congregation at this special time. In other words, he adapts his text to the needs of the hour.

That does not mean that he alters anything in the text. He does not press a word or thought in it beyond its native meaning. He reads nothing into the text. Nor does he pare down a word or a thought and make them mean less than they actually mean. Homiletical adaptation dare not degenerate into exegetical or homiletical falsification. "He that believeth not shall be damned." That is true for ever, just as the Savior said it. In no way does the preacher tamper with it.

Adaptation is the effort to get out of a text the very things needed for a congregation at the time. It answers the question, What has this text to say to me and my people to-day? Certain thoughts in the text thus assume a special importance for the new sermon. And all the thoughts of the text will group themselves accordingly.

This adaptation may be seen most plainly when a text is used at one time for a funeral, at another time for (say) Easter, and at still another time for an ordinary Sunday. An old lady dies near Easter time. Her text might well be Job 19, 23-27, as voicing the *comfort* of the resurrection. The same text could be used at Easter, preferably Easter evening or the Sunday after Easter (which is made part of the Easter festival in the church year). The emphasis now would not be on comfort, but on *assurance* and the *triumph* of faith. Yet this text would also be quite appropriate for one of the last Sundays of the church year, when the Church thinks of "the last things," death, resurrection, life everlasting. The emphasis now would be on our great Christian *hope*. Adaptation takes into account the specific purpose the text is to serve.

Such adaptation dare never be forced. In fact, it ought, in most cases, to be obvious to the hearers the moment the text is read. Sometimes the appropriateness of a text for the day for which it is set, or for the occasion for which it is chosen, is not at once apparent. The preacher may even ask, Why this text? In such a case only a few words should be necessary to make the hearers see the fitness of the text and the points in it that clearly adapt themselves to the day or the case. As the sermon unfolds, all this becomes still clearer.

Properly adapting the text and its contents to those who are to hear the sermon, really expects a great deal of the preacher. Like an able physician he must know all about the medicine he administers, as well as all about the patient whom he is to treat. How can he properly use his text for his people, when he has not fully mastered that text and its real contents? Or how can he make the text say what it ought to say to his hearers when he does not know their needs as he should?

Take the great text, Abraham sacrificing Isaac, during the Lenten season. Once a preacher built on this text the admonition to copy Abraham's faith. He misconceived his text. He failed to perceive the great incongruity between Abraham's altogether exceptional trial and any trials of Christians to-day; for who of us will ever be called by God to slay his son? He also misconceived the need of his people at the time. During Lent they need the sacrifice of Christ, the Lamb that was actually slain, and not even admonitions to faith can serve as a substitute. — Too often preachers see in their texts only the idea of service, and then apply the whip of the law to their people to drive them to this service. Their entire diagnosis may be, and nearly always is, wrong. Yes, there is great lack of service, of activity, of prayer, benevolence, and good works in general. But this is only a symptom. What the congregation really needs is more faith and spiritual strength. A man, sick and weak, cannot render much service. Make him healthy and strong, and he will delight to run the way of the Lord's commandments. If the preacher knew his congregation aright he would offer it the Christ, the divine grace, the quickening, healing, strengthening Gospel in his texts. He would feed, and not shout and lash. In other words, he would adapt his text.

A bungler in this matter is a depressing infliction on a congregation. The worst feature about it is that there is hardly a way to correct him. An expert, using his text to build up the spiritual life of a congregation, is a joy and delight, for which no congregation can be thankful enough to God.

Poor and faulty text adaptation helps to empty the pews. Masterly adaptation has the opposite effect.

## FOURTH CHAPTER

## MASTERING THE TEXT.

Nothing less will do. The preacher must not merely study his text more or less, he must master it.

We are quite safe in saying that a good deal of the weakness and ineffectiveness of the sermon is due to insufficient and improper text study. Somehow the opinion prevails that a good sermon may be preached even if the text is not mastered.

Some rely on their gift of eloquence, and certainly that is not to be despised. But eloquence must have the proper material to work upon. Why waste eloquence on poverty of thought? Give eloquence the fullest, richest, and very best material. Only then can it produce its maximum effect. One may, however, listen with real pleasure to an ordinary speaker, provided he comes into his pulpit with a text fully mastered.

Some rely on their general knowledge of the Bible and of the doctrine of the Gospel for success in preaching. There is no question that this is necessary and helpful. Yet general knowledge raises the preacher but little above common-places. The substance of his preaching will be ordinary. Moreover, the task is long. It will not do to repeat endlessly a number of commonplace ideas. The fund with which the preacher starts must constantly be replenished, or he will grow stale.

Some rely for their success in preaching on material drawn from extraneous sources, books on illustrations, anecdotes, etc., general reading, or things that come to mind and are more or less interesting in life. An intelligent preacher will find his own worth-while illustrations. He will scorn anecdotes altogether. The funny ones are the stock-in-trade of lecturers, who speak for an hour or two, and must permit their audience to unbend by allowing them to laugh occasionally. Anecdotes take too long to tell in a sermon. Their truth cannot be vouched for. In most cases the little story has not much of a point. But worst of all, it will nearly always be the mere story that sticks in the hearer's mind, not the point of truth it is meant to illustrate; and so the anecdote defeats its own purpose. Pity the preacher who suffers from anecdotage! Cullings from the preacher's reading of papers, magazines, and popular books may give his sermon a literary show, but it will be no more. To quote such material is a mistake. Best of all are a keen eye and a keen ear, and an understanding heart that sifts, tests, and works up what it sees and hears. But all that is thus acquired is not to be used as a substitute for text mastery, but only as supplementing the most precious material gained by such mastery.

A substitute for real text mastery has never been found.

### 1. *Begin with Prayer.*

The right understanding of the Word, or of any part of the Word, is a gift from above. The pride of learning must be turned into the humility of prayer. Luther's rule will ever hold true, *Fleissig gebetet ist ueber die Haelfte studiert*, Diligent prayer is more than half the study.

Some men kneel in their studies and pray at length. Others bow the head over their desks and breathe a prayer. The chief thing is the prayerful attitude, which must permanently fill the heart.

Many a special difficulty has yielded to prayer. Great mental effort and arduous research may fail, prayer leads to the solution. If the author may refer to his own experience, he can testify that often a text seemed hopeless. All at once, like a gift from heaven, the text crystallized, the form of the sermon stood out in the mind. One prayerful sigh had followed another, and had not been in vain.

### 2. *Let the Text Act Directly on Heart and Mind.*

Take the text before you and read it with all your mind and heart centered on its every word. Keep it a while before your eyes. Drink it in slowly, deeply. Then take the original Greek or Hebrew. Read the original and the translation side by side. If you know only a little Greek and Hebrew, thank God for what you have of it, and use it, absolutely use it! If you know neither of these languages, get at least an interlinear Greek New Testament, and begin to learn something of the Greek New Testament.

At this stage the sole object is to let the text, and the text alone, act upon your mind. The deeper this direct impression, the better. Just so you understand the text, that is all. You may want to look up some of the words in the original the better to grasp the sense of the translation. Little more will be needed, unless the text be exceptional.

Now carry your text with you. As you go about your duties turn it over in your mind. When the mind is free for a little while meditate on the text.

Get thoroughly wedded to it. Perhaps quite soon, perhaps a little later, you will be ready to put down your thoughts as they have grown out of your impressions. The entire scheme of your sermon may spring forth almost as of itself. If thus the iron should suddenly become good and hot, forge it. Do not delay, forge it! It is a pity to let it get cold again.

Keep your hands from commentaries at this first stage. And never, never, never read any man's sermon on the text this early! There is nothing like the direct action of God's own inspired words and sentences on your open and unprepossessed mind. As you love God and your work, get the full benefit of this effect.

With your mind saturated with the text at first hand,

### 3. Work Through the Text Exegetically.

Now study the text by means of the best commentaries, dictionaries, and grammars. This, of course, means an exegesis of the Greek or Hebrew original. The man unable to read the original is deprived of the finest possible source material for preaching. He must bend every effort to make up for his loss as much as he can, by using the best and fullest commentaries he is able to procure. Before he presses a single term or statement in the English, he must make sure that the original warrants such pressure. The danger is that he may stress in the English what is not stressed at all in the original; or vice versa. Again, he dare not rely on the picture seemingly implied in an English word, for there may be no picture at all in the original word, or an entirely different picture which the English was unable to reproduce. And he must try, by means of his helps, to get the real pictures in the words of the original.

In Rom. 3, 25 "propitiation" is really "mercy-seat," ἱλαστήριον, the lid of the ark of the covenant, beneath which lay the two tables of the law. On this lid the blood was sprinkled, so that God looking down would see the blood-sprinkled mercy-seat hiding the accusing law. — "Forgiveness" is ἄφεσις, a sending away of our sin and guilt, "as far as the east is from the west," i. e. so that it will never be found. — "Sin" is "a missing of the mark" set by the law, ἁμαρτία. The Bible is full of picture words — all material of pure gold wrought with heavenly skill, away beyond any trivial anecdote of doubtful origin, any secular quotation however apt, even far beyond any pious thought from godly writers. It is God's gold from heaven.

We cannot furnish in this place a complete treatise on exegesis. We confine ourselves to the following:

1. Every sentence in the Bible has *one meaning*, and only one. We dare not give up until that one meaning is discovered and fully established. That may take time and effort, but both are well spent.

2. Authorities often differ greatly. They flatly contradict each other. The preacher may feel that he is quite helpless to act as judge between them, especially when they speak with such a show of learned assurance. Let him remember that no man, however great and learned, is infallible. Great names and great numbers are not decisive. Hide behind no man's skirts. There is always one decisive criterion, *Scriptura ex Scriptura explicanda est.* Interpret

Scripture by Scripture. In doing this, be sure to get in each case *all* that the Scriptures offer.

3. Never accept an interpretation that contradicts *the Analogy of Scripture*. In certain small, as well as great, things the Scriptures markedly speak in one way only, and not in another. For instance, they never speak of the Holy Ghost as an instrument which we use. Of course, one must know his Bible to apply this principle in text study. It is a valuable safeguard.

4. Never accept an interpretation that clashes with *the Analogy of Faith*. This is even more valuable than the former test. The Analogy of Faith is composed of all the main *sedes doctrinae* and their doctrinal contents. If I find that my text says something seemingly contradictory to this Analogy, I know at once that I am not reading that statement in my text aright. There is a mistake somewhere, and I must find it. For in no incidental statement do the Scriptures ever contradict what they say in the great important doctrinal portions. If I cannot, with my best efforts, discover my mistake, one thing is certain, I dare not read a single statement in my text in contradiction to the assured doctrines of the Scriptures.

Acts 2, 27 reads in the English as though the soul of Jesus had been in hell during the time between His death and His resurrection. Even the Greek, read superficially, may sound that way. Yet elsewhere the Evangelists tell us positively that the soul of Jesus was in His Father's hands in Paradise. The whole matter is cleared up when it is discovered that the expression does not mean "leave my soul in hell," but "abandon my soul unto hell." Good commentators have been gravely misled on this passage.

### 4. *Catechize the Text.*

Does it speak literally, or does it contain figures of speech? If there are figures, what are they? What is the *tertium comparationis* in each? Get the exact answer, and never stretch a figure beyond the point of comparison.

Among the questions that help to bring out the full information contained in the text are the following.

Inquire for

> The speaker.
> The person spoken to.
> The person spoken of.
> The subject spoken of.
> The place involved.
> The time indicated.
> The occasion dealt with.
> The scope of the text.
> The emotions running through the text.
> The context and connection.

Apply any other questions to probe the text.

Take as an example the emotions in a text. They are often overlooked. Commentators as such tend to be coldly intellectual and often preachers are that way. Yet hundreds of texts throb with intense feeling. They are highly dramatic, at times tragic. Take Luke 12, 16-21, The Rich Fool. Whoever penetrates to the emotions in this text will not preach on commonplace themes like The Proper Use of Riches. He will see the tragedy in the text — a man proud and happy in nothing but great earthly prosperity, his soul called to judgment that very night. All the Greek classics contain nothing that equals this one parable. Thus the whole range of human feeling runs through the texts one meets in the Bible.

5. *Uncover the Truths in the Text.*

A truth is the divine reality itself. A genuine fact is a truth. Any adequate statement of such a reality or fact is a doctrine.

Sometimes churches and preachers say that they do not like doctrinal preaching. If they know what they are saying, they surely pronounce judgment upon themselves. For the opposite of truth is unreality, that which is not a fact, which is not so. Lies are unrealities posing as realities. Fancies are unrealities, offered in place of truth. No greater crime can be committed than to offer in the pulpit lies and fancies under the pretense that they are God's Word. This is the devil's work, for he is a liar from the beginning, and the father of lies. John 8, 44. He lied to Eve that she would not die if she ate of the forbidden fruit. They who scorn to preach and to hear doctrinal sermons, thereby say that they desire only lies and fancies, and not the realities and facts that are decisive for their souls.

We may classify the truths that are stated in Scripture texts as follows.

Such as *instruct,* inform, simply enlighten, and make known certain great spiritual facts. John 3, 16 is an example. It is the Gospel, or "great news," compressed into a single statement.

Such as *refute error,* expose its lying character. In Matth. 22, 23-33 Jesus explodes the Sadducean error that there could not be a resurrection of the dead.

Such as *admonish,* like the law with its commandments, and the Gospel with its appeals, John 14, 1,

"Let not your heart be troubled: ye believe in God, believe also in me."

Such as *rebuke faults*, vices, and all forms of ungodliness. Texts like this *forbid*, "Let no corrupt communication proceed out of your mouth." Eph. 4, 29. They *urge against* a wrong act or course, "Think not to say within yourselves." Matth. 3, 9. *They warn*, "He that believeth not shall be damned." Mark 16, 16. Jesus warns Peter, Mark 14, 29-31. They *threaten*, "If ye walk after the flesh ye shall perish." Rom. 8, 13. Jesus threatens the Jews, John 8, 21; the Sanhedrim, Matth. 26, 64.

Such as *comfort*, "Blessed are the poor in spirit," etc. Matth. 5, 3 etc.

Many texts contain a variety of truth, often plainly marked.

*6. Study the Arguments in the Text.*

Sermons, however, are not arguments. To preach is not to argue, but to testify. No man can argue the sinner into repentance, faith, and salvation. Against every argument a shrewd mind can bring a counter-argument. Testimony is a totally different thing. By its very nature it is either true or false. You cannot argue with testimony. All you can do is either to believe and accept the testimony, or refuse to believe it and call it false. Hence our divine commission is to be Christ's witnesses, Acts 1, 8.

Argument is addressed to the intellect. The sermon addresses the entire man, intellect, feelings, and will. It is a failure if it does not reach the will. One may win a debate, and yet not convince his opponent.

> "A man convinced against his will
> Is of the same opinion still."          *Hudibras.*

And yet texts are full of arguments. The term arguments, however, is here used in a specific sense. Ordinary arguments are reasonings. In ordinary arguing one line of reasoning is pitted against another line. No sermon dare descend to this low level. We testify to the truth. But the truth, just because it is the truth, has convincing power. Every man who meets the truth *ought* to believe it. He knows he ought. If he refuses he stands self-condemned. In this sense the truth to which we bear witness is full of argument, namely full of convincing power. Being truth, i. e. reality and fact, all counter-argument is cut off. A man who attempts to argue against truth and reality and its convincing power, by that very act proclaims himself a fool.

To seek the arguments in a text means simply to look for those features in the truths of the text which reveal their convincing power. There are always features in every truth which aid in driving that truth home. The preacher's duty is to discover and use those features. Men may still reject the truth so presented in its convincing power, but by doing it they are doubly condemned.

Some of these arguments are *plainly stated.* "Avenge not yourselves, etc.; for it is written, Vengeance is mine," etc. Rom. 12, 19. Here the second truth supports the first (which is in the form of admonition). — Many of these arguments are *hidden.* They are like masked batteries. They shoot suddenly from an unexpected quarter, and are thus the more effective. They thus help to make the sermon strong. "Have no fellowship with the unfruitful works of darkness." Eph. 5, 11. There are powerful arguments in the two terms "unfruitful" and "darkness." Who wants to keep cultivating a field which never raises as much as a single grain of corn? Who wants to be identified with works, which, the moment the light shines on them, stand revealed as damnable? In 1 Pet. 1, 4 God is praised who has begotten us again "to an inheritance incorruptible, and undefiled, and that fadeth not away." Each of these three great modifiers is convincing as to the supreme excellence of this inheritance, and thus shows why we should praise God.

Again, the nature of some arguments is *direct proof*. One or more truths are stated, each of which helps to convince us of the reality of some other truth (which, of course, may be stated in any form; see point 5 preceding). "Take heed that ye do not your alms before men, to be seen of them (stated as an admonition): otherwise ye have no reward of your Father which is in heaven," Matth. 6, 1 (stated as a fact). The second statement proves the correctness of the first. — "Take no thought, saying, What shall we eat? or, What shall we drink? or, Wherewithal shall we be clothed?" Matth. 6, 31. Two proofs are added, 1) "For after all these things do the Gentiles seek" (negative proof): 2) "for your heavenly Father knoweth that ye have need of all these things" (positive proof). The Bible is full of such proof. In each case it consists of testimony to a further truth.

The other type of argument is *elucidation*. It intends to make clearer and thus to show the convincing power of a truth more fully. This can be done in a variety of ways, for instance, by a fuller repetition; by exemplification; by pointing to the contrary, or to what is similar; by removing an objection, etc. In the epistles the connective γάϱ, "for," is extensively used for introducing elucidations. It is quite proper to translate it with "for," but the preacher ought to state for his own clear apprehension just what this connective conveys in each case. Thus one "for" may mean, "in order to repeat and state more fully"; while another may mean, "in order to show by an example"; etc.

Is. 55, 10-11 begins with an elucidation, "As the rain cometh down and the snow, etc., so shall my Word be," etc. The analogy of the rain and snow makes clearer the truth about the action of the Word. In Romans 4 the example of Abraham is used *in extenso* in elucidating justification by faith. So also Elias in James 5, 16-17 as an illustration of effectual fervent prayer. In Rom. 3, 21-24 there are two elucidating "for" statements, "for there is no difference" (negative), and, "for all have sinned" etc. (positive).

*Metaphors* are condensed similes and in many cases have the force of illustrative argument. In James 1, 6 a simile is introduced by "for," while in 3, 2 the metaphor is used, "to bridle the whole body," i. e. to control it, which verse 4 elaborates more fully.

### 7. *Last of All Glance at Other Men's Sermons.*

It is dangerous to look at sermons too early. You may happen upon a good sermon, which, if read too early, may so fasten itself upon the mind as to prevent your getting away from it and working out something good independently. Glancing at sermons toward the end of the work of mastering a text should help in two ways.

1.   The preacher sees what other men have done with the text.   Having mastered the text he is in a position to read any sermon on the text critically, i. e. with a mind free enough not to be enslaved by the other man's work.   He is thus able to see weaknesses and faults, as well as excellencies.   Such reading stimulates.

2.   If the sermon thus read is a poor one, the preacher will at once feel that he is able to produce one that is superior to it.   That is a pleasant feeling to have.   The main point in this situation is that the preacher gauges the high level he should reach with his own effort.   If the sermon thus read is an excellent one, the preacher has the necessary high mark set for him.   And he should feel that he, too, must and can, by his own independent effort, reach an equally high mark.

Too many are content to aim too low.   It was Lowell who wrote, "Not failure, but low aim, is crime." All true homiletical study ought to raise our ideals about sermons.   If your ideal is high enough, and tends to rise, nobody need fear about the character of your sermons.   Get rid of salving your homiletical conscience with excuses.   All of them are hollow.

Never plagiarize.   A sermon thief should be the last man to stand in the pulpit.   An occasional quotation is, of course, quite proper.

It is always a mistake to follow human authorities.   To base our convictions on them is to have only a human foundation.   At best they are helpers, aiding us to see what the Word really contains that we may stand entirely on that Word.   When Dr. Eck was asked whether he could refute Luther, he replied, "Not with the Scriptures, but with the fathers." His questioner replied, "Then the Lutherans are *in* the Scriptures, and we are *beside* them." Every preacher must so ground himself on the Word in all his preaching, that he will never be caught merely *beside* the Bible. He must always be altogether *in* it.

### 8. *Other Aids in Mastering Texts.*

Mention must be made of parallel passages of all kinds. It is highly advisable to look up all such passages, and to study them in conjunction with what the text itself contains. It is an excellent rule to follow, always to seek out *all* that the Scriptures say on any one point. It is the only safe way.

Great aid is derived from the study of sound Biblical Dogmatics and Ethics. For it is the business of these theological branches to gather together from the Scriptures all their dogmatical and ethical teaching, and to present it as the Scriptures themselves lay it before us. Both rest on the most complete exegesis. Both utilize all the main passages of Holy Writ. Both aim to restate exactly the contents of these passages and to summarize what they contain. Both treat at length all the important questions that thus arise. Neither Dogmatics nor Ethics can thus be set aside or neglected by the preacher, unless he actually decides to impoverish himself and make his preaching unsafe and shallow for his hearers. If there were no Dogmatics and Ethics we preachers would have to build them up ourselves for the purpose of our work. While both branches in their full elaboration go beyond the ordinary requirements needed for sermonizing, by doing so they give to the preacher that fulness and balance of knowledge by means of which he becomes a safe interpreter of the Word.

Finally, we must mention spiritual experience. The preacher must believe his own message. He himself must live the life to which he would by God's Word and grace lift others. Young men have less of this experience, which cannot be helped. As the preacher grows older he tests the promises of God more and more, tastes the truth of the Gospel, conquers temptation, shakes off doubt, learns his own weaknesses and how and where to gain strength, and thus becomes "a witness" who preaches what he himself has tested. As he advances in life his experience with men will grow. The deeper his knowledge in this direction becomes, the more able will he be to meet their needs from the divine source of help, from which to minister unto men God has called him. The supreme need of every Christian pulpit is a man who carries Christ in his own heart and whose life is filled with the power of divine grace in the Word.

# PART TWO

# THE DIVISION

FIRST CHAPTER

## ART IN THE SERMON.

### I.  The Question of Art in the Sermon.

The moment we begin work on the actual sermon
we face a question of fundamental importance.  Our
answer to this question determines practically everything we do in constructing the sermon.

Are we merely going to collect a lot of Biblical
and Christian material?  If so, then we need but little
instruction in our work.  The Bible is a great store-
house — go in and take what comes to hand.  And
there is Christian life, individual and congregational,
as found in this world of sin and evil.  It affords a
thousand thoughts to any observant preacher.  Let
him go and take upon what his mind happens to light.
It will not require much effort to pile up enough for
a half hour's speaking.  If sermons are merely loose
collections of pious Christian thoughts, there would
be no need of Homiletics.

There are actually those whose idea of a sermon
is nothing more than "a pulpit talk."  They begin
anywhere in general, and they end nowhere in particular.  They might just as well have begun elsewhere, and ended somewhere else.  For there is no
directive, no control of any kind.  Nevertheless, even
if the sermon degenerates into a mere "talk," most
men will at least put a little order into what they say.
Very likely they will combine related things, instead of
just jumbling them.  Furthermore in their presen-

tation they will, in all probability, try to state one thing or another in a telling manner. But the moment they attempt and achieve even this much they are using the first tiny elements of homiletical art. By the application of ever so little of this art, preachers of this lowest type reveal that they have a glimmering of the great homiletical principle that governs, and always ought to govern, all preaching. What is this principle? As between two ways of doing a thing discard the one that is inferior, choose the one that is better.

In all sermon construction the sum and substance of Homiletics amounts to what is contained in this little word "better." Choice after choice presents itself to the preacher, and in every case he should take what is "better." And the aggregate of these choices, a score, a hundred of them, constituted homiletical excellence. The best sermon is therefore the one which in every alternative adopts that which is better. There will be alternatives in which one thing or one way is only a little better; but there will also be alternatives in which one thing will be much better than the other. The sum total of all the little "betters" and all the big "betters" will result in what is best.

It is better to use a text than to do without one. It is better to have a unit text than one that merely offers a subject or a key thought. It is better to have a full, rich text, than a mere scrap or pretext. So in all that has to do with texts. Likewise, it is better to have arrangement than mere loose material; better to have a subject than no subject at all; better to have a real theme than a mere subject; better to have a true division of the theme than haphazard cutting up of material. So in all that pertains to the outline. It is better to have homogeneous material than heterogeneous; it is better to organize this material than to work it in loosely; it is better to focus this material than just to string it out. Always and always it is the *better* that counts.

The one grand duty of Homiletics is to show us all along the line the things and the ways that are better. The student in the Seminary is to learn the better way to begin with. It is a pity to see men in late life still handicapped homiletically by their early inferior training.

Yet a strange streak of perversity runs through the preaching fraternity. The inferior is often adjudged the superior, the better scorned as the worse, and a twenty-five percent is figured as a hundred percent. Perverted ideas usually stick tighter than burrs. Not that it is easier to do a thing in a poor way — generally it requires more work. Once the better way is acquired, it, like all mastery, is followed by greater ease. But to reach mastery requires strenuous effort, the very effort many refuse to put forth. But in whatever way homiletical inferiority may be explained, the explanation does only one thing — it discredits the inferiority.

The moment we apply the homiletical principle described, and discard the inferior for the better in building the sermon, we are using art in the sermon. Art in Homiletics is simply choosing the better in sermonizing.

The art here meant does not stand alone. It is but an integral part of all that belongs to public Christian worship. One may, of course, worship out-of-doors or even in a barn. But Christian congregations, since early days, have, whenever and wherever possible, built beautiful churches. Study a structure of this kind. You will easily find a hundred points, some great and vital, some small and minor, in which the plan of the building, its construction, and its details, all reveal the one sustained effort, to achieve what is better. Hence there is art, architectural and ecclesiastical art, in the church building. Congregations usually go to the limit of their financial means in this respect.

These beautiful churches are built for us to preach in. Must not the sermon match the church? Should not the sermon show the same striving for what is better in substance as well as in form and arrangement? If cost and effort are not spared in the building, which is but an earthly house and shell, effort and skill dare not be spared in the sermon, which is the scriptural substance.

As the church, so the worship — all its parts should be beautiful. The hymns are poems wrought with great skill and selected from a great mass — only those that are better having been chosen. From the prelude and the Introit to the Doxology and the postlude all is arranged beautifully. Liturgics, in a long line of development, has discarded what was inferior and retained what was superior. We have the great pipe organ, because there is no better instrument for worship. We have forms of prayer, of confession and absolution, of versicles and responses, just these, and just in this combination, because none better have been found.

Into this lovely form of worship a slovenly sermon

does not fit. We use a gold setting for some precious jewel, such as a diamond or emerald, not for a cheap pebble. In fact, the sermon should crown the worship. If anything, it ought to be the most beautiful part of the entire worship. The art in it ought to be of the highest order.

The Bible itself is full of art and spiritual beauty. Some of the Psalms are like the rarest gems, exquisitely wrought; all of them are "a joy for ever." The Parables of Christ are incomparable. They have been imitated, never equalled. Isaiah 40-66 is the grandest dramatic lyric ever written. It is like a vast cathedral, all of the finest material, and wrought with supernatural skill. Study the structure of the books of the Bible — every one appears with a plan of its own, aimed at one grand impression, with its details all fitted to harmonize. There is Genesis with its ten sections, each starting with the expression, "These are the generations." There is St. John setting forth the divinity of Christ in what has rightly been called the "crown gospel." The structure of Romans is significant. Remove the epistolary greeting at the beginning, and the personal greetings at the end, and you have the greatest apostolic sermon that was ever preached.

Thus we might instance Christ's Sermon on the Mount, St. Paul's address on Mars' Hill, Stephen's Defense. In every sermon in the Bible, and in every sermon summary, we will find the power of the Word combined with the appropriate type of spiritual beauty in presentation.

The preacher who lives in the midst of it all should certainly be responsive to it all. The beauty of holiness in the Bible should certainly find an adequate reflection of genuine spiritual beauty in his sermons.

## II.  The Art Features Native to the Sermon.

There are two kinds of art, sacred and secular. The two dare never be confused. The difference is in their inner quality. The one draws its inspiration from above, the other from below. The one lifts the soul to God, the other leaves it in the world, and perhaps draws it down into the lusts of the world. The one is spiritual, the other at best non-spiritual, at worst anti-spiritual. The quality of each can best be judged by the effect.

It ought to be easy to distinguish the sacred art features appropriate to a sermon from the secular art features used in ordinary lectures and speeches. The difference, as already stated, lies in the inner quality, and appears in the effect. We must not look for the difference in the art features themselves. Sometimes there is confusion on this essential point, to the extent that art in sermons is decried and spurned. Because men of the world make so much of art, the godly preacher may draw the wrong conclusion that he is to do without art. There may also be the opposite case. A preacher may load his sermon with art for art's sake, disregarding its quality, admitting unspiritual art features and disregarding the unspiritual effects. Both are wrong.

The sermon that markedly spurns art is greatly inferior and offends intelligent hearers. Good bread and meat may to some extent be relished, even if carlessly served. Yet, when we are invited to dine, we rightly expect a clean table, plate, knives, forks, and the other things that make the dinner palatable and pleasant. But a sermon that loads on art affects us the other way. The glitter and polish of phrase and sentence, the dramatics of form, the elegance and fastidiousness of detail attract attention to themselves and to the esthetic and literary preacher, spirituality wanes and grows cold. Dainties alone make a slim meal for a hungry man.

Genuine art used for spiritual ends will always have its place in our churches and our worship, and this necessarily includes the sermon.

In describing this art let us begin at the top. It is the art that is *native to divine truth*.

By its very nature all truth is beautiful. Divine truth, being the highest of all, a revelation direct from God Himself, has the quality of beauty in the highest degree. It is the business of the sermon to present some part of this glorious truth. To do that in a way that is at all adequate means to display the beauty inherent in the very substance of truth.

On the other hand, all lies are ugly and hideous. That is why lies need to be decorated. They must appear with painted faces and false hair, and with every other means to cover up their ugliness.

Because truth is beautiful, it satisfies, clarifies, ennobles, exalts, and thus attracts. Especially divine truth. Lies degrade, corrupt, deceive, damage, destroy, and thus repel. Especially spiritual lies.

Truth needs no argument or propaganda. All it needs is to be revealed as what it is. By its very nature it captivates and wins. It never uses any other means. Lies must have false arguments and propaganda to make them pass. The worst thing that could possibly happen to a lie is to have some one reveal it as what it really is. By its very nature, when stripped of its mask, a lie repels and offends. Only liars love lies, and yet they would not admit that they are what they are. Truth-lovers love truth, and are happy to admit that they are what they are.

Jesus Christ, true God, begotten of the Father from eternity, and true man, born of the Virgin Mary, is the central substance of all our preaching. He Himself has said, "I am the truth." In all the world there is none like Him in beauty. His character, life, teaching, deeds, suffering, death, and glorification are absolutely supreme in their attractiveness. Who can preach Christ and yet keep out of his sermon all the rays of this beauty?

The entire Gospel and doctrine of salvation is the absolutely highest truth with which human souls may come in contact. In all the universe there is nothing lovelier than the love of God in Christ Jesus to us fallen sinners. In all human experience there is nothing so happy and blessed as the restoration of a fallen soul to childhood and hope of eternal life with God. Who can preach all this truth without making its beauty shine forth radiantly from his sermons?

Moreover, this divine truth is living. It is not a set of dead facts. It pulsates with life and power. It is the embodiment of love, grace, and mercy, the living presence of righteousness and holiness. Ever and ever you can meet it anew, and find it ever new, ever more winning, more satisfying, more uplifting. It is the special privilege of the preacher so to meet this living truth in text after text, and by his preaching to aid others in meeting it likewise. He surely cannot do this without letting the abounding heavenly beauty of the living truth of God shine forth in his sermons.

Genuine science also has truth, and is seeking for more of it in slow and painful progress. But its truths are facts, just facts, and they are dead. In their way they, too, have a beauty, but as scientific facts only for the mind (science means knowledge only). They never warm the soul with love and grace; they never lift the soul to love and holiness. There is a fragment here, and a fragment there, to be pieced together as best we can, and to use for our earthly existence. God's saving truth in Christ Jesus is all-perfect and all-complete; it is God Himself reaching down into our souls to let us have life, and to have it ever more abundantly.

In the second place, the sermon must use the art which naturally goes with *the transmission of divine truth*.

The pulpit is intended for this transmission. It faces an array of pews, filled with an audience. The preacher is not alone, in his study, contemplating the divine truth in its native beauty, his soul enraptured and uplifted by its lovely power. He is a channel, in the pulpit, pouring the truth into the souls of his people. There is a living contact between heart and heart, and the point of contact is in the divine truth coming from the preacher's lips. Christ chose preachers of the Gospel, not just a book, and not just readers of a book. In other words, the divine truth is not to be transmitted in an impersonal, set and stereotyped form. Preaching means that the preacher receives into his own heart and mind the divine truth, there to mold it anew for transmission. And this molding of it is to be personal, serving the needs of his hearers. This means, that all the loveliness and attractiveness naturally inhering in the truth are to shine forth in the preacher's transmission, namely those captivating features which at the time of the preaching are to win and hold the hearts of the hearers.

In this transmission the preacher is a painter. He takes the specific truths in his text and makes them stand out for his hearers. There is clearness, definiteness, plasticity. That is beauty and art. It may be done in a simple manner, but it will be of a higher order in that case. The heart of the hearer is satisfied, lifted up, blessed. The opposite of this form of art in the sermon is the presentation of abstractions, abstruse ideas and reasonings, confused notions, loose and rambling remarks. These can neither grip nor captivate the heart. They strain and lose the attention.

Again, the preacher, in transmitting the divine truth to his hearers, resembles a fine musician. That is because he must employ the medium of living speech. There is constant movement, the flow of speech. Now the flow will be calm and measured, again it will rise and grow intense with power. There are all kinds of variations, but all of them directed to one goal, namely the heart of the hearer. Now one side, now the other side of some needful truth is shown, until the whole stands forth in perfect harmony. The very process is beautiful, doubly so when the character of the truth thus transmitted is considered in connection with the transmission. The opposite of this feature of art in the sermon is monotony, commonplace talk, loud harangue, working oneself up into a spurious effort at effect, all insincere eloquence, and the like. None of these are true music, all of them either weary the mind or jar upon the feelings.

The second feature of sermon art here described often appears in secular speeches, and may be highly effective, for instance, when hearth and home, blood and life are at stake. But even when dealing with such great issues, they are on a lower level, of the earth only and this life. When the soul is at stake and the issues are spiritual and eternal, we move on the highest possible level, and the character of the transmission must be equally noble and high.

In the third place, the sermon must use *the art of Rhetoric*.

While Homiletics demands a thorough knowledge of Rhetoric, from the art of composing a complete discourse down to the details of choice of words, etc., Homiletics cannot teach Rhetoric, just as it requires but does no teach Logic, Psychology, languages and other branches of learning which every preacher should know. So we need to say but little here on this art-feature as it applies to sermons.

Let us note that of all forms of public address the sermon is most subject to *the law of order*. There are many parts, but they must all be symmetrically combined into a unity. Each part must be placed where it naturally belongs. All the parts must be kept in due proportion to each other and to the larger unity which they form. Moreover, as these parts are combined and unfolded, there will be now a rising with intensity, now a calm spreading and broadening, and again a compact concentration. In other words, a properly compared sermon has built the material it

uses into a structure, the focal point of which aims to
produce a unit effect on the hearer. A discourse of
this kind cannot be built without using art in its structure, namely the art of rhetorical composition naturally
required for the purpose of the sermon.

To the extent that these natural principles are
ignored or violated the sermon becomes inferior. A
man may preach on "Faith and Love" if his aim is to
present the relation of these two to each other. But if
he intends no more than to say something first on
faith, and then on love, he sacrifices unity. His product
will result in two brief dissertations, pasted together,
each of them on a mere general subject on which a
great deal may be said. Organization will be lost
completely, and unity of effect become wholly impossible. A few fundamental art considerations would
lift him above this low level.

A theme like Pierson's "Four Rules of Christian
Living" is inferior for the same reason. It could at
best produce only four little sermonettes strung together. Besides one cannot but ask, Why just four
such rules for this sermon, when there are surely more
than four? If these four are in the text, why are they
thus combined? Why does the preacher fail to show
the unity that divides into four such quarters? This
criticism applies to all sermons which use numerals
in their themes. They are twins, triplets, etc., not
units. All of them make the impression that the
preacher did not understand one of the basic features
of his art, or that he has been too indolent to work
out what was necessary. In addition, when we examine one of these little sermonettes by itself it will
appear without a real theme. "Faith" is not made a

theme by merely setting "Love" beside it; so also "Love." "A Rule of Christian Living" is an indefinite thing, and is not advanced to a theme by merely adding a numeral.

But Rhetoric supplies much more in the line of art. We may mention all the forms of language in endless variety. From them all the preacher will choose in each case the most adequate and telling expression. There is the wide field of figures of speech. It is inexhaustible for combined beauty and power. The law of choice will select what is simple, pure, noble, in perfect harmony with the lofty subjects that are to be presented. For the simple ways of saying things are most beautiful, not the ornate, verbose, complex and involved. Pureness and nobleness of speech are beautiful, not slanginess, coarseness, and rudeness. All this means art. The Bible is full of it, and thus becomes our perfect model.

SECOND CHAPTER

# THE TEXT AND THE SERMON.

## I. Clearing up the Subject.

Should the sermon have parts? Nearly all preachers would answer in the affirmative. Yet in reality they are not agreed. Everything depends on our conception of what sermon parts are or ought to be.

The man who preaches on a mere subject or topic, attempting what is called "a topical sermon," will probably treat two or more sides of his subject. He may call these the "parts" of the sermon. They are parts, however, only in the sense that he has made them such. He might just as well have treated other sides of his subject, and they would have been the "parts." In other words, the parts in a sermon of this type, when added together, do not equal the subject or topic. Just as the subject is the free choice of the preacher, so these parts are the free choice of the preacher from among the possible sides or features of the subject.

Again a subject or topic may be elaborated after a fashion in loose essay style. The material arranged under the subject is split up into sections, and each section receives a sort of sub-title, its wording drawn from something contained in that section. The essay form is the freest, or we may say lowest, of all forms of sermonizing. It is an attractive form when put into print for reading, and is much used for written composition. It is not nearly so effective for speaking. The sub-titles that look well on a printed page, cannot be used at all in speaking. Should the attempt be made, nevertheless, to use them in speaking, they would not sound well, and generally would appear odd. Moreover, such sections under sub-heads could be called "parts" of a sermon only in a very broad sense of the word. This free essay style is a product of nothing more advanced than college training, even when it is used by homiletical teachers in a theological seminary or by graduates of such a seminary. In the author's judgment preachers should rise far above it in building sermons.

When a preacher uses a theme, instead of a mere topic, he will require parts in a more real sense of the term. There are some who have advanced to the idea of a theme, and who yet fail to unfold a theme in the manner which this really requires. They treat the theme in a loose fashion. They arrange "parts" under it, but they still do so by following only a general line of thought. When the "parts" they select are added together they do not equal the theme. They present only some of the thoughts which the theme at the time happens to suggest. Other "parts" might be substituted. In fact, the preacher himself, after more mature reflection, might wish he had used other "parts."

The best type of sermon is that which uses a genuine theme, and then splits that theme so that the resultant parts when added together actually equal the theme. It is somewhat like an orange. The peeling that encloses the edible part resembles the theme, for the entire sermon is embraced in the theme. The meat in the orange consists of cells full of juice, but these are divided into sections which can be pulled apart and laid side by side. The sermon parts resemble these sections. When they are put together, they form the orange. No one section could be left out if the orange is to be complete. And no section from another orange could be wedged in among the original sections. This may serve to illustrate what we mean by genuine parts. All true themes present organisms, more or less complex; and the essential and natural portions of each organism are its real parts. A tree has roots, a trunk, and branches. These are its parts. A building has a foundation, walls, roof, if we go no farther. A book has but two parts, the cover, and the leaves. A machine has many parts, according to its complexity. Sermon themes that embrace only a few grand parts are best, starting with two and extending at most to six, seven, or possibly eight. There is a natural limit, due to the time usually allotted to the sermon.

## II. Essentials of a Discourse with Parts.

Every discourse, deserving the name, has some kind of logical arrangement, and the better the arrangement the better the discourse. When there is no arrangement the sermon is like a lot of building material dumped helter-skelter on the ground. An ill-arranged sermon is like a botched house. One well arranged is like a first-class house, a delight to the architect and the owner and to all who see and pass through it. The preacher's business is to construct only the latter kind.

Some one has divided sermons into two classes, the vertebrate and the molluscan. There are sermons whose beginning and end could be reversed, or in which one might interchange any of its so-called "parts," and the sermon would lose nothing, in fact it might actually gain a little. It is well enough to have drapery. But words, beautiful phrases, and fine sentences and sentiments are not enough. There must be a skeleton underneath, not a mere stick, unless, as one has remarked, you desire a scare-crow.

And yet, despite all these caustic remarks of the best homiletical experts, proper skeletonizing is not deemed necessary by a good many preachers. They nail a few sticks together, put on voluminous drapery to hide them entirely from their hearers, and call the result a "sermon." When the better way is shown them they deny that it is the better way. Wrong ideas, when imbibed early, have a persistence that is truly astonishing.

Of course, it is true that an excellent sermon may be preached without an excellent inner structure. The preacher may have a fine personality, an excellent voice, natural force, trained eloquence, and scattered through his sermon he may have pearls of truth and a striking way of putting things. Such features may make his sermon excellent. But none of these, not even all of these, features excuse the structural fault. Excellence in one or more points never makes up for inferiority in other points. In fact, a flaw in a great diamond is more deplorable than the same flaw in a cheaper stone. That excellent sermon would be still more so if the structural fault were eliminated. On the other hand, if the principle of thus excusing a fault in one serious point were consistently carried out, faults might multiply and extend to other points as well. Soon the sermon would cease to be at all excellent. The right way is to eliminate all faults, not to discount them by means of a few excellencies. An excellence never looks well hitched up with a fault.

The essentials of a properly arranged discourse, which includes the sermon in its front rank, are three, 1) Unity; 2) Organization; 3) Progress.

1. *Unity.* — While nearly all are agreed that this is the very first essential requirement of a well arranged sermon, there is considerable difficulty about settling definitely what really constitutes unity. Of course, it is not duality — an easy thing to poke fun at, as some have done. But what then is it?

The trouble again lies with the conception of the sermon. We have instanced four types of sermons from the structural point of view, 1) the topical sermon treating several sides of a subject; 2) the essay style of sermon with sub-heads for different sections; 3) the theme sermon with loosely arranged parts; and 4) the theme sermon with strictly arranged parts. Now it will be almost impossible to define sermon unity and cover all these types of sermons. For the first three types the idea of unity would have to be stretched, while for the last type the idea of unity would have to be employed in a strict sense. This, however, is only another way of saying that there are sermon types, the very structural nature of which shows that they lack the very first essential of a properly arranged discourse. So we decline to define unity in a way that might apply to all these sermon types.

There is no real unity when merely several sides of a subject are elaborated, such as the preacher may happen to choose at the time.

There is no genuine unity in an essay-sermon with a number of interesting sub-heads for the sections of thought that have been selected.

Nor is there a unity when a theme is treated under parts that merely tell us more or less of what is in that theme.

We can speak of real unity only when a theme is divided into its component parts. Putting it in the simplest way, unity is, 1) that there is *one thing*, the one named by the theme; 2) *all the parts* of that one thing, each in its place, none missing. A sermon of this type is a unit in the true sense of the word.

When homileticians speak of a secondary unity, one of *aim* and of *tone*, this is not another kind of unity, but really only a natural feature of the essential unity of a sermon. Take as an illustration a dining table. It is made to place dishes and food on, for us to sit at and to eat from. That is its purpose or *aim*. It has legs, an upper frame, and a flat top. These are the parts. They harmonize in regard to the aim. They are thus one in *tone*, though each part is different from the other. Every sermon with essential unity *aims* at one great purpose, for it is one sermon, not two sermonettes, or more. Its natural parts are all there, and all agree, though quite different from one another. Aiming to accomplish one thing, their *tone* naturally is one.

When a sermon has essential unity we need not fear that one portion of it will point in one direction, and another portion in a different direction. Divergent aims only show that there is no real unity. So with the one tone. It is there if the unity is there. If there are diverse tones, say only two, the sermon has no unity whatever.

2. *Organization.* — Unity and organization are really quite closely allied. Unity calls for one thing, the whole of it, and all its parts in place. Organization looks at the thing from the other side — there are certain component parts, and these must be properly fitted together, so as to accomplish one definite result.

Organization requires much more than mere order. The alphabet is an example of order, so are the numerals one, two, three, etc., but neither is an organization. A filing system is intended merely for an orderly arrangement of a variety of documents, facilitating immediate access to any one of them. There is no limit to the compartments it may have.

In organization there is a controlling principle. For the sermon this is embodied in the theme. This principle dominates all the parts. It allows only such parts as are vital to the principle, and demands rejection of all extraneous material, however valuable and attractive it may be in itself. When building an arch the idea of the arch controls. Only such stones are selected as will fit this particular arch. All other stones, no matter how fine, are rejected.

Secondly, the controlling principle combines the material or parts so that each piece gets the position that best helps to express that principle. Not only must all the necessary pieces be there, each one of them must also be put exactly where it belongs. It is the controlling principle which decides the place of each piece. Take an army on a grand parade, infantry, artillery, cavalry, and all the rest of it. All that is required is an unbroken line. Whether there are more or less regiments, etc., makes no difference. Which are in the van, which in the rear is quite immaterial. All that is wanted is order. An army in battle array is quite a different thing. There is a plan of attack — the controlling principle. In closest accord with that plan there are just so many troops of each kind, and every detachment has its particular place. It makes all the difference in the world which troops are in the front line, which are in the rear; where the artillery is placed, where the reserves are stationed, etc., etc. Here we see the army as an organization. The sermon is not a review of troops, but a battle carried to victory.

Here is a very simple illustration of order:

You may have as many more of these triangles as you please, for there is no control. A sermon with its material thus arranged lacks organization.

Here is a first step in organization:

Only four triangles can be used in this design, not five, not three. They are combined in a certain way, and no other way will do. Yet even so the idea of organization is incomplete, for the design would be perfect, no matter which of the four triangles is at the top, at the bottom, or at one of the sides. But take a tree with 1) its roots; 2) its trunk; 3) its branches.

None of these three could be interchanged. The roots must be in the ground, the trunk rising out of it, the branches radiating at the top. This is complete organization.

In reality organization goes still farther. The controlling principle dominates even the sub-parts of a sermon, both as to what they shall be, and just where each shall be placed.

Stating thus what organization is may leave the impression that it is a difficult thing to achieve in a sermon. Quite the contrary. Find a proper theme, and the parts of the sermon will in all probability organize themselves under its control. Of course, having only a subject or topic, a key thought or a striking expression, or even a theme minus the knowledge of what it really stands for, anything like proper organization will be either out of the question entirely, or filled with difficulties too great to be overcome in a satisfactory way.

Lack of organization makes for ineffective sermons. Parts that are only little trains of thought placed one after the other cannot make a strong sermon. People, too, are not to feel that they are again and again coming to a point, and then running back to do it all over again in a little different way, finally calling it finished. They are to realize that they are filling in a set of angles, the last one closing and completing the design. Or, using another illustration, they are to see the house from cellar to attic and come away with a distinct picture of the accommodations it affords.

3. *Progress*. — The sermon is movement. From the address, "Dear Friends" to the close with "Amen"

there is no halt. But this is only because speech is movement. Progress connotes a goal. Every step in the direction of that goal is progress. Aimless or desultory walking around is movement well enough, but it certainly cannot be called progress.

The goal is set, either openly or by implication, in the theme. With unity in the theme and the sermon there will, of course, be but one goal. It amounts to the same thing when we say that the controlling principle in organization sets the goal. That principle is expressed in the theme and reaches clear through the sermon, and naturally will be only one, not two or more. So the goal demanded by progress is furnished already by the unity and the organization.

Progress then is the thought movement that climbs to the goal set in the theme. The parts are the stages of approach. Yet each one of them is within sight of the goal, and thus vivid with interest. It is somewhat like climbing a mountain. In the introduction we leave the foothills; then we go on up over the first great rise, over the next, till finally we come to the very top, where, of course, we may linger a little in the last sermon part or in the conclusion. That which made the climbing so attractive was that we had a view of the peak from the very start and at every stage of the journey. Reaching the peak is the climax of the pleasure in seeing it from below.

Several things should now be clear. To withhold the theme from our hearers is like refusing to tell what the goal is. It is a psychologic mistake, though some think it a piece of sermon wisdom, and practice it as such. Using mysterious expressions for the goal is only one form of this mistake. There are curious persons who will wonder what the preacher is really headed for when he couches his theme in words of mystery. But curiosity is at best a low motive for attention. It is effective in novels, not in discourses and sermons, that deal with really serious personal matters. When you and I are asked to take a journey, about the first thing we want to know is the destination. If that is not revealed, or if we cannot safely surmise it, we will refuse to go along. But if the destination is some highly attractive place, we will be keen to go and enjoy every step of the way. Just going around in a circle, even though it be a circle of thought, is no pleasure. So also swinging like a pendulum becomes monotonous almost from the start. Running off on side-roads is another mistake. Who cares for side-roads when the goal of our excursion is climbing to the top? The worst of all is not to get to the attractive destination we expected to reach at all, but to be left stranded somewhere on the road, or to land at some other place. It leaves a bad effect on the hearer when the sermon sends him away disappointed.

As with organization, progress is easy to attain. Determine exactly where you are going, then go there — and the feat is accomplished. Choose a highly desirable goal and move straight toward it — and your sermon will be good. One secret is that your goal must be specific. One may say he intends to climb the Rocky Mountains, but that is too indefinite a proposition. Take one peak; there is not time and strength enough to ramble over the entire mighty range. Even when you are specific, be specific enough. The Glory of Christ is a grand subject, but not specific enough. You will be able to treat in a sermon only one or the other side of His glory, as for instance the glory of His death, or of His suffering.

### III.   The Text and the Essentials of the Sermon.

Perhaps very soon in his meditation on the text the preacher will begin to seek for a proper theme and for the main points of an outline, by means of which to unfold in a telling sermon what the text contains.   He is bound to face this task, at least by the time his study of the text is well advanced.   He must seek in his text for a sermon unity with organized parts progressing to a goal.   What will he be likely to meet?

1.   In a good many cases he will find what he seeks without special difficulty.   The text, being a unity itself, presents this unity for the sermon.   At first the preacher may catch only the general idea of this unity, when he asks the text what the main thing is that it has to say.   The main parts under that unity also appear.   Theme thought and parts appear simultaneously, or nearly so, and the point of the theme, the goal of the sermon, together with the course that must be traveled to reach that goal, is clear to the preacher's mind.   This is always a happy situation.   All that is left to be done is the work of formulation, namely filing the outline with skill and patience into the most perfect form.   With all the basic ideas ready to hand this seldom takes long.

Having occasion to preach on the work of the ministry as a calling inviting young men, the author chose Matth. 28, 19-20 as a text.   The theme thought was at once apparent, namely the work of making disciples.   So also the parts — 1) a work in the highest sense Christ's own; 2) to be performed with His own means; 3) for saving immortal souls; 4) assured of success by the Lord Himself. Culminating in the last part, but already apparent in all the other parts, as they stood in the rough, was the idea of the attractiveness of this work. It was easy to put into simple form.

**The Greatest Work in the World,** as such forever attractive to us all, and especially to those who may have a leading part in it. Think of its greatness in connection with

I. *Its heavenly Founder.*
II. *Its divine means.*
III. *Its assured results.*
IV. *Your own blessed part in it.*

2. But sometimes *the multiplicity* lies, as it were, on the surface, while the dominant unity seems to be hidden, and the controlling principle is not apparent. In a case like this the natural way is to evolve the unity from the multiplicity, by organizing the varied thoughts. This may take some time. It is usually achieved by intensive meditation on the parts that lie open in the text, combining them in a natural way and then seeking to express as exactly as possible what the combination really signifies.

The old pericope text, Luke 15, 1-10, with its two parables, is a text of this type. At first one may be tempted to divide it horizontally, 1) Jesus seeking the lost sheep, 2) the woman seeking the lost coin. Presently one sees that in both parables there is 1) the lost, 2) the seeking, 3) the finding, and 4) the rejoicing — four distinct and cumulative parts, the order of which also cannot be changed. One feels, too, that there is a unity, but what is it? A look at the next parable, the Prodigal Son, helps. In this third parable Jesus illustrates what happens *in* the lost sinner's heart when he is found. In the first two parables He illustrates what is done *for* the sinner in order that he may be found or saved. This is the unity of the text. Now the preacher may proceed to organize and formulate. Here is an effort along that line.

**No Wonder There is Joy in the Presence of the Angels of God!**

I. *Think of the love that goes out to the lost!*

II. *Consider the effort that is put into the search!*

III. *Appreciate the success that marks the finding!*

IV. *Then join in the joy and praise that resounds in heaven!*

3. Sometimes *the unity* in a text stands forth quite distinctly, but the multiplicity into which this unity naturally divides is at first not at all apparent. The temptation usually is to take the unity thus presented, and to divide it abstractly and independently of the text. Those who are ready to preach topical sermons will be satisfied with this procedure. There are always a few general things that may be said on any Biblical unit idea. But a sermon of this kind does not stick to the text, to say nothing about exhausting the text and adapting it adequately to the hearers. In other words, getting only a unity out of the text results in a sermon of inferior type.

The problem presented by a text which seems to have only an outstanding unity, is to find the necessary multiplicity for a genuine division and organization. This problem calls for analysis of what lies hidden in the text. Dig into the text, study all its details, lay it out before you piece by piece. Even a short text will reveal great and weighty concepts, which, if the unity has been properly apprehended, are bound to split that unity into component parts.

Acts 21, 8-14 has a plain unity, which even the text itself states in the words, **"The will of the Lord be done!"** But how about a division of this theme? There seems to be nothing that readily meets the eye. Eventually these division thoughts emerge: Submitting to the Lord's will means 1) that we give up all self-will. One kind of self-will is described in the text, Paul's friends dissuading him from going up to Jerusalem. Submitting to the Lord's will means 2) that we put our full trust in the Lord. And Paul himself is the example in the text, ready not only to go up to Jerusalem, but also to die there if it be the Lord's will. Really submitting to the Lord's will means 3) that we find in him true comfort and support. We see this in Paul's friends, at first grief-stricken, at last comforted and sustained, realizing that the Lord's will is best. This should make an effective sermon.

John 14, 21-24 evidently deals with love for the Lord — the unity of the text is plain. In working out the sermon it was found necessary to concentrate on the main concepts in the text, namely ἀγάπη, the love of comprehension and purpose (not of mere liking); λόγος, His meaning or revelation, and λόγοι, the different parts of His revelation; ἐντολαί, the Gospel behests (not the law of Moses); τηρεῖν, keeping, in the sense of guarding. This study of the concepts helped to produce the following outline.

### Lovers of the Lord.

We all want to be called that. When are we truly our Lord's lovers? We are His lovers when, first of all, we realize what He means by *love*, namely a comprehension of His person and His work, and a purpose to embrace both. Secondly, when we realize what He means by connecting His love with His *Word*, by which He comes and reveals Himself to us, namely His "behests" (commandments), and His teachings (sayings, λόγοι). Thirdly, when we realize what He means by *keeping* His Word, etc., namely guarding it against any perversion, and guarding it by fully believing and obeying. Fourthly, when we realize *the conclusions* to be drawn from all this. Where the Lord says "he" write your own name, and then let all those who do this see that they are one body. This is our spiritual union. Those who keep not His "sayings" disrupt the union. Here then lies the healing of our diseases, etc. Repentance for lack of this love, and strengthening of our love for Him, for His Word, for keeping it inviolate. Blessed are such lovers of our Lord! — The sermon was addressed to a general convention of the church when disunion disturbed it and empty treasuries hampered it.

4. Most troublesome of all are texts in which *the unity and only a part of the necessary multiplicity* appear. It is vexing to lack an important piece for completing a pattern of thought. What will you do when you have all the parts of a beautiful chair before you except two of the legs, or except a leg and a piece of the back?

Perhaps the missing pieces are there, only the preacher has not found them. More study, with close analysis, will usually tell. If, however, the missing parts cannot be found, then there is only one alternative — give up the partial multiplicity that lies on the surface, and seek a different division.

A case in point is Luke 15, 11-32, the parable of the Prodigal Son and his Brother. It is easy to divide and organize the story of the younger son. The preacher may tell **The Story of the Prodigal.** There are three plain chapters, 1) Here is sin in its wretchedness; 2) Here is repentance in its sincerity; 3) Here is grace with its fulness of comfort. But how shall we bring in the older brother? We cannot complete the pattern we have begun; it is already complete, the addition would only mar it. There is only one thing to do — we must drop the three parts we have made, and try something entirely different. Here is a solution:

**The Parable of the Two Sons that were Lost.**

I. *The son who left and returned.*
II. *The son who remained and would not come in.*
III. *The father who opened his heart to both.*

Another solution would be to put the father into the theme, and show how he treated the two sons (two types of sinners — the openly wicked; the secretly self-righteous).

### THIRD CHAPTER

## ANALYSIS.

### Introductory

There is a wide range in outlines. To be well equipped for his pulpit work the preacher ought to be thoroughly acquainted with the possibilities offered in this part of his work.

Variety has been called the spice of life. *Variety* is a good homiletical principle. If there are a half dozen excellent ways of doing a thing, it would be folly to repeat endlessly only one of these six ways. Homiletical narrowness is inferior. A violin has four strings. It is true, a good violinist can play a fine piece of music all on one string, or only on two. But if in forty or fifty years of playing he would confine himself to just one or two strings, he certainly would not be called a master of his instrument. Yet there are preachers, even homiletical teachers, who build all their sermon houses after one stereotyped pattern. They may attain great excellency in handling this one pattern, but they can certainly not claim mastery in their work.

In advocating variety we, of course, do not mean that the preacher should use an excellent way, and then vary this by using an inferior way. Apples of all grades are sold on the market, the prices varying accordingly. The variety in sermons we have in mind is not of this type. We want no mixture of sermons, some excellent in structure, some medium, and some faulty. All our sermon fruit is to be of the highest grade. There are varieties of apples. We want them all, but only the highest grade of each variety. So with sermons. We want all the types worth having, and for each type the most perfect outline attainable.

An excellent teacher of Homiletics, the author of a good book on the subject, issued a volume of Old Testament sermons — every sermon with exactly three parts. How he did that is a mystery. Another teacher of Homiletics, also the author of a work on the subject, confessed that he preached only analytic and no synthetic sermons. This, too, is strange. Nevertheless, variety is unquestionably better. This principle applies in various ways. It breaks up what might be called homiletical traditionalism. It is merely traditionalism to use only two or three parts in every sermon. Let us have more parts occasionally as texts afford opportunity. It is traditionalism to cut up a text into two or three parts, and then to preach on each piece consecutively. It is traditionalism to announce every text in the same way; to use the same versicle after the reading of the text; to use the identical form of addressing the hearers; to use only one set of gestures; to end every sermon by recapitulation; etc. A certain preacher used "my beloved hearers" thirty-two times in a sermon — one of his members made the count. Another employed "brethren" with almost equal frequency. The author was caught overworking the adjective "excellent." Another always braced himself with his hands on both sides of the pulpit near the Bible, when he read the text. Still another prostrated himself in prayer on the Bible before reading the text. And one kept making a spasmodic gesture with his right arm during the entire sermon, raising the forearm, with fingers clenched, from the pulpit frame to his mid-body. These are mannerisms. All offend against the principle of natural and attractive variety.

There are *three first-class types of outlines*, the analytic type, the synthetic type, and the homily.

All three are "textual," as over against "topical"; likewise all three are "expository." They all stick to the text, exhaust it, and adapt it. No other types measure up to these three. While this statement will be disputed, perhaps violently assailed, the author would not for a moment consider modifying it.

The question is not one of mere taste, it is one that goes far deeper. It is not one of dialectics, style, or eloquence, for all of these find the maximum of room in the types of outlines here to be presented. These types are superior, because they utilize the text in ways unequalled by any other types. It is in vain to dispute the fact. As to form, these types are of a higher class in every way than any other types ever produced. Finally, as regards effect on the hearer, these types are more telling, spiritually more penetrating and satisfying, than the other types. Therefore we abide by these three. It is the one duty of Homiletics to show the things that are genuinely better. If, like Socrates of old, it be accused nevertheless of presenting the worse as the better, like that old philosopher Homiletics must remain true to itself, win its disciples, a Plato for instance, and others, and having done its duty, rest content with that.

## Analytic Outlines.

There are two vital features which distinguish an analytical outline.

The first is, that the unity of the text is made the unity of the sermon. Summarize the text, and sum up the sermon — the two sums are identical in an analytical sermon. The outline, of course, is merely the framework of the sermon. In the sermon the unity derived from the text is expressed in the theme.

The second distinguishing feature of an analytical outline is, that the parts of the text which constitute its unity are used in the same way and in the same order to constitute the parts of the sermon under the theme.

Suppose that a text contains three main thoughts. Their sum is the theme of the sermon. And the three main thoughts in the text form the three parts of the sermon, each thought formulated accordingly.

This type of outline is always *simple*. Its very simplicity is its strength and effectiveness. This ought to be strongly emphasized. The grandest works of architecture are adjudged to be such because of the simplicity of their lines. This is true of all works of art, painting, music, poetry, etc. Perfection is lost as simplicity disappears beneath ornate complexity and intricacy of design.

This type of outline is *natural*, devoid of anything artificial. We need hardly say that this is an attractive virtue. Naturalness is always preferable to artificiality. Here again there is strength.

The analytical outline is *strictly textual*, in the sense that it takes the text as it is and in that way impresses it upon the hearer. Some may be curious to hear what "the preacher" has to say, how he stands on a question, what he will make of a situation. It is vastly better for the hearer, as well as for the preacher, to have the former desire to know what "the text" has to say, how the Word answers a question, or sheds light on a situation. The preacher is safest behind the fortress of his text, not when he steps outside of it into ideas or argumentations of his own, and certainly not when he roams far from his text.

The analytical outline is *logical*. It puts two and two together, and we all see that this makes four. By its very structure this form of outline holds the preacher to the point. If he should stray none the less, the text is there to show that he is straying, and the hearer knows it, or ought to know. There is great force in the logic of texts. Spiritual men always bow to it.

One of the best advantages in outlines of this kind is that they are *easy* to construct. Probably this is the reason why they are so popular with preachers. Of course, a virtue can be overdone. Not every text can be treated analytically, and some that might be so treated yield better results when handled synthetically. Because analytical outlines are the easiest to build they are usually recommended to beginners. In seminary work they are the student's first task. When properly worked out, sermons with analytical outlines are always acceptable to the hearer, and can be made as effective as any other form of sermon, and with less effort. They are easy to carry away and to remember, a virtue by no means to be despised.

There are various

## Ways of Constructing an Analytical Outline.

Everything depends on the contents of the text.

1. A text may contain a number of *primary, coordinate subjects.*

Example Matth. 13, 31-35.

### The Kingdom of Heaven in its Wonderful Power.

I. *Like a grain of mustard-seed in the field.* (Open and visible power.)
II. *Like a handful of leaven in three measures of meal.* (Secret and hidden power.)

Another example, Luke 15, 11-24.

### How the Sinner Comes into the Kingdom.

Simply tell the story chapter by chapter as furnished by the text in order.

I. *The folly of the sinner.*
II. *The deception of the world.*
III. *The sensibleness of repentance.*
IV. *The blessedness of pardon.*
V. *The joy of reception.*

Let us add a more extended example. Jeremiah 31, 31-34, undoubtedly deals with The New Covenant. This, however, is only a bare subject, and not yet a theme. We get a simple theme when we note that we have before us **Jeremiah's Description of the New Covenant.** The idea of a "description" naturally calls for a presentation of the main features or marks of this covenant. These are exactly what the prophet furnishes us. All we need to do is to elucidate them in due order. This New Covenant

I. *Differs from the old;*
II. *Is wholly inward;*
III. *Furnishes knowledge to all;*
IV. *Rests on the Lord's forgiveness.*

We may file this into better form. Since the first point is general we may weave it into the other three. Jeremiah tells us that

### The New Covenant Will be Graced in a Superior Way

by
I. *Holiness;*
II. *Knowledge;*
III. *Pardon.*

Thus the three primary and coordinate subjects in the text, under their natural unity, become the three parts of an analytical sermon. The goal of the sermon is the need of the hearers to realize what they possess and enjoy in the New Covenant in which they now live. The sermon should attract those who are still outside this Covenant, and make those who are in it cling more firmly and joyfully to this Covenant.

2. A text may contain two or more *genera* suitable for sermon parts.

Example, Matth. 6, 24-34, Christ telling us not to be anxious for earthly things (one genus), but to be concerned about the kingdom of heaven (another genus).

### The Lord's Admonition in Regard to Our Chief Concern in Life.

I. *He warns us not to make earthly things our chief concern;*
II. *He bids us seek first of all the Kingdom of God.*

This outline is not a model, but only an elementary illustration of a division of the genera in a text. After a satisfactory rough cast is made, the work of filing it into better shape begins.

3. A text may also contain a number of *species* suitable for analysis.

Example, 2 Pet. 1, 3-8,

### The Things That Are Necessary to Life and Godliness.

I. *Add to faith — virtue;*
II. *To virtue — knowledge;*

   III.   *To  knowledge — temperance;*
   IV.   *To  temperance — patience;*
    V.   *To  patience — godliness;*
   VI.   *To  godliness — brotherly kindness;*
 VII.   *To  brotherly kindness — charity.*

It is much better to use these seven parts presented by the text itself, than to try for two or three parts, just because the smaller number of parts is more usual (traditional). The more main parts, the fewer sub-parts.

    4. Analysis may use *the arguments* in a text when these are sufficiently prominent. We have discussed the question of arguments. Some arguments are open, some are masked. Texts which may be treated analytically because of the arguments they present, can usually be made to answer the question, Why? And the reasons drawn from the text can be made to begin with, Because.

    Take Psalm 1, Why is the godly man who shuns the wicked and clings to God's Word blessed? Two answers lie on the surface, 1) He is like the tree, etc.; 2) He is not like the chaff. This is a rough statement, merely showing that the text contains divisible arguments or reasons. Moreover, we have done no more than put the negative reason beside the positive one, which is a low type of division. A positive formulation would be better. Also, we do not need to keep the formal "why" and "because" (unless we wish to do so); we may simply imply them. Here is an example.

### The Blessedness of the Godly Man.

In reality we are asking, Why is he blessed? The text gives three positive reasons.

     I.  *He is blessed through the Lord's Word.*
    II.  *He is blessed with the Lord's prosperity.*
   III.  *He is blessed by the Lord's acknowledgment in the*
               *Lord's judgment.*

Of course, we might begin each part with "because," provided we put "why" into the theme,

> I. *Because of the Lord's Word;*
> II. *Because of the Lord's gift of prosperity;*
> III. *Because of the Lord's acknowledgment.*

Another example is Matth. 5, 3-12, where after each beatitude, there follows a formal "for" stating the reason.

Some texts simply imply arguments or reason. Studious meditation brings these arguments to the preacher's mind. Again, he has the alternative of formally stating the reasons, or of omitting the formal "why" and "because." Example, Ps. 75, 4-7.

### The Blessedness of True Humility.

In substance this theme asks why humility is so desirable. Four reasons may be drawn from the text. Humility

> I. *Frees from the senselessness of pride.*
> That is certainly worth a great deal.
> II. *Places into the right attitude toward God.*
> That is always the vital thing.
> III. *Faces with courage all who are proud.*
> Warning them in no uncertain way.
> IV. *Is crowned and honored by God.*
> This exceeds all that pride could possibly secure.

6. There are *other features* which invite analytical treatment, such as the truths in a text, the doctrines, the pictures or illustrations, etc. If the text is a story, we may find the chapters in that story and readily use them as analytical parts.

Example on the doctrines, Jer. 23, 16-19.

### How to Use the Great Doctrines of the Lord for the Protection of Our Souls.

> I. *The doctrine of divine Inspiration.*
> II. *The doctrine of the divine Wrath.*
> III. *The doctrine of the divine Omnipresence.*
> IV. *The doctrine of the divine power of the Word.*

Example on the illustrations used in a text, Ps. 23, 1) The sheep resting in perfect peace; 2) The traveler on the right road and safe even in danger; 3) The banquet guest feasting in undisturbed joy; 4) The life led by goodness and mercy up into the Lord's house. The theme will have this substance, David pictures his own blessed life in the Lord's care. The preacher should have little difficulty in dressing down this analytical material.

Stories are always interesting, and yield easily to analytical treatment. Example, Acts 9, 36-43.

### The Little History of Dorcas, the Dressmaker.

  I. *Her heart was filled with faith.*
  II. *Her eyes were open to the need about her.*
  III. *Her hands were diligent in works of love.*
  IV. *Her work was highly appreciated by the church.*
  V. *Her whole life was signally approved by God*
      (namely by raising her from the dead).

7. There is one more type of analytical treatment that deserves special mention. Instead of drawing the analytical parts for the division from the text as such, *the analysis is superimposed on the central thought of the text,* but always in harmony with all that the text says, and often employing hints or directives in a text.

Example, Job 14, 1-5. Job voices the great truth that our life is short and troubled. But he misuses this truth to murmur against God. This leads us to inquire on our own part concerning this truth.

### The Great Truth:
### That Man is of Few Days and Full of Trouble.

  I. *We must know it well.*
  II. *We must not use it to justify ourselves.*
  III. *We must let it lead us to God's grace and mercy.*

We thus take the great truth and tell analytically what we ought to do with it.

Take Luke 10, 38-42, on the One Thing that is Needful. Instead of trying to analyze this One Thing, we analyze what we ought to do about it, namely 1) Know it fully; 2) Seek it simply; 3) Grasp it firmly. We are thus not attempting to divide anything in the text itself, although in the elaboration (not in the division) we may freely refer to Martha, Mary, and Jesus. Our analysis is super-imposed.

The thing may be done in another way, by centering on the One Thing Needful, and asking

### What is the One Thing Needful?

We have very little in the text itself, and therefore use an analysis of our own.

    I. *God's Word — not our work.*
    II. *God's grace — not our merit.*
    III. *God's gift — not our giving.*

In treating short texts an analysis of our own is often very helpful. This is not done in an abstract way, but with a view to our hearers. Thus, Rev. 22, 11-14, for a funeral.

### Hear the Word of Christ, Who is Alpha and Omega, the First and the Last: Behold, I Come Quicky!

    I. *Recognize and feel His greatness!*
    II. *Note and take to heart His warning!*
    III. *Appreciate and taste the sweetness of His promise!*

## FOURTH CHAPTER

## SYNTHESIS.

There is more confusion about synthetic outlines than about any other type. Even writers on homiletics at times are in doubt just how they are to be constructed. Young preachers thus go out from the seminary inadequately equipped in regard to this part of their work, and often never discover what synthesis is. Yet there are texts which can be treated satisfactorily only by means of synthesis; and many texts that might be handled analytically could be made more effective by means of synthesis.

What is the synthetic treatment of the text? Let us begin with

### I. The Simplest Form of Synthesis.

In a purely analytical outline the coordinate parts of a text are used in their original order as parts also for the sermon. It is the simplest form of synthesis to change this text-order. Suppose a text presents three coordinate thoughts, A, B, and C. The analytic outline takes these three thoughts and converts them into sermon parts, leaving their order, A, B, and C. But there may be a good reason for a different order in the sermon. The preacher is free to make a change, for instance C, B, A; or C, A, B; or any other. The moment he does this he has taken the first step in synthesis.

Example, Jer. 31, 31-34, **"Jeremiah's Description of the New Covenant."** Jeremiah tells us that the new covenant will be graced in a superior way by I Holiness; II Knowledge; III Pardon. This division is purely analytical, because the three thoughts are presented in the text itself in this order. But as the preacher studies these parts he begins to see that in the experience of the Christian the order is different. So he rearranges, **The New Covenant Blesses Us in a Superior Way** I With light; II With pardon; III With a new life (holiness). Or he may prefer this order, Jeremiah tells us that the new covenant I Delivers our souls (pardon, or justification); II enlightens our minds (illumination); III Directs and controls our hearts (sanctification, holiness). It is the simplest form of synthesis to make transpositions like these. When this is done there may also be changes in formulation, as we have indicated in this example.

Some writers on homiletics prefer to call such rearrangements of the coordinate parts of a text in the construction of a sermon, analytical-synthetical outlines. It seems better to use a designation like ours, namely the simplest form of synthesis, for this is exactly what it is. Only the parts are rearranged in a new logical order. The substance of the theme and of the parts is left unchanged, although in the rearrangement their formulation may be altered. — But synthesis may go a step farther.

## II.   The Intermediate Form of Synthesis.

The second type of synthesis still deals with the coordinate parts of the text, but now it alters the theme. As the preacher contemplates the great thoughts of the text, one of them rises above the rest, and this he converts into a theme. The rest of the thoughts he arranges in order under this theme.

Let us take the same text, Jer. 31, 31-34, and the same basic text thoughts 1) holiness; 2) knowledge; 3) pardon.

We drop the theme, "Jeremiah's Description of the New Covenant." Instead, we use the second thought in the text, namely knowledge, as the theme. We make the theme, "The Blessedness of Really Knowing the Lord." That leaves us two main text thoughts for the sermon parts, namely 1) holiness; 2) pardon. We use them as the parts of the sermon.

### The Blessedness of Really Knowing the Lord.

*I. Knowing by our own experience his pardoning grace.*
*II. Tasting by our own experience the excellence of his ways.*

Part one deals with pardon, yet in this arrangement with the experimental knowledge of pardon. Part two deals with holiness, but now with our experimental knowledge of this holiness, namely the excellence of the Lord's holy ways.

Thus any one of the three great text thoughts in Jer. 31, 31-34 may be elevated in the theme. Take the last, pardon.

### Our Supreme Treasure — The Forgiveness of Sins.

*I. Think of its value!*
*II. Appreciate its fruits!*

When we think of its value, we have the right knowledge (the second text-thought). When we appreciate its fruits we have holiness (the first text thought).

Now let us elevate the first great part of the text into a theme, namely holiness. Introduction of the sermon: What is wrong with the world of men to-day? Their hearts are devoid of God's law, their inward parts are rotten with sin. They know not what holiness means. What is the cure?

### I Will Put My Law in Their Inward Parts.

That means,

*I. By His pardoning grace God frees us from the curse of sin.*
*II. By His sanctifying grace God makes us to know His will.*

The idea of holiness is used in the theme (first text thought). The idea of pardon forms part one (third text thought).

The idea of experimental knowledge is used in part two (second text thought).

In all this work of outlining there must, of course, be flexibility of formulation. In other words, the preacher must be able easily to word his thought, so that theme and parts are expressed naturally and put into proper relation to each other. — We now proceed to

### III.   The Advanced Form of Synthesis.

In the simple and the intermediate forms of synthesis we operate with the coordinate text thoughts in building the outline, just as we do in analysis. We do one thing with these coordinate text thoughts in the analytical outline; another thing in the simplest form of synthesis; and still another thing in the intermediate form of synthesis. Now in advanced synthesis we go beyond the main coordinate text thoughts.

The first step is to *take apart all the thoughts in the text*. They may be major or minor thoughts, it makes no difference, coordinate or subordinate. Put them side by side. Make a catalog of them. The number does not matter, and the order in which they occur is immaterial. We simply want all the thoughts in the text so that we can easily survey them in their totality.

The second step is to *synthesize the text thoughts* which we have discovered. Take the list before you, and let your mind dwell on it as intensely as possible. Pay no attention to the unity of the text, as one must do in striving for an analytical outline. The unity you need for the sermon will take care of itself. Presently, when the intense meditation on the list of thoughts has gone far enough, something that we might call crystallization takes place. The thoughts listed will combine in a new way to form a new pattern with a new unit idea underlying this pattern. Sometimes this crystallization takes place as in a flash. It is like a gift from above. Sometimes it comes slowly, after prolonged effort. At first one or the other inferior or faulty rearrangement may come to mind, only to be discarded because on further meditation it appears inferior or faulty. Patience and perseverance are necessary. In the end the goal will be reached, and even the efforts that brought no definite results at first will net helpful points.

It is evident at once that this advanced form of synthetic outline building is more *difficult* than constructing analytic outlines. It takes more brains. On the other hand, all forms of synthesis vastly *increase the variety of sermon types,* and thus greatly enrich the pulpit. There is really no end to the variety of sermon structures which may be attained by means of synthesis. Here is *room for homiletical skill,* calling forth the best that is in the preacher. A man of parts will hardly content himself with repeating endlessly the fixed and rather stereotyped pattern of bare analysis. Synthesis holds out to him ideals that grow and constantly beckon to his skill.

Yet synthesis is just as exact as analysis, only in another way. It uses the thoughts of the text, and thus builds as truly on the text as does analysis, only the structures are different and generally more beautiful. Thus synthesis is just as *textual* as analysis.

Real synthesis, just like analysis, operates only with the material in the text, not with anything added

to the text from the outside. It is a false definition
of homiletical synthesis to think that it consists in
combining the text with something that lies outside
of it. Any aversion to synthetical outlines, based on
this idea of the process involved, is a serious mistake,
an error in judgment.

We all use texts for some specific occasion or case,
a dedication, a funeral, etc. Thus to combine a case
with a text, shaping the outline accordingly, is not
what we mean by synthesis. For we can preach an
analytical sermon for any given case or occasion, just
as well as one that is built synthetically. It would
be wholly wrong to call all casual sermons (those intended for a case or an occasion) synthetical.

Advanced synthesis is rather more difficult to explain
theoretically than to work out practically. Here, too, examples
are better than mere precept. Deut. 18, 15-19 will not submit
to analytical treatment, for the simple reason that this text
cannot be divided into consecutive coordinate parts, — there
are no such parts. The substance of verse 15 and verses 18-19
is identical; and verses 16-17 contain only a subordinate historical reference. Anything resembling an analytical treatment,
i. e. a division of the text into coordinate consecutive parts,
would thus be arbitrary and abnormal. Even to superimpose
an analysis upon the central thought of the text would be a
useless attempt. Synthesis alone offers the solution.

We therefore take the text apart. It contains the following thoughts:

1. When the covenant was made on Sinai Israel asked
   for a mediator.
2. God commended that and made Moses the mediator
   of the covenant.
3. Thus Moses came to excel all the other prophets
   Lsrael afterwards had.

4. God saw farther than Israel. He looked to the new covenant, and thus promised a still greater Prophet and Mediator than Moses.
5. This was to be God's Son, yet of Israel's brethren.
6. In His office He was to resemble Moses, and yet to exceed him.
7. He was to bring Israel the supreme revelation.
8. This consists of God's own words — what He shall order Jesus to say — all that is spoken in the Lord's name.
9. In a supreme way this requires faith — "unto Him ye shall hearken."
10. The warning and threat against unbelief are equally strong — "Whosoever will not hearken," etc.

This is the timber — what shall we build out of it? In other words, how shall we synthesize, recombine in a new logical plan under a theme covering this material? We must meditate and concentrate the mind on what lies before us. Presently from our contemplation there rises the thought of *a grand resemblance between Moses and Christ.* We find, on trial, that under this controlling idea all the ten thoughts of the text can be arranged by combining those that are related. A little further consideration shows that in this resemblance *Christ is by far the greater.* The rest is easy, mostly a little skill in formulation to get the best form.

### Moses Reflects the Greatness of Jesus.

   *I. Both transmit covenants — Jesus the final one.*
  *II. Both convey revelations — Jesus the highest.*
 *III. Both are made mediators — Jesus the supreme one.*
 *IV. Both deserve faith — Jesus most of all.*

The study of the text thoughts may, however, take a different turn. It all depends on the preacher's keenness of mind and spiritual versatility, also on his perception of what material in the text may fit the need of his hearers. As his mind dwells on the thoughts in the text, he may be struck by a vision of the *doctrines* embedded in it. So he scans his

text closely to see whether he can treat it from this angle.
Here is the result:

**When God Promised the Prophet Like Unto Moses He Revealed
the Great Doctrines of Salvation.**

    *I.   The Virgin Birth.*
    *II.  Divine Inspiration.*
    *III. Atoning Mediation.*
    *IV. Justifying Faith.*
    *V.  Final Judgment.*

The order of the doctrines is the preacher's own, simply a
logical onet. Part one rests on the word "of thy brethren."
Part two on " will put my words in his mouth." There would
be no sense in doing this if the Lord's words would not be
preserved most exactly for all generations. Part three rests
on the words "Prophet like unto thee," i. e. Mediator-Prophet.
Parts four and five are obvious. When the Final Judgment is
reached the circle of doctrines is definitely closed. — The illustrations herewith presented on Deut. 18, 15-19 do not by any
means exhaust the possibilities of advanced synthesis on this
text. With ten or more thoughts in a text, some of them of
greatest weight, different preachers adept in synthesis will be
able to construct a goodly number of most excellent synthetical
sermons.

## IV.  The Highest Form of Synthesis.

The mechanical part of the operation in this type
of synthesis is the same as in the advanced type. The
text thoughts are listed as completely as possible and
subjected to intense meditation, more or less prolonged
as the case may be.

But now the truth, or truths, of the text are visual-
ized from some pronounced angle of present need.
What is in the text "for our learning," and what is
in the preacher's heart in the way of vivid apprehension of his people's need, begin to fuse and melt

together. The living power of the text and its contents rise to meet and satisfy this need.

It is not because text and need meet that we call this type of sermon synthetic. It is synthetic, just as the other forms are, because the text thoughts are rearranged and synthetized.

The powerful impulse of some keenly felt need only makes a special group of these sermons. The need, by controlling the synthesis, puts these sermons in a class by themselves, namely the highest of all.

In advanced synthesis something in the text itself arrests the preacher's attention, so that the thoughts of the text crystallize about this center. In the highest type of synthesis some need fuses with the gold in the text. The text thoughts synthesize accordingly.

In other words, when we study the text thoughts *by themselves,* they *by themselves* fall into this or that pattern under a unity to match. This is advanced synthesis. Again, as we study the text thoughts *with some need* filling the preacher's heart, *that need* causes the text thoughts to assume a certain telling pattern. This is the highest type of synthesis.

In this process certain thoughts assume the central position, the rest become subordinate. Often the latent ideas in a text, the vital implications back of the text thoughts flash out when touched by the need. Thus the thoughts crystallize into the new pattern.

Not all texts can be used in this way. It would be a grave error to force a text to meet a need, for, being forced, it would not really meet the need. This means that we cannot reach the same homiletical height in every sermon. Our homiletical wings will not always carry us to the very top. Yet we must know about this fusion of text and need in the glowing heart of the preacher, so that when the hour arrives we may rise to the great opportunity.

We have an example on a small scale in the way Jesus handled Ex. 3, 6 and 16, when the Sadducees tried to turn the resurrection into an absurd impossibility, Matth. 22, 23-33. Ordinarily in preaching on the words, "I am the God of Abraham," etc., we would set forth God's covenant relation to Abraham and his people. But the need of refuting the falsehoods of the Sadduccees made the lips of Jesus flash out this theme from the text, "God is not the God of the dead, but of the living." The latent truth in the Exodus text blazed forth, like a masked battery, and annihilated the Sadducees' denial of the resurrection. This illustrates the main point in the highest form of synthesis, the text meeting and fusing with the need. If Matthew had reported Christ's complete discourse on this occasion we would most likely have had a complete illustration of how all the thoughts in a text are combined to focus on the need.

Peter's sermon on the day of Pentecost is a fuller illustration. He used Joel 2, 28-29 to clear away the doubts of his hearers regarding the Pentecostal miracle and to set before them the glorious truth of the mission of the Holy Spirit.

Jer. 31, 31-34 furnishes an example. We may preach analytically on this text; we may also use the simplest form of synthesis. But, as the preacher dwells on the prophet's words he may see how they completely smash the spurious idea of *progressiveness* in religion as voiced by the Moderns. They call this idea up-to-date Christianity. Well, the prophet gives us a picture of

**The Genuine Up-to-date Christian,**

I. He is past the point of mistaking *the religious notions of men* for divine realities (v. 34, the Word).

II. He is no longer deceived by *mere morality* as over against *the new life* (v. 33, the new obedience).

III. And he has left far behind *all schemes of saving himself* instead of trusting in *God's own pardon.*

A second example from the same text. Filled with deepest sorrow at seeing so many men wrecking themselves religiously by steering a wrong course, the preacher may use his text to show

**God's Compass for Your Soul-Journey Through Life.**

It points to the fact, that

*I. Nothing can take away sin but God's own pardon.*

*II. Nothing can bring you to God save His own revelation.*

*III. Nothing can please God except the new heart which He Himself creates.*

## FIFTH CHAPTER

# THE HOMILY.

In ordinary speech the word "homily" means "a plain sermon." In Homiletics we use "homily" to designate a sermon constructed in a particular manner.

In analytical, as well as in all forms of synthetical outlines, the theme is really the *logical* unity of the parts. In a homily the theme is only a *descriptive* unity of the parts.

Analysis, as well as synthesis, in outlining, by their very nature end up by fitting parts together into a *strict* symmetry of thought. Each main thought has its necessary place in the scheme of thought that is chosen, and it is shaped and molded so as to fit that special place. It would mar the design produced by analysis or by synthesis to drop out a part, to change the order of the parts, or to formulate them each in an independent way. In a homily this is different. There is no theme with such strict control of the parts, and no strict pattern to which each part in its place must conform if the pattern is to be carried out symmetrically. Instead of strict symmetry there is *free* development. As in a natural scene there are hill and valley and stream or lake, trees, meadows, cultivated fields and a cluster of houses, sky and earth, sunshine and shadow, so in a homily there are its component features. We describe the scene in nature, whatever it is that lies before our eyes. If we went a mile farther,

of course, the scene, and the description of it, would
be different. So the text that happens to lie before
our eyes. The homily merely describes what appears
in the text as the trained eye passes over it. If we
read a bit farther and used that portion as a text,
the description would be different according to what
the eye would then meet.

Because there is no logical or strict control, and
the text is taken just as it is, no rearrangement of its
natural features is necessary by means of synthesis.
It is better to describe things as they really are in the
text, than to make any kind of change. Hence we
find no synthetical homilies as distinguished from
analytical ones. Homilies all follow the same natural
course.

The unit idea, however, is not dropped, for the
simple reason that the text itself is a unit, and any
description of the features that make up the text results in presenting that *unity*. The freedom in constructing a homily is not in the theme, save as to its
formulation, but in the presentation of the parts,
including even their formulation. We take the parts
as they naturally come in the text. We attempt no
coordination, which would be a logical control. We
seek for no balance, no design or pattern in laying
them out. We do not say of a scene, This mountain
must be here, this valley there. For we are not composing a scene on canvass, we are merely painting the
one that lies before our eyes in the text.

That, too, is the reason why a homily has *more
parts* than other sermon types. A homily cannot be
constructed with only two parts, or three. Such an
outline would not be a homily. One could not really

describe a scene by just noting a few of its features, say a hill and a valley. A description requires that you include all the features of the scene before you. On the other hand, one should not become too minute. It would be a mistake to lose oneself in detail. Thus in a text, you could not stop to elucidate every concept in it, explain every implication, and follow every application. Take one of the works of a great painter. An artist could lecture on it for hours, but he has only about thirty minutes to tell you what the great painter has achieved. Those thirty minutes can be made very valuable to you by his skillful treatment. He will touch some of the details in the painting, but never every line, every bit of color, every light and shadow. So the preacher when by means of a homily he shows his hearers what is in the text.

It seems easy to produce a homily. And it is, — but only for the pulpit master! On reading an excellent sermon of this type the preacher may think that he can equal it without difficulty. But there is something deceptive about constructing homilies, — they are *the most difficult* of all the sermon types. That is why so few homilies are actually preached, and still fewer put into print. Some preachers never even attempt this form of outline. No need, then, to say, Do not use this form too often lest you become monotonous. In fact, the majority of texts are unsuitable for homilies, and some that might do for a homily do still better for analysis or synthesis.

A homily easily degenerates into a Sunday School lesson, in which one verse or thought after another is commented on by the teacher. If the text should include a few more verses, the comment would go on and cover these also. A sermon in this style would be decidedly inferior. Then, too, the effort in constructing a homily may easily degenerate into a series of little side excursions starting out in various directions from the text, a string of baby sermonettes, as one has called them. Instead of following a straight unit line to a fixed goal, little branching lines are followed, and at the end of each the preacher jumps back to the text in order to get a new start. This makes a heterogeneous sermon. There is no harmony or homogeneous unity. A text is like a fine painting, and the man who describes and explains the painting must be an expert in composition, just as the preacher who elucidates a text by means of a homily.

We may say that in general the art of good description is not sufficiently cultivated and used by preachers. Many a Biblical scene should be painted in our sermons, yet how few preachers even try to paint them? Now a good homily is in the nature of a grand painting. Not that it consists of mere descriptive matter. Yet it does consist of a harmonious description of the truths of a text, a description shot through with significance for the hearer. No wonder it is difficult to do, and model samples are scarce.

The best texts for homilies are such as permit a series of natural steps, one rising above the other till the top is reached. These are far better than texts which seem to move along only on a horizontal line of thought.

Example, Luke 15, 11-32, the Parable of the Prodigal. The theme is the least difficult thing to decide on. It merely summarizes the story which the preacher intends to retell. The steps are indicated in the parable itself, and one rises above the other. 1) The son's foolish decision; 2) The gay life while it lasted; 3) The wretched swine-herd; 4) The great resolve to return home; 5) The meeting of the father with his son; 6) Perfect pardon; 7) The other son, at home, yet lost; 8) Did the father succeed in finding this other son?

Observe how the steps in the sermon will rise till the top is reached. The unity of the structure is plain, even as the parable itself is a perfect unity. Only there are two climaxes, yet both are in place. The one is declarative, namely the perfect pardon of the younger son; the other is interrogative — did the father succeed with the older son? The question is purposely left open in the text. — But in thus following the natural course of the text, every step in it must be filled with significance for the hearer. It would result in a shallow sermon to picture only the story of the two sons in the text. The sermon would be inferior if to each portion of the picture an application to the hearers were attached. The masterly way is to weave together the parts of the story and their significance. Each part is thus focused from the very start.

Another example, Matth. 11, 28-30. The theme intends merely to summarize the text, permitting the parts to unfold freely. "The Lord Extends His Hands and Invites Us to Come to Him." 1) The invitation to come. — The right and the power to come lie in this invitation. Come means trust (faith). In the end all depends on whether we did come. 2) To me, Jesus. — He alone has saving power as the Redeemer and divine Helper. His love and grace; the folly of spurning it. 3) All ye that labor and are heavy laden. — The burden of guilt and wretchedness. What it means to be relieved of it; what it means to go on staggering under it. 4) The promise of rest. — This is peace through pardon. Then assurance amid affliction. The highest possible gift for the soul. 5) The new yoke. — It is easy and light, bearing us, rather than we bearing it. What an exchange from being heavy laden! The meek and lowly Savior leads us on till we enter the rest above. — Here again there is unity, for the last part closes the text as well as the sermon and leaves no more to be added. Yet the unfolding of the parts is free, each step following in its own way. All we need is to mark the steps, i. e. make them stand out distinctly.

The preacher must know how to strike the right tone from the start. If then he unfolds the parts naturally, without wandering, just letting the text, as it were, speak to the hearer, a lovely and highly effective sermon should be the result.

# FAULTS IN OUTLINING.

We doubt our ability to list them all. So we shall content ourselves with mentioning only the more obvious. Moreover, in this chapter we restrict ourselves to the sermon parts as distinct from themes, touching these only where necessary.

1. There are *divisions that suit any text*. For that very reason they should be discarded. Here is an ancient one, 1) We shall explain our text; 2) Then we shall apply it. Or, 1) What the text means; 2) What lessons it teaches.

To use a division of this kind is to betray lack of brains. No more needs to be said. — Regarding application to the hearers, this should never be packed into just one part, even when there are only two. Whatever application is made, connect it at once with the substance of the text that is elucidated.

2. Avoid using a text for the *"lessons"* that may be drawn from it. The very word "lessons" is out of place.

There is no unity in "lessons," for one may always squeeze out another "lesson," if he looks closely enough. Even to promise only "the main lessons" is a mistake, for why discard the minor ones?

But this practice of drawing "lessons" and making "applications" is a far graver fault than most preachers are aware of. The Scriptures contain two great elements. The one consists of God's great saving acts, plus the great saving doctrines by means of which they are presented. These acts show what God has done *for* us, what He offers and gives us. They embody His redeeming, atoning, pardoning, quickening grace. All of them aim at *faith*. We simply receive, possess, enjoy. When the preacher presents these acts (or doctrines) he uses *homiletical Appropriation,* by which he helps us to believe, receive, possess, and enjoy. And this is the supreme part of the preacher's work. — Then there is the second element. This consists of the examples in the Scriptures, plus the doctrines connected with them. They are intended to produce something *in* us, namely in making our *life* more holy and Christlike. Any presentation of this element in the Scriptures is *homiletical Application,* by which the preacher stirs us up to exercise our love and Christian virtues, and to get rid of our flesh, our worldliness, our ungodliness of life. This is the secondary part of the preacher's work.

Absolutely always homiletical Appropriation outranks homiletical Application. Absolutely always homiletical Application rests on homiletical Appropriation. First preach the Christ *for* us, then preach the Christ *in* us. If a text seems to have only the latter element in it, remember that this text is part of a Biblical book in which the supreme element is the foundation. Our Christian life must thus be based on Christian faith. Every "good work," as the dogmaticians call it in harmony with the Scriptures, is only the outgrowth and fruit of saving faith.

What a mistake then for the preacher to look at a text only for the "applications" and "lessons" it may

contain! What a mistake to overlook the Christ **for**
us, the grace for us, the saving gifts for us! Preach
the Redeemer first, then the Example. Preach first the
faith by which men receive the Redeemer and salvation, then the love by which they follow Him. This
will correct the everlasting search for mere "lessons"
in texts. This will put both Appropriation and Application into their proper relation and places.

Where "works," "service," and the like are made
too prominent Protestants fall back into the old Rom-
ish error, and the mere name "Protestant" will not
save them.

3. Avoid *categories* in dividing themes. By
categories we understand the questions that begin with
"what," "how," "who," "which," "why," "when,"
"where," etc., etc.

It takes no brain power to divide by means of
categories. They are useless even for theological students in seminaries, for no one can learn anything
worth while from them. Anybody, on any subject or
theme, can ask two or more category questions. All
idea of unity is lost when categories are used. For
always some additional question of this type can be
added. Why stop with "why" and "how"? Why not
ask a few more? Moreover, any text can be divided
in this way, if one cares to call this sort of thing
division.

Now it is true, categories have been used by
preachers, even by eminent ones. We regret to admit
it! When an eminent man does a poor, weak thing,
certainly that is not to his credit. Preachers have
perpetrated more than one faulty and even wrong
thing in sermonizing. When we catch them at it, we

should shun their example, not foolishly follow it. Often their faults go back to their early training. Their Homiletics should have been better in the start.

Categories belong in the workshop of the study, not in the finished product in the pulpit. Quiz your text by means of category questions when you are busy absorbing its contents. Do not let us see you doing your preparatory work in the pulpit.

Perhaps when you have been ill or completely upset during the past week, unable to do any high grade work on this account, you may as a last resort use a few category questions. We will excuse you — we cannot praise you.

4. Beware of *switching the parts* from the line of thought in the theme. This is often done inadvertently and unconsciously. The way to do it is to run in an oblique connective word or expression between your theme and your parts. Without realizing it, you thus turn a corner down the wrong street, instead of going straight on along the main avenue of your theme. Sometimes the switching is done only mentally. If you really want the sermon to head the way you have switched the parts, then start in that direction beginning with the introduction and theme.

Example, 2 Cor. 7, 10, theme "The True Repentance." Inadvertantly the preacher switched the parts and described four prevalent misconceptions of repentance, literally preaching on the very opposite of this theme, namely on "False Repentance."

Example, John 8, 23, theme "The Truth Shall Make You Free." According to this theme the preacher should either describe to us how the truth sets us free; or he should prove to us that the truth sets us free. Instead of doing either, he slips in the little word "what." 1) "What is truth?" 2) "What is Freedom?" Thus switching off into two sermonettes loosely strung together.

5. It is even morally wrong *to break the promise* made in the theme of the sermon. Every theme is a promise, and at that made entirely voluntarily, to speak to the hearers on what the theme naturally includes. The parts should redeem that promise, even redeem it fully. The pulpit is a sacred place, and the preacher is in the presence of God. In that place he should be the last person to break his promise.

It is only an evasion to hide the theme and to leave the hearers in doubt as to what he intends to preach. If the theme is worth while at all, it is worth while stating it clearly. An excellent theme, perfectly carried out in the parts, is a great satisfaction to the hearers.

6. Homileticians generally raise the question whether the theme and the parts should be openly stated. Some are in favor of hiding at least the parts. After preaching for almost forty years, and after hearing all kinds of sermons especially during fifteen of these years, our conviction is fixed, that it is a great mistake *to hide the sermon theme*, and an equally great mistake *to hide the parts*.

One might as well hide also the text. That would put the hearer completely to wondering what the sermon is about. By hiding the theme and the parts the burden of figuring them out and formulating them in some way is thrown upon the hearer. Unless some very special interest attaches to the sermon, few hearers will accept this burden. They will soon tire of paying close attention, and that is always fatal to the effect of the sermon. It is sound psychology to state the main points of a sermon with all due clearness and precision. Haziness is weakness, not strength.

In this respect sermons are much like newspapers with their headlines. Many an item is read in the daily paper because the headline seems interesting. In journalism headlining is an art in itself. Striking sermon parts likewise stimulate attention, arouse interest, keep the hearer keyed up to the last. Of course, trivial and uninteresting headlines in a newspaper cause the reader to skip the items that are thus marked. Perhaps that is the reason why preachers do not wish to state the parts of their sermon. If so, they condemn themselves. Let them build up their sermons with captivating parts!

The objection that stating the parts to the hearer, in common language, "gives away" at the start what the preacher intends to say, and thus loses any further interest on the part of the hearer, is not sound. Even if stating the parts does what the objection claims, it at least enables the hearer to know just where the preacher is in his sermon, and this is always a satisfaction. Clearness in things that we already know is never a disadvantage. But well formulated parts, just like good themes, arouse attention. The hearer wants to know what the preacher has to say on that theme, or on that part under the theme. Besides, all well stated themes "give away" only a part of what the preacher intends to say. That is what arouses the hearer's mind.

Brilliance in rhetoric, striking expressions or passages, plus eloquence in general, never make up for loss of clearness in letting the hearer see the entire sermon structure. And most preachers are not peers in eloquence, and only occasionally flash brilliantly. It is true, drapery is good, but all first-class artists also know anatomy. If we cannot distinguish an arm from a leg in a painting, the painter's work is abominable. The same thing is true of a sermon.

In hiding sermon parts for fear of allowing the "skeleton" to protrude, a plain psychological effect is overlooked — the hearer begins to fear that the preacher has no "skeleton" at all beneath his sermon drapery. The hearer may even go a bit farther and think that the preacher lacks ability to construct a good "skeleton," else he would do so and let the thing be sufficiently seen; or that the preacher in this instance neglected a part of his task. Our hearers are indeed often more friendly to us than we really deserve, yet a good many of them have rather keen minds and exercise them even when friendly disposed toward us.

7. Avoid *mannerism in stating theme and parts*. There are hundreds of ways of stating both — use them. We ought finally to discard formulas like this, "And now by the help of the Holy Spirit and on the basis of our text, let us consider" etc. Likewise, the invariable "firstly," "secondly," etc. Learn flexibility. Several parts can be stated without enumeration, and yet every hearer can be made to know what each is, and how many there are.

Sometimes, yet not always, it is advisable to state all the parts in a cluster right after, or shortly after, stating the theme. It all depends on the substance of the sermon, and the preacher must be the judge. Those who condemn this procedure fail completely to perceive that there are marked cases in which a statement of the parts greatly helps the entire sermon. We even feel like asking more. Suppose there are three or four parts and the preacher states them distinctly — well, and good. But when now he starts preaching his first part it would be a good thing for him to state it once more. For in listening closely to the statement of all the parts, the mind — as we have found by repeated experience — often does not at once recall what the first part is to be.

It is a mannerism always to state the parts in advance. One good way is to state each part as it is reached. The hearer thus watches the process of building up the sermon, which should be interesting.

There is another way, scarcely ever used, but certainly to be recommended as excellent in some cases. The theme is duly announced — then a sufficient pause. The preacher now begins building up his first part, and does not express the sum of this part until he reaches the climax of it. Or, he builds up the part completely, and announces at the end just what he has built up. So with each succeeding part. Rightly done, this is an excellent way.

To these different way of acquainting the hearer with the parts must be added the endless variety of form in statement. Using both, the different ways and the manifold forms, sermons will always seem fresh and interesting.

8. The unity must always be *a true unity of the parts, and vice versa* the parts when put together must constitute the unity, and no more, and no less. No part dare appear as an appendix, tacked on and superfluous. Likewise, there dare be no gap in the structure.

9. The parts must be *coordinate*. In other words, they must be of equal or nearly equal weight. That

does not mean that they must all have identical length.
They may vary in this respect. But no minor or subordinate thought dare be handled as a major part.
All the parts, by being equal in weight of thought,
ought to balance.

10.    Each part must occupy *the place naturally
due* to it in the organism presented by the sermon.
In constructing a sermon that is like the tree, I dare
not put the roots where the branches ought to be, or
the trunk where the roots belong. To do a thing like
this is to make the sermon structure a freak. In a
logical arrangement abide by the logic. If the parts
carry out a figure, keep to the figure. Build no abnormal structure.

11.    The space allowed to each part must be according to its relative importance. Build no *lopsided*
structures. The preacher is often tempted to over-
develop his first part, then finding that he has used
up most of the time allotted to the sermon he cuts down
and dwarfs the remaining parts. But whatever the
part, do not let one part overshadow the rest or crowd
them to the wall.

12.    *No part dare be the theme itself* either in
form or in substance. Example, "The Blessedness of
Love, 1) What it is; 2) How it may be attained."
Sermons like this still persist, yet part one is really
the entire theme, and part two is merely an addendum
to the theme.

13.    *Each part must be essential to the theme*,
so that its omission could not be allowed. This natural
and even self-evident rule is often transgressed. Sermons are preached with parts not at all essential to

the theme. Parts are pasted on, simply, it seems, because it is traditional to have two or three parts. There is an entire group of such sermons, all for festive occasions, and all with practically just one theme, namely the way to rejoice on this festive occasion (whatever the occasion happens to be). One preacher discovers two or three ways, while another knows of five or six. The theme to begin with is trivial, especially for a festival, when we have the right to look for something better than ordinary didactic animadversions. If, however, the text does state something specific about our way of celebrating a given festive occasion, this belongs in the theme, which then should be properly divided. Parts arbitrarily put together under a loosely formulated theme are always out of place.

Another common violation of this requirement is found under themes that express a judgment. Example, "It is Necessary to Bridle the Tongue." This theme requires that we state reasons in the parts. But some will divide as follows, 1) What does it mean to bridle the tongue? 2 How necessary this is. Part one is out of line entirely, and part two covers the entire theme. If we desire to use two parts like this, the first offering explanation, the second proof, the theme must be arranged accordingly, "St. James Tells us to Bridle the Tongue. 1) What it means to bridle the tongue; 2) How needful this is."

14. There must be *no overlapping* of the parts. Inadvertently the parts may be so formulated that one infringes upon the other, or that there is no clean-cut division between them. Overlapping usually takes place when the division is too close. Only a keen mind

and most careful thinking could handle parts naturally
close to each other.  Usually the parts run together in
the elaboration, or each part is elaborated arbitrarily
in order to keep the parts separate.  Either alternative
is bad.

15. The parts should not rest on a *misapprehension* of what is really meant by the theme.  There
are entire groups of themes subject to misapprehension
as to just what they mean, hence also as to just how
they should be divided into sermon parts.  Take, for
instance, declarative themes in any form.  To the un-
trained mind themes like this at times seem baffling.
How shall we split "The Love of God for the Sinful
World?"  It would be no division to say 1) The sinful
world needs God's love; and 2) God's love went out to
the sinful world; for part two is equivalent to the
entire theme, and part one is a sliver chopped from
the theme.  In cases like this the preacher must first
of all determine exactly what he means by this theme.
Legitimately he may intend to *describe* God's love for
the sinful world.  If so, let him proceed with parts
that picture the astonishing things God has done and
still does for the sinful world.  He will thus really
satisfy his theme.  Many declarative themes may thus
be adequately handled.  In the case before us the
preacher has an alternative.  Legitimately he may
intend to *prove* the love of God for the sinful world.
If so, let him proceed with parts that set forth the
evidence or proof of this wonderful love.  Thus in a
different way he would satisfy his theme.  Whatever
his intention may be in this case will, of course, be
stated in the introduction of the sermon, especially in
the way the theme is introduced.

PART THREE

# THE THEME

## FIRST CHAPTER

# THE VALUE OF A THEME.

A theme completely outranks a mere subject. Why? Because a theme contains a subject and much more besides. There is also a predicate, either expressed or implied. The connection of the subject and the predicate constitutes a judgment. To preach on a theme as thus described offers so many advantages that there is no question as regards preference.

The essays which college students are required to write are generally called "themes." They elaborate subjects, and the essays themselves are denominated "themes." When used of a sermon the word "theme" designates, not the elaboration, but only the unit idea, properly formulated, on which the elaboration is based.

It is really immaterial whether we speak of a "theme" or of a "proposition." The former is derived from a Greek term, θέμα from τίθημι, while the latter is from the Latin *propositio*. Efforts to distinguish between the two in homiletical use have not been successful. It would be arbitrary to say that "theme" signifies merely the idea, and "proposition" the formulation of the idea. The idea and its formulation are practically the same thing.

By a sermon theme we understand the definitely formulated sentence (or its equivalent) in which the unity of the sermon receives its adequate expression. Themes should divide naturally into parts, hence in a discussion of themes there will always be reference also to the parts. A theme that cannot be properly divided is in reality no theme.

1. The value of a theme becomes apparent when we think of *the sermon*. Beyond question, the sermon should constitute a unity, never merely a series of thoughts strung together. This unity ought to be organized, and should aim at a goal. The very nature of the sermon thus requires that at the most fitting place the unity which it intends to present and unfold ought to be clearly and adequately stated. This means that the sermon should have a theme, and that the theme should be duly announced.

If it has no theme the sermon sinks to a lower level. This level is often a very low one. If there is a theme it is a great mistake to hide it. Hiding the theme is like running a store without indicating in any way what the store offers for sale. There is no sign above the door, the show windows are empty, and inside the building the goods are all behind curtains. Or, to use another illustration, hiding the theme of a sermon is like cutting all the headlines out of a newspaper.

Even a brief sermon or a short address ought to have its theme. A small unit is proportionately improved by organizing its few thoughts effectively under a guiding theme. Some may dignify a few loose "remarks" with the title: "address"; in reality they do not deserve so fair a title.

2. The value of a theme is seen when viewed in connection with *the text*. We have already discussed the true character of a text. A proper text is always a unit, rounded out and complete in itself. It may have two or more distinct parts, but these are

always viewed together under the one thought that covers the entire text. It is the preacher's duty to state in a clear, definite, and telling way just what the text means to convey. Only by doing so will he do justice to his text.

If the preacher tries to evade this duty he fails in the most essential part of his task as regards the text. By merely rambling through the text he betrays that he does not treat it seriously enough. He creates the suspicion that he has not given it sufficient study, or that he lacks the necessary ability for sounding the depths of his text. Texts are not as docile as some preachers imagine; they have a way of charging the men who try to preach on them with laziness, superficiality, or lack of ability. Anyone can tell with little effort what the general subject of a text is. We hardly need a well-trained preacher for that. The formulation and announcement of an adequate theme is a thing quite superior. It reveals mastery of the text, sound theological and, in particular, also homiletical training, and this training diligently applied. The man who works out a good theme gets far more out of his text than the man who does not attempt to obtain such a theme.

3. A theme has great value for *the preacher*. The work of constructing, dividing, and elaborating sermon themes constitutes the highest type of mental and spiritual discipline for the preacher. Building up his thought structures into well organized and progressive unities puts to work and develops all his higher faculties. Since these structures are all built out of divine truth, the effort spent in formulating or organizing this truth in the most perfect fashion

trains the preacher's spiritual power of grasping, penetrating, combining, and expressing this truth. Working thus every week with themes brings an exceedingly blessed experience to the preacher.

Those who prefer to work on lower levels necessarily forego the higher benefits. They grow more and more accustomed to lax methods, until at last they are actually unable to rise above them. They may even get to admire their own inferior work. They resemble the poor cook, who "slaps" her meals together and serves them in the commonest fashion, yet expects to be complimented and well paid for her lack of skill. We might put up with her in the kitchen and dining room. When it comes to the pulpit in a beautiful church we expect the highest type of efficiency.

For the preacher there is a practical side to building real theme structures. Once the design of such a structure is sketched out, the sermon is practically completed. The work of elaboration is greatly reduced. Thus time and effort are saved. Working thus in an efficient manner, there is a psychological reaction on the preacher. The very feeling that he is turning out an excellent piece of work puts an enthusiasm into his heart which will lift his entire effort, even on through the delivery of such a sermon, to a higher plane. All labored efforts work in the opposite direction. Instead of psychological uplift, assurance, and joy, there is a feeling of strain, of discouragement, of secret dissatisfaction in spite of all striving, which affects even the delivery in the pulpit. The man who knows deep down in his heart that he has a well-built sermon will preach his best, while the man with the opposite feeling, be it ever so secret, cannot possibly preach his best. The hearer's intuitions are almost always keen. He may not be able to analyze and to tell exactly what the trouble is, yet he will instinctively know the difference between a good and a poor sermon.

It is easy also to memorize a well-constructed theme sermon. There is no better aid to memory than natural combination and logical coordination and subordination of thought, especially when accompanied by exact formulation. The hardest thing in the world to retain in the memory is thought imperfectly and irregularly connected. It is like trying to carry a lot of loose sticks in your arms — they always try to get away. Lay the sticks in order and tie them with a rope — you may carry them with one hand. That laying together and tying up is using a theme.

A good theme, properly divided, is a great help for memorizing a written sermon. We have never heard a sermon read in the pulpit that we cared to listen to. Even the best reading is weaker than free delivery. A preacher may think that once his sermon is written he is safe as far as memorizing is concerned. He is, but only as long as he uses his written pages as a crutch in the pulpit. If he does not want to use such a crutch he must build a structure that is naturally fitted together, i. e. a theme with true parts and sub-parts. If he writes merely as thoughts come to him, he will leave little gaps, or make odd turns and connections. These are often deadly pitfalls for the memory. As he eloquently moves on in his delivery, his memory will suddenly refuse to leap some gap left in the writing, or to make again the odd turn that was unnoticed at the time of writing. Suddenly he finds only thin air to tread on — a painful, and at times tragic, experience. In other words, it is not safe to preach from memory without having a manuscript in the pulpit, unless the sermon is built upon the actual line along which the mind naturally moves.

Once the president of a church body, in preaching the official sermon, was caught in this way. He found himself unable to go on. He came down from the pulpit, got his manuscript from the sacristy, went up again, and only thus, aided by his written sermon, finished the sermon. You may imagine the painfulness of the experience. Others, when their memory leaves them in the air, go on with anything they are able to grab at the moment.

A case like this happened at a large convention of preachers. The preacher went on beautifully, until unfortunately his manuscript slipped from the Bible and fell to the pulpit floor. The man did not wish to pick up his sermon, and so labored on as best he could' for a few minutes, then said amen. Thus the memory will act when attempting to recall what has been written.

Now, all beginners ought to write their sermons for about ten years, yet never so as to really need the manuscript in the pulpit. That means as perfect an outline as possible. Nothing trains like writing. Nothing develops versatility of expression like writing. Nothing produces finish and finality like writing. The man who uses too many words to say a thing, who is inclined to repeat, to string his sentences out, to ramble and to digress, has not written enough. Yet to get the most out of all the drudgery of writing necessitates that the preacher work only with a true and sound **outline.**

Once this apprenticeship has been served the preacher should arrive at the happy stage where his sermon is composed almost wholly in his mind. He will need only the outline on paper, and may even dispense with the paper. Yet he will never reach this stage, or never be safe when he thinks he has reached it, unless he has mastered rather completely the work of building genuine outlines. No loose ends; no gaps; no odd turns; no twisted connections. Just a straight line to the goal; each link of the chain in place. For this the long years of writing were to train him. Now, having attained his goal, preaching becomes a real joy. There is only trained mental concentration. Each mental reproduction is far better than the preceding, and the reproduction in the pulpit the best of all. It is like a Pullman limited gliding along on its rails. The rails are the theme and the skeleton naturally unfolding it. The switches are all closed, the signal bars and lights all in place. The destination is reached smoothly and on time. This is what theme preaching, properly practiced, will do for the preacher. Nothing better has ever been devised or tried.

4. A theme has great value for *the hearer.* The longer a man preaches, the more difficult will it be for him to put himself into the position of the man in the pew who is to do the hearing. After years of practice in hearing sermons the author has reached the conviction that good hearing is also an art and must be learned by practice. It is the preacher's great business to aid the hearer in his task of really getting the sermon and taking it away with him.

There is the matter of sustained attention. Preachers often wonder why their hearers, at least a part of them, soon become rather inattentive. I can speak for them. It is almost impossible to give close attention to a sermon of about thirty minutes, if the preacher does not give the hearer certain necessary and natural hand-holds by which to grasp and retain the sermon contents. The better the hand-holds, the easier it is to keep up the strain of attention. It is, of course, a strain to preach, but it is also a strain to hear with full attention.

The theme is the supreme handhold. If no theme is offered, the mind of the hearer soon drifts. For a little while he may beat around in his mind in trying to discover what the preacher is really attempting to do. Then he gives it up, his attention flags. The main parts when properly announced, either simultaneously, or in succession, are the next great hand-holds for the hearer's mind. To deny the hearer this help is letting him get lost in the sermon. Presently he does not know where he is. He makes a few efforts to find out, then gives up. The sermon rolls on, but the mind that ought to receive it has begun to drift. It may retain a bit here and there, if the preacher says something very personal or otherwise startling, but as a whole the sermon is not received. It is the preacher's own fault.

It is no pleasure to get lost in a sermon. There is only one comfort, namely that the misery will not last much beyond thirty minutes, though minutes often lengthen out unduly while one is waiting for the amen. Without wanting to do so I have become drowsy during such preaching; or when mentally alert I have solved problems of my own. It would have surprised the preacher if he had known with what my mind was busy while my eyes were looking at him. Perhaps I had a feeling of guilt in not getting the sermon I had come for, or to get so little of it, but this did not improve the failure.

Most preachers use only two or three parts, as if there were a law against using more. Yet a part that lasts from twelve to fifteen minutes is too long to grasp readily unless it is split up and the sub-parts are made visible. How many preachers forget this? If there are no sub-parts that the hearer is able easily to detect, the effect is a blur on the hearer's mind, and he loses to that extent.

The greatest aid for the hearer in apprehending a sermon is clearness of structure plus interesting form and formulation. Even old and simple truths offered in this way will delight the hearer and send him away gratified.

One more point should be added in regard to the hearer. Properly built sermons are educative. Not a few of them will linger in the mind long after they have been heard.

## SECOND CHAPTER

# DIVIDING THE THEME.

The theme is intended to express the unity of the sermon, but always so that this unity can be properly divided. The latter is quite essential.

A theme is far more than the title of a sermon. While a brief theme may also serve the purpose of a title, usually the general subject of the sermon is preferred for this latter purpose; for instance, when a sermon is printed, or when the subject is posted on a bulletin board. But in actual preaching we need the theme as the carefully formulated unity of the sermon placed at the head of the division. And again we need it as an expression of the unity that we are about to divide into its component parts. There is no difference in this respect between the theme of an analytic or that of a synthetic sermon. Even the theme for a homily partakes of this characteristic, although the homily allows more freedom in presenting the parts.

Knowing that we intend to divide the theme, the best way to formulate it is to take this into consideration from the start. It is a waste of effort to formulate an awkward theme, and then to puzzle our heads about dividing it. A theme that cannot be readily divided is very likely no theme at all, or is a faulty one. The preacher must train himself to formulate good divisible themes readily. It is always a satisfaction to operate with a theme the division of which is at once easy and natural.

It is the theme that we must divide, always the theme. Any dividing of the text is a matter for itself, preliminary to the task of forming the theme. Once we decide on the theme, we concentrate on that, and see to it that its character is such as to offer us the natural parts which properly combined equal the theme.

A theme, in order to be divisible, must possess two features:

1. A line for the direction of the division.

2. Marks of cleavage for the parts to be made by the division.

## I. The Line of Direction.

The essential difference between a mere subject or topic and an actual theme is that the former in no way indicates in what direction the division is to be made. If I set out to preach on "Repentance," "Concerning Faith," "Justification," or any bare topic like these, I fail to indicate in what direction I intend to take my hearers. If after all, instead of just making loose remarks on my topic, I divide it in some way, the division can only be arbitrary. With equal right and propriety I might have used some other division — there is nothing in my subject to prevent me from doing this. I may treat two or three important sides of the subject I have selected; but I may also treat several minor sides of it. I have simply placed myself and my hearers in mid-sea, and I may steer in any direction at random. I have a limited time to steer hither and thither, and that is all. I am headed for no port and do not intend to reach one, or I would have said so at the start by using a theme and not taking a mere subject.

It does not change matters that some preachers like this sort of thing, and imagine that their hearers are best served by it. As regards the latter, they may not know better. Yet to trade on their ignorance is not treating them fairly. Preachers ought to rise above such a procedure in the pulpit with a Bible text open before them. It is such an inferior way of preaching, no matter what may be said in its favor.

The moment we add even as little as an attributive modifier to a subject, we narrow it down and give it at least something like direction. Take as an example "True Repentance." While not a theme in the full sense of the word, yet the attributive "true" indicates that the preacher is not going to say anything or everything he may happen to think of on "repentance," but is going to confine himself to a description of genuine repentance as opposed to the different forms of spurious or sham repentance. Note, too, how the interest is heightened psychologically by thus pointing the subject in a specified direction. Every normal person prefers to hear about "true repentance" as over against "repentance" in general. It is the old law of Homiletics, namely presenting that which is better — always that which is better.

Adding a second noun and turning the subject into a possessive modifier has the same effect. Instead of preaching on "Faith" in general, let us say that you confine yourself to "The Fruits of Faith," or to "The Power of Faith," or still more specifically to "The Saving Power of Faith." Again the subject is pointed in a given direction. It is narrowed down, invested with a more specific interest, and is thus made decidedly better.

Directive terms thus mark out a course for the sermon-ship. And it is always better to sail along a given course, than to drift or sail around at random. Every directive term is like an arrow ————>; it points in one, and only one direction, namely the one we have carefully chosen. If the arrow word or words are sufficiently definite we travel between fixed banks, either down or up the stream.

We may use another illustration which will appeal to those who have at any time wielded an ax in splitting blocks of wood for a stove. The ax must descend exactly in the line of the grain. That is the natural way to split a block. It will not split at all if the ax descends obliquely. It will only split off in slivers or chips if the ax hits the block a glancing blow. An expert at splitting needs to exert himself but little to

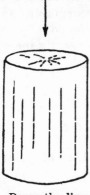

Down the line
of the grain.

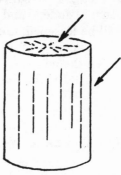

Oblique, or
glancing.

halve a block for he makes the ax follow the grain. A bungler, who strikes oblique or glancing blows, uses up a vast amount of energy, and his results are certainly not in proportion to his strenuous efforts.

It is exactly the same when it comes to division in sermonizing, only that we ourselves must furnish the block of wood with its natural grain running straight down through the block, or theme. Why take some knotty, twisted, crooked piece, and then maul it around with our homiletical ax — perhaps a dull one, with a poor and loose handle; when we can pick out a neat, clean block with straight grain and no knots, and take a perfect ax, and with one true stroke down the grain halve and quarter the block? The homiletical woodpile is full of the finest kind of blocks. Homiletics furnishes the best possible ax, and even tells us just how to swing it so that the blow falls true. Why argue to the contrary? Why waste time and strength and end with the poorest kind of results?

The directive line is indicated in several ways. We ought to shape our themes accordingly, and of course, understand exactly why we do so. The work will be lessened, and the satisfaction greatly increased.

The line of direction is most frequently marked in the theme

1. By the *emphatic* word;
2. By the *limiting* word;
3. By the *logically important* word.

## The Emphatic Word Marking the Line of Direction.

The first way to secure direction in splitting a theme is to insert a word or an expression which naturally bears the emphasis. The preacher must, of course, know the purpose for inserting such a word, and must use the emphatic word accordingly. It is a pity to have an emphatic term in the theme, and then blindly try to split the theme in some other direction.

The emphatic word may be an adjective, a noun, a pronoun, a verb, an adverb, etc., or an expression equal to any of these, such as a genitive, a phrase, or a short clause. English is not flexible enough to permit more than a very brief clause in a theme; longer clauses make the theme too heavy and involved for the English ear. All emphatic expressions are like arrows pointing in a specific direction.

Sometimes a word or an expression bearing a secondary emphasis is found in a theme. This points in the same direction as the term that carries the primary accent, and thus acts merely as an auxiliary in determining the direction in which the division should move.

Example, Matth. 12, 38-42, "The *Significant* Deliverance of Jonah from the Belly of the Great Fish." It is taken for granted that the sermon will deal with the general account of Jonah's deliverance. But how is the sermon to utilize this deliverance? The arrow word, in this case an adjective, tells us — we are to hear about the *significant* deliverance of the prophet. His deliverance was full of great significance, and the sermon intends to show us this specific significance. To make the matter as clear as possible we here add the parts secured by this directive term: Jonah's deliverance, first of all, prefigured the passion and resurrection of Christ — it was highly "significant" in this respect. Again, his deliverance foretold the coming of the Gospel — it was very significant in this respect.

Finally the prophet's deliverance calls upon us to prepare for the judgment to come — its significance was marked also in this respect. These three parts exhaust the significance of Jonah's deliverance. There is nothing further that we can add. Christ, Gospel, judgment form a complete whole.

Example, John 7, 40-53, "The *Reception* Jesus Found Among Men." Here the emphatic word is a noun.

Example, Acts 3, 22-26, "How *we, too,* are children of the Prophets and the Covenant." The pronoun "we too" is emphatic.

Example, Matth. 9, 9-13, "The Kingdom of God a Kingdom *for Sinners.*" The emphasis is on the final phrase "for sinners."

It is always a mistake to overlook or disregard the emphatic term in a theme. Take the last example: "The Kingdom of God a Kingdom for Sinners." That means, we are going to speak on this wonderful characteristic of the Kingdom, namely that it is wholly and altogether for sinners. In treating this theme we ought not to wander off in any other direction. For instance we are not to divide,

1.  What is meant by the Kingdom?
2.  All sinners need the Kingdom.
3.  The way sinners get into the Kingdom.

A division such as this is no real division. It is only an exhibition of crooked thinking. The emphatic phrase in the theme emphatically tells the preacher to go one way, namely the right way; but no, he must wander off on several wrong ways. If he were a banker I would certainly not entrust my money to him. Instead of following emphatic directions to invest it in the right way, he might persist in investing it in quite another way. Or, if he were a physician, he might not see the emphatic symptoms of my disease and administer the right medicine, but merely experiment around on my case according to vague notions of his own.

Now, the thought that the Kingdom is wholly one *for sinners*, should receive a division something like this:

    *I.   At its head stands the great Savior of sinners.*

    *II.   Through its portals none but poor sinners go.*

    *III.   In all its domain hosts of pardoned sinners praise God.*

## The Limiting Word Marking the Line of Direction.

Instead of some emphatic word or expression we may place into the theme a limiting word or phrase and allow that to act as the arrow pointing the direction the division should take. The limiting word, of course, limits, narrows down, and thus makes a groove or channel, marking the course of the division. The limiting word may also be the emphatic word in the theme, thus in a double way pointing the direction.

Example, Luke 18, 9-14, "The *Biggest* Fool in the World." There are many fools in the world, but this sermon is to be limited to the biggest one of them all, as the Lord Himself described him to us. He is the biggest, for he fools himself in the greatest matters, in the most wretched way, with the most deplorable results, when even a poor publican knew the way of wisdom for himself.

Example, Micah 5, 2-4, *"Micah's* Message Concerning the Christ-child." Here the limiting word is the genitive "Micah's." In his writing he has one great message concerning the coming Savior. The contents of this particular message are to engage our attention in the sermon.

Example, Is. 63, 7-16, "How Israel *Finally* Forfeited the Lord's Lovingkindness." The limiting term is the adverb "finally." Everything in the development of the sermon must point to this finality of loss.

Example, Sam. 3, 22-32, "The Godly Man is One Who is Able *to Wait*." Here the limiting term is the infinitive "to wait." The godly man is able to do many things, but this sermon will treat only of his ability to do one thing, namely to wait.

Limiting words in a theme are exceedingly helpful when properly noted and employed. They compel the preacher to look in one direction only. Our minds are so much inclined to look around in every direction, even when we know it is futile. For instance, when we mislay something, instead of thinking just where we may have put the article, we often start our search anywhere and everywhere, even where we know we could not possibly have put the lost article. It is often so in seeking divisions for sermon themes. We look in a dozen useless, hopeless, helpless directions. The true direction may escape us altogether. Look only in the direction of the limiting word, if there is one in the theme, and soon you will find just what you need.

Take the theme just mentioned, on Israel finally forfeiting the Lord's lovingkindness. In endeavoring to split this theme one might look 1) at the lovingkindness; 2) at what is meant by forfeiting it; 3) and then at Israel who did forfeit it. Now it is true, the lovingkindness, the forfeiting, and Israel's action, will all have to be handled in the sermon somewhere and in some way. But these three points are certainly not the parts that divide this theme. At best they only saw the theme into sections, chop it into lengths. Such handling shows that the main cue in the theme has been overlooked. The adverb "finally" plainly points the direction for the parts.

    *I. Israel continually abused the Lord's loving-kindness.*

    *II. Israel's rebellion even vexed the Holy Spirit and made the Lord an enemy.*

    *III. Thus Israel lost the Lord's grace forever.*

    *IV. And no intercession, however heartrending, can bring that favor back again.*

These parts can be filed into better shape. Our aim here is merely to show how the parts must all take direction from the limiting term "finally." That is the way the wind blows in this theme, and all the parts like flags must wave in the same direction.

### The Logically Important Word Marking the Line of Direction.

    The logically important word sometimes has no emphasis or other distinguishing mark. Although it lacks prominence, yet like the rudder of a ship, it swings the entire theme in just one certain direction, and all the parts must swing in the same way.

    The logically important word in the theme indicates whether we are dealing with a question, an assertion, a narrative, a command, etc. By doing so it points out the direction which the parts should follow.

    *The Question Form.* — This form is used quite frequently. It always implies pertinent answers, and naturally the parts at once furnish these answers. — Example, Luke 10, 38-42, *"What* is the One Thing Needful?" The logically important word is the interrogative "what." Here the answers may be given in something like the following way: The one thing needful is really so great that we must look at it from

various sides. It is 1) God's Word — not our work;
2) God's grace — not our merit; 3) God's gift — not
our giving. — There are many themes of this type.
We append a few:

> *When* shall We Find Rest for our Souls?
> *Whereunto* shall We Liken this Generation?
> *Are* your Talents at Work?
> *Will* you Be Faithful unto Death?
> *Could* you Watch with the Savior one Hour?

We have underscored the logically important word in
these questions, but that does not mean that the word is to be
emphasized.

Instead of an outright question we may have the
equivalent of a question, which, of course, also points
in the direction of answers. Thus:

> *Why* we Worship Christ as Our King and Priest.
> *How* an Old Man Celebrates Christmas (Simeon).
> *When* the Guest Turned Host in Bethany (i. e. what then?)

In question-themes the question itself may be split
up and thus passed on to the parts, leaving the answer
for the elaboration. It will always be some great
question that is thus divided. And the questions in the
parts must, when taken together, equal the great question in the theme.

Example, Rom. 1, 16.

### Why Was St. Paul Not Ashamed of the Gospel?

We get the answer when we ask,
  I.   What he knew of the Gospel.
 II.   What he had experienced of the Gospel.
III.   What he had done for the Gospel.
IV.   What he expected of the Gospel.

Another example, Luke 12, 16-21,

**Saul, Saul, To Whose Voice Are You Listening?**

I. *Your own voice of folly? or*
II. *God's voice of wisdom?*

Occasionally a question theme is divided into its parts by making the parts bring forward the vital points that condition the answer. The answer itself recedes into the elaboration. Example, Is. 61, 1-6, "Have You Ever Realized the Overwhelming Greatness of the Work of Salvation?" This question may be furthered in its answer by pointing out the vital points involved in the answer. 1) Salvation — think what the task means. 2) Salvation — think of the Savior this requires. 3) Salvation — think what agencies must be put to work (Gospel, Church). — This is a rare type of outline. It may be used with implied questions, and is effective in holding something back, thus stimulating interest.

A variant type is the question, direct or implied, with opposite answers. The opposite conditions may be given at once in the parts.

Example, Is. 63, 7-16,

**Will the Lord's Lovingkindness Last Forever?**

I. *No, it will not, when men obdurately abuse that lovingkindness.*
II. *Yes, it certainly will, when men in faith embrace that lovingkindness.*

But the conditions for the two opposite answers may also be left for the elaboration. Example, Zech. 7, 4-10,

**What Benefit Has the Lord of Our Good Works?**

I. *None whatever.*
II. *A great deal.*

Never use a trivial question. If the answers are too obvious the question theme is not interesting enough. Raise no question which you cannot properly answer. Jesus often had to correct the questions asked him, before He could profitably answer them.

*The Assertion Form.* — An almost endless number of themes appears in the form of simple assertion. The logically important word is the verb. Example, Acts 5, 1-11.

### There is Nothing More Dangerous Than Sham Christianity.

(The logically important word is "is.")

  *1) Sham orthodoxy.*
  *2) Sham faith.*
  *3) Sham piety.*
  *4) Sham salvation.*

An assertion means to state *a fact.* A good many preachers, however, are greatly puzzled by such themes, and often fail to divide them. There are really three ways for diving assertion or fact themes. 1) Divide the fact itself, and by doing so show that it is a fact. 2) Furnish two or more decisive proofs that the theme is indeed fact. 3) Combine these two, by first unfolding the fact in part one (the unfolding takes place in the sub-parts), and then proving the fact in part two (the separate proofs forming the sub-parts). These are the logical ways of handling all fact themes.

Take the theme for Acts 5, 1-11: There is Nothing more Dangerous than Sham Christianity. Logically you may mean: I intend *to show* you this fact as a fact. Then you will divide in the way indicated above. But you may also mean: I intend *to prove* this fact. If this is your meaning you will at once offer proofs.

Example:

**There is Nothing More Dangerous Than Sham Christianity.**
("Is" states the fact. )

    *I. It substitutes a show of truth for the essence of truth.*

    *II. It substitutes obedience to Satan for obedience to Christ.*

    *III. It substitutes hypocrisy for holiness and good works.*

    *IV. It substitutes hell for heaven.*

These four parts are a complete circle of proof. Each part may therefore also begin with "because."

If we desire to combine the fact with the proof we may use this manner:

**There is Nothing More Dangerous Than Sham Christianity.**

    *I. Let us see what sham Christianity looks like* (sham orthodoxy — sham faith — sham piety — sham salvation).

    *II. Let us learn why sham Christianity is so dangerous* (it uses the Word as pretense — it tries to fool God — it deceives and destroys itself.

Here part one unfolds the fact of sham Christianity in detail, and part two gives the proof in detail.

Other themes in which the verb states a fact and thus points the direction of the parts are the following: Matth. 6, 1-8, the fact divided:

**Our Father Seeth in Secret.**

("Seeth" indicates fact.)

    *I. He penetrates every sham.*

    *II. He discerns all sincere devotion.*

John 15, 17-27, the fact proved:

**It is Impossible for a Christian to Go Through the World Unscathed.**

(The verb "impossible to go through" points to the fact.)

    *I. Because of Christ Himself.*

    *II. Because of the world.*

> III.  *Because of ourselves as true followers of Christ.*
> IV.  *Because of the work Christ has assigned to us as His followers.*

Luke 17, 7-10, fact and proof combined.

### We Are Unprofitable Servants.

> I.  *It is good for us to know it* (here elucidate the fact).
> II.  *It is foolish for us to dispute it* (here furnish the proof).

In many assertion or fact-themes *the verb is omitted.* These constitute the majority. They are often more puzzling than the themes that contain their verbs. While thus actually the logical word is absent, virtually it is there, namely by implication. The way for the preacher to manage these themes is to restate them for himself so that the proper verb appears and the direction in which it points is clearly seen. This is done in the study, not, of course, in the pulpit. Example, Acts 6, 8-15.

### Stephen, a Man Full of Faith and Power.

> I.  *In his successful labors.*
> II.  *In his sereve trial.*
> III.  *In the heavenly light which shone upon him.*

This theme with its verb inserted reads: Stephen *was* a man full of faith, etc. The fact is put before us as a fact, though the verb in the theme is left out. The parts thus properly furnished the details of that fact.

Example, Acts 13, 38-43:

### Your Case and My Case in the Court of Heaven.

> I.  *Desperate when we look at our sins.*
> II.  *Hopeless when we count on our good works.*
> III.  *Completely changed when we bring in Christ.*
> IV.  *Triumphantly certain when we come with faith.*
> V.  *Gloriously won when we hear God's sentence of pardon.*

The theme really is, How your case and mine *looks* in the court of heaven. This indicates the direction for the parts. It looks 1) desperate; 2) hopeless; etc., according to what our case is made to rest on in that court. — Other themes of this type:

"The Sinner's Only Hope Before God" (there *is* only one hope for the sinner before God).

"The Glory of the Christian Church (there *is* such a glory).

"The Open Sepulcher" (it *is* open — a wonderful and significant fact).

"The Feast of the Soul" (there *is* such a feast, and that means "soul-hunger," "soul-bread," "soul-eating," "soul-life").

"God's Use of Men of Faith and Power" (He *uses* them — show how).

"The Ox and the Ass on the Sabbath Day," Luke 13, 10-17 (what is done with them on the Sabbath *has much to say* to us — state what).

*The Narrative Form.* — The logically important term which points the direction for the parts is sometimes one that indicates a narrative or story. We may divide according to the main points of the story. Or we may call the parts chapters in the story. Example, Acts 9, 36-43,

### The Little History of Dorcas, the Dressmaker.

   *I. Her heart was filled with faith.*
  *II. Her eyes were open to the need about her.*
 *III. Her hands were diligent in works of love.*
 *IV. Her work was highly appreciated by the church.*
  *V. Her whole life was signally approved by God (by her resurrection).*

The term "history" shows that a story is to be told. — Example, Acts 17, 10-14.

### The Shining Example of the Men of Berea.

  *I. They went to the Bible.*
 *II. They sought for certainty.*
*III. They found salvation.*

The word "example" points the direction. — Example, Acts 13, 44-49,

**The Tragic Story of the Hardening of the Heart Repeated in the Jews at Antioch.**

    I.   The first chapter — *God graciously brings the Gospel of salvation to lost sinners.*

    II.  The second chapter — *God is met by the wicked closing of men's hearts and ears against the Gospel.*

    III. The third chapter — *God is compelled to withdraw His Gospel and leave the hardened sinners to their fate.*

    IV. The fourth chapter — *God always finds others in whom His Gospel succeeds with its blessed work.*

Or, more briefly put,

    *I.   The Gospel comes.*

    *II.  The Gospel is spurned.*

    *III. The Gospel is withdrawn.*

    *IV. The Gospel is sent to others.*

The word "story" shows that the narrative form will be used in the parts. — Example 2 Kgs. 5, 1-19,

**Once Upon a Time in Damascus and Samaria.**

    *I.   There was a mighty general, who was stricken with leprosy.*

    *II.  There was a little Jewish maid, who knew her religion.*

    *III. There was a foolish Israelite king, who forgot his God.*

    *IV. There was a wise prophet, who voiced the Word of God.*

    *V.  There were sensible heathen servants, who helped their foolish master.*

    *VI. There was that mighty general again, who now believed and confessed the true God.*

The story form for the parts is pointed out by "once upon a time." The theme really means to say that "once upon a time in Damascus and Samaria" there were certain interesting persons who did a number of interesting things.

The narrative form is easy to use with texts that contain a real story, or material that may be turned into a story. And everybody likes a story, if it is well presented, which means that the main points be strikingly put and arranged in the order of a climax.

*The Imperative Form.* — The logically important word is the one in which the command is given. This form is always dramatic, and can be made highly so.

The command itself may be split so as to show fully *what* it contains.

Example, Acts 17, 10-14,

**Search the Scriptures as the Bereans Did.**

I. *Know what they say.*
II. *Believe what they say.*
III. *Adhere to what they say.*

"Search" indicates a command. Or,

**Learn in Berea What the Bible is For.**

*I) To preach; II) To believe; III) To apply; IV) To spread.*

"Learn" denotes a command.

But the command may also be divided by presenting the different convincing *reasons* for it. For with certain commands we will naturally ask *why* we should obey them.

Example, John 12, 12-19,

**Hosannas and Palms for the Savior King.**

This means, *bring* them. But why?

I. *For the King's own sake.*
II. *For our own sakes.*
III. *For the sake of His foes.*

These reasons are purposely incomplete, in order to sustain interest.

There are still other directives which the preacher may employ in his themes. For instance *exclamatory* themes, which also are dramatic. The reason for the exclamation points the direction. Then, too, the many *figurative* themes, either a text figure, or one used as an auxiliary concept in the theme. The figurative term points the direction. We shall elucidate the use of figures in themes in other connections.

THIRD CHAPTER

## DIVIDING THE THEME (Continued).

### The Marks of Cleavage.

The line of direction for dividing the theme is very valuable. Once we see in what direction we must proceed with the work of dividing much of the difficulty disappears. Yet we need something more, namely the natural marks of cleavage, which show us just where the split is to be made, how many parts we should have, and what these ought to be. The old writers on Homiletics called these marks of cleavage the *fundamentum dividendi*. By putting a line of direction into a theme plus the natural marks of cleavage, and then making use of both in the work of dividing, all arbitrariness in dividing is removed. We secure the right kind of division, in fact, the right division. There is no question about it any more.

While the line of direction and the marks of cleavage are distinct from each other, and are treated accordingly in Homiletics, in practice the two nearly always coincide. In other words, the eye that notes the direction in which the theme should be split, nearly always notes at the same time the marks of cleavage. Or, proceeding the other way around, the mind that projects a theme with an arrow word in it will nearly always also project it in such a way that the necessary marks of cleavage are found in it. Thus by getting the right form of theme the preacher at the same time obtained the natural and correct division of the theme.

### I. What Are the Marks of Cleavage?

By the marks of cleavage we understand the thought in the theme which points to the division peculiar to that theme.

It is imperative so to construct themes that they will cleave naturally. It is equally imperative to see the marks, or clearly grasp the thought containing the marks, which indicate how the theme unfolds in its parts. Once we have the marks of cleavage, a division will result which is natural, logical, beautiful, satisfying, and, being a true division, complete.

We can now see what is wrong with many sermon divisions. Some of them appear abitrary, merely due to some notion that happened to enter the preacher's mind at the time. At another time he probably would divide the same theme according to some other notion. Some divisions are artificial — since there must be a division, a division is made, whether it really divides the theme or not. Again, some divisions are just efforts — the preacher tried earnestly, but really did not know how.

The illustration of splitting a block of wood, which we used to show the line of direction, may also be used for the marks of cleavage. Those who have split wood know that sawed blocks dry out and show tiny fissures radiating from the heart of the block. It is an easy matter to sink the ax, not merely in the general line of the grain, but right into one of these fissures. A well placed blow of the ax, even without very much force, causes the block to fall apart. On the other hand, if the ax follows only the line of the grain, but misses the fissures, the split is much more difficult to make. So with sermon themes. The homiletical ax must sink into the natural fissures of the theme, then the split is true, **and** also easy to make.

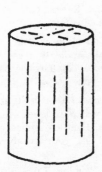 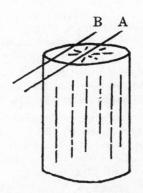

Showing the marks of cleavage.

A — the split according to marks of cleavage.

B — failing to follow the marks of cleavage.

A block of wood is not highly organized; we may only halve it and split the halves. There are thousands more highly organized objects as well as creatures. Each has distinct natural parts of its own. The lines where these parts meets are the marks of cleavage for a natural division. You may cut an orange through arbitrarily, but its natural structure is in segments which may be easily pulled apart. A chair has a seat, legs, and a back. A building has a foundation, walls, and a roof. A chariot has a body, wheels, an axle, and a tongue. A human being has a trunk, head, arms, and legs. So every theme has its natural parts. It should be built to have them, and the marks indicating them should be instantly recognized and used in making divisions.

Example, "The *Way* to Peace with God." This is equal to saying, *Whereby* may we attain peace with God? The theme thus points to certain *means* for reaching this peace. The marks of cleavage are thus brought to view. They are *the objective means* of grace, namely Word and Sacrament; and *the subjective means* of appropriation, namely faith.

Example, "What *Will Happen* when You Make a Fearless Confession of Christ? The marks of cleavage indicate a series of happenings: 1) The world will oppose you. 2) The Father will protect you. 3) The Lord will accept you.

Example, "Come *Unto Me*, All Ye that Labor and are Heavy Laden!" Why unto *Him?* Why we who labor etc., unto *Him?* The *reasons* for our coming unto Him are indicated by the marks of cleavage. 1) I will end all your troubles. 2) I will give you rest.

Example, "When God Promised the Prophet Like unto Moses He Revealed *the Great Doctrines of Salvation*." The italicized words show the marks of cleavage. The division must consist of these doctrines. The text, Deut. 18, 15-19, presents 1) The Virgin birth; 2) divine Inspiration; 3) atoning mediation; 4) justifying faith; 5) final judgment.

In many instances the marks of cleavage are not indicated by a special word or expression in the theme. But this lack should not cause much difficulty. The marks are there nevertheless — if we have a real theme to deal with. They are in the thought which the theme expresses. To see just what parts the theme calls for, restate the theme as exactly as possible in simple words. This is frequently done in the actual preaching of the sermon, perhaps right after the formal theme has been announced, perhaps also at the beginning, or at the end of the different parts. It is a very helpful thing to do in the study when the outline is under construction. All that is required is to answer this question, Just what do I mean to say by this theme? At times this question may induce the preacher to reformulate his theme. He may perceive that he does not wish to preach on what the first formulated theme really says. He may see that he can secure a far better theme by turning the thought in a different direction.

Example, John 9, 24-41. This text deals with the enlightening of the eyes. One might start out with the theme, "How a blind man was brought to faith." In trying to divide this commonplace theme, the preacher may hit upon the steps by which this man was led to faith. Presently the preacher will see that he can drop the special reference to the man's former physical blindness. He centers the theme on the steps he has discovered in studying the plainer theme with which he started. He summarizes these steps, and arrives at an outline like this, "Faith's Normal Pathway: it proceeds 1) From experience; 2) Through knowledge; 3) In confidence; 4) Unto adoration." In other words, it starts with an experience; advances in that way to knowledge; goes on by means of that to confidence; and in the fulness of that confidence rises to its goal — adoration. The theme could also be, "Faith's Normal Pathway as Illustrated by the Blind Man the Pharisees Cast Out."

Example, Mark 10, 17-27, "The Kingdom of God and Earthly Riches." Here the thought shows the marks of cleavage, for this theme promises that the preacher will show us *the relation* of the Kingdom and riches. The text helps us, in that it shows us on the part of the rich young ruler the wrong relation, and on the part of Jesus, in what He told the young man, the right relation. Hence the theme may operate with these parts, 1) The two are often antagonistic; 2) The two can be truly combined.

Example, John 15, 1-8. This is a text on "fruit." But this word taken by itself has no real marks of cleavage. Further study may, however, easily lead to what is needed. So presently the preacher will arrive at a theme like this:

**Fruit:**
**Required in the Kingdom of God:**
**The Fruit of the Heavenly Vine.**

In three striking ways Jesus shows us that such fruit is required. He lets us see

I.    *The branch on the vine.*
II.   *The pruning-knife in the husbandman's hand.*
III.  *The withered branches in the red blaze.*

The branch is on the vine only in order to bear fruit, not merely to grow and draw strength for no purpose. The knife is meant to prune and thus to induce fruit. And the burning dead branches are a warning against failure to bear fruit.

Example, Matth. 28, 1-10, and the favorite theme, "Jesus Lives!" We see the marks of cleavage when we restate the theme in a simple way, What does it *mean* for us that Jesus rose from the dead and now lives? Now it will not be difficult to arrive at parts like these,

### Jesus Lives!
That is
I.    *A fountain of joy for you this Easter morn.*
II.   *A source of strength for you in your entire life.*
III.  *A stream of grace for you in the Holy Sacrament.*
IV.   *A well-spring of hope for you in the face of death.*

The parts consist of an analysis superimposed on the central thought of the text, yet in full harmony with it (see above Part II, Ch. III, Analysis, 7). This type of division permits part three, namely a reference to the Sacrament so generally celebrated on Easter Sunday.

## II.  Groups of Cleavage Marks.

A study of good outlines will show that we can make a number of groups according to the marks of cleavage that happen to be employed. It is, of course, impossible to group all outlines in this way. Yet the groups that can be made are helpful in various ways. They are useful for the beginner by showing him a great number of patterns and designs for dividing, which have been used by able men. They help to train the eye and the mind when now a text confronts us and we are to project a theme with marks of cleavage in it. These groups are helpful for any preacher in showing him patterns of cleavage which he, perhaps, has not been using in his work.   We all tend to narrowness, like the men who use only analysis and not synthesis, or like the men who use only two or three parts and never think of four or more.   It is well to refresh the mind occasionally by looking at cleavage groups which we might just as well use occasionally as not, but which, except for a list like the following, would not occur to us.

1.   *The Dogmatical Group.* — Scores of divisions are used in Dogmatics, which are useful and suggestive also in Homiletics.   They may be technical in Dogmatics, and as such unsuitable in a sermon, for we cannot use technical terms in a popular discourse. Yet even in Dogmatics some are not at all technical — anyone at once understands them.   And those that are technical can often be reproduced in untechnical language and thus applied in dividing themes.   Since Dogmatics deals with the substance of the Christian faith, and uses all the products of sound exegesis, this group is extensive and exceedingly useful.   Here are a few examples:

**Our Epiphany Joy, as We See the Heavens Open Above Jesus.**

> *I.   It centers in Jesus Christ.*
> *II.   It extends to the Father and the Spirit.*

The text is Matth. 3, 13-17.   The doctrine of the Holy Trinity is used, since all three persons appear for our joy in this text.

**The Glory of God Revealed in the Birth of Christ.**

> *I.   The glory of His love.*
> *II.   The glory of His wisdom.*
> *III.   The glory of His truth.*

The text is Matth. 1, 18-23. The glory of God consists of the manifestation of His attributes. Here three of the attributes shine forth. Dogmatics teaches us what the attributes of God are.

### What Gives Us Courage and Power to Pray?

*I. The Father's love.*
*II. The Son's promise.*
*III. The Spirit's grace.*

The text is Luke 11, 5-13. The doctrine of the Holy Trinity is used in the cleavage.

### Your Case and Mine in the Court of Heaven.

*I. Desperate when we look at our sins.*
*II. Hopeless when we count on our good works.*
*III. Completely changed when we bring in Christ.*
*IV. Triumphantly certain when we come with faith.*
*V. Gloriously won when we hear God's sentence of pardon.*

This outline, on Acts 13, 38-43, presents the actual doctrine of Justification, and the marks of cleavage are naturally dogmatical. But the technical expressions are avoided, while their substance and sense is retained. Note the dogmatical cleavage in the use of these five terms in the five parts: "sins" — "good works" — "Christ," i. e. his merits — "faith" — "God's sentence of pardon."

2. *The Ethical Group.* — This, too, is an extensive group and furnishes any number of divisions. As to technical phraseology, the remarks under the first group apply also here. Examples follow.

### Remember What Spirit Ye Are Of!

*I. The spirit of unflinching obedience.*
*II. The spirit of sanctified zeal.*
*III. The spirit of Christlike love.*

"Obedience," "zeal," and "love" are ethical concepts. The text is Luke 9, 51-56.

**Let Mary of Bethany Lead Us in Honoring Our King!**

    *I.   Come with a heart like hers.*

   *II.   Come with devotion like hers.*

  *III.   Come with bravery like hers.*

The text is John 12, 1-8, and the comparison with Mary is made by means of inner analysis, hence the ethical points "heart," "devotion," "bravery."

**King David's Portrait of the Godly Man,**
**And the Question:**
**Is This a Portrait of You?**

    *I.   His heart and mind filled with the Word of God.*

   *II.   His life rich with the fruit of spiritual prosperity.*

  *III.   His associates the company of the righteous.*

  *IV.   His blessedness the divine approval from beginning to end.*

The comparison in Ps. 1 is made on the ethical points of a mind and heart filled etc.; a life rich etc.; associates of a certain kind; and divine approval.

**Daniel's Model Confession of Sin.**

There is in his confession, as there must be in ours also:

     *I.   Deep grief for the wickedness of sin.*

    *II.   Complete admission of the guilt of sin.*

   *III.   Genuine feeling of God's wrath for sin.*

   *IV.   Not the least effort to pay for sin.*

    *V.   The mercy of God as the only escape from sin.*

The text is Dan. 9, 15-18, and the description of true repentance follows ethical lines.


    3.   *The Psychological Group.* — This is very frequently used, and often furnishes cleavage that results in attractive parts.  The bodily organs, eyes, ears, hands, heart, etc., are at times used symbolically in a psychological sense.  Examples:

**One Thing is Needful.**

I. *Know it fully.*
II. *Seek it simply.*
III. *Grasp it firmly.*

Luke 10, 38-42. The actions named in the parts are psychological.

**The Man Who Thinks He is Independent.**

There is something wofully wrong with him, namely

I. *His heart is wrong.*
II. *His brain is wrong.*
III. *His life is wrong.*

The division here, on Prov. 16, 1-9, as the terms "heart," "brain," and "life" show, is psychological.

**Job's Sermon to Us on the Significant Brevity of Human Life.**

The sermon puts the brevity of human life before us th it we may

I. *Think of it.*
II. *Understand it.*
III. *Draw the right conclusion from it.*

Job 14, 1-5. To think, understand, draw a conclusion, are all psychological.

**"When I Have a Convenient Season."**

I. *An evasion.* Which means
II. *A refusal.* Which means
III. *Complete opposition.* And what this means need not be said.

Acts 24, 24-27. Evading, refusing, and opposing are psychological acts. — We add an example on the bodily members used psychologically in a symbolic way, Acts 9, 36-43.

**A Little History of Dorcas, the Dressmaker.**

I. *Her heart was filled with faith.*
II. *Her eyes were open to the need about her.*
III. *Her hands were diligent in works of love.*
IV. *All that her heart, eyes, and hands thus did was a help to the church and approved of God.*

4.  *Juxtaposition of God and Man, the Divine and the Human.* — The cleavage indicated by these two factors is one naturally expected in sermons, for they all deal with these two — God and man.

### The Lord is Come to Call Sinners to Repentance.

I.  *He calls.*
II.  *They come.*

Another example from Luke 24, 1-12.

### The Blessed Easter Light.

I.  *It shines forth in the risen Savior.*
II.  *It is reflected in the hearts of all believers.*

On the same text, again putting Christ over against us, we may outline:

### The Glorious Easter Message of the Open Tomb.

I.  *What does it tell us about Him who died?*
II.  *What does it tell us about us who shall live?*

A three part division may result when the human part is split into faith and unbelief, as on Acts 13, 44-49.

### Whose Fault is it When Men Refuse to Believe?

I.  *We have an answer when we look at God and His Gospel.*
II.  *We have a fuller answer when we look at those who will not believe.*
III.  *We have the complete answer when we look also at those who do believe.*

A variant of this type of cleavage is found in the *Juxtaposition of the Objective and the Subjective.* Either of these, or both, may also be split, thus making more than two parts.

Take Luke 18, 1-8.

### Why Does the Christian Pray Without Ceasing?

I.  *Because the Lord's promise is sure.*
II.  *Because we feel our need so deeply.*

The Lord's promise is objective; our need, and especially our feeling of it, is subjective. — Here is another example from John 11, 20-27.

### The Hour of Need in Bethany.

    *I.  The need at its worst.*
    *II.  The help at its best.*

Part one is subjective, for it describes the feelings, doubts, and conflicts in the hearts at Bethany. Part two is objective, describing Christ's great plans and actions. — A three part division results when the subjective joy that resulted is described in an additional part.

    *I.  It was an hour of need indeed.*
    *II.  It became an hour of grace through Jesus Christ.*
    *III.  It ended as an hour of joy.*

We add a four part cleavage from John 1, 35-42, where the first two are objective, and the last two are subjective.

### "Behold the Lamb of God!"

    *I.  God hath provided It.*
    *II.  It has borne the world's sin.*
    *III.  Our hearts must trust in It.*
    *IV.  We must lead others unto It.*

5.  *Juxtaposition of Time and Eternity, of the Earthly, and the Heavenly.*  This closely resembles the foregoing, sometimes in the form of a contrast between opposites, sometimes only in a comparison. Each of the two contrasting elements may also be split, making more than just two parts.

Example, Luke 17, 20-30, the first element (time) divided into two.

### Between the Two Great Advents.

    *I.  Behind us the cross* (time).
    *II.  About us the Kingdom* (time).
    *III.  Before us the glory of the end* (eternity).

John 6, 24-29 offers a good example, combining time and earthly things, and eternity and spiritual things.

**A Thanksgiving Question: What Meat Do You Labor For?**
> I.   *The meat which perisheth?*
> II.  *Or the meat which endureth to everlasting life?*

Luke 12, 4-9 is well in point, putting eternity and time over against each other.

**Keep in View the Day When You Shall Appear Before Christ and the Angels of God.**
> I.   *On that day you surely want Me to confess you* (eternity).
> II.  *Then in these days you surely do not want to deny Me* (time).

6.  *The Yea and Nay Group.* — We may also call it the affirmative and the negative group, or the positive and the negative. Affirmation over against negation necessarily runs through all our preaching. We constantly urge life instead of death, light instead of darkness, heaven instead of hell, etc. This natural, and even necessary, cleavage may appear in the sermon parts. But there is a cheap and superficial way of using the yea and the nay in division, namely when it amounts to this:

1.  What the thing we are speaking of *is*.
2.  What the thing we are speaking of *is not*.

Or, the nay first, and the yea second. The thinness of this proceeding is apparent, because it can be applied to any text or any subject. It is deceptive, too, because in many instances when the positive side is expounded the greater part of the negative is already used up, and vice versa. For there are any number of positive ideas which cannot be properly presented without at once weaving in the negative, and vice versa. Even when the two are strictly kept apart, merely putting "no" and "not" into one of the two parts of a sermon, makes no workable division, because it would be merely formal. In other words, just to repeat a statement, a paragraph, or still worse an entire part of a sermon, with a lot of "nos" and "nots" running through it, is a hopeless proceeding. We must avoid this sort of cleavage.

There is, however, a fairly wide field in which affirmation and negation may be effectively employed. This field is found where we deal with so-called opposites. It embraces all those cases in which the negative must be separately described as something that stands out by itself.

Example, John 7, 10-18.

### Can I Really Be Certain in Regard to the Doctrine of Christ?

> *I. No — if I listen to men.*
> *II. Yes — if I do what Jesus says.*

Note the two opposites "listen" and "do." Here we have more than "listen" and "not listen," or "do" and "not do" one and the same thing. — Another example, Luke 16, 10-17.

### The Church Member and His Money.

> *I. Your money is to be an aid in your church-membership.*
> *II. Your money dare never become a detriment to your church-membership.*

The theme, of course, deals with the relation of the church member to his money. The parts show the positive and the negative cleavage. For "to be an aid" is positive; "to become a detriment" is negative. Yet note how "to be an aid" is not merely negatived in part two by "not to be an aid," which would be useless for division. — Example, Acts 18, 24-28.

### In the Tent-Maker's Home in Ephesus.

I. *Here we find a man who knew much, and yet knew all too little.*

II. *And we find others who knew little, yet knew altogether enough.*

The expanded theme reads, What do we find in the tent-maker's home in Ephesus? In other words, the theme invites us to look into Aquila's home to see what is so interesting there. This interesting thing is the contrast between Apollos, and Aquila and Priscilla. The cleavage is on the yea and the nay, namely "much" and "not much," i. e. "little." The beauty in the arrangement, however, is that the yea and the nay is doubled. There is "much" and "little" for Apollos; and then, reversed, "little" and "much" ("enough") for Aquila and Priscilla. — Examples, Zech. 7, 4-10.

### What Benefit Has the Lord of Our Good Works?

I. *None whatever.*

II. *A great deal.*

The elaboration explains each part. Both are true, though they seem contradictory. 1) The Lord of hosts, who is all-perfect, all-blessed, cannot be given a thing by all the best and holiest good works in the world, such as are mentioned in verses 8-10, to say nothing of sham works like those in verses 6-7. 2) Yet He is greatly pleased to see by our good works that His saving Word and grace have actually changed our hearts and made them new; and He is greatly delighted to see His justice and mercy reflected in our lives as His true children, even as His joy is to make us at last perfectly like Him.

7. *The All and the One Group.* — Like the foregoing this group must be restricted to those cases in which it is worth while to place side by side "all" and just "one." If the same thing is to be said of "all" as of "one," there is no cleavage, but only repetition; likewise, if what is true of "one" is identical with what is true of "all." Ruling all these cases out we

have left a few in which a treatment of "all" combines well with a treatment of "one."

Example, John 21, 15-19.

**How the Risen Savior Cares for His Own.**

*I. The single sheep.*
*II. The entire flock.*

Jesus' dealing with Peter is one illustration of His care; while His commands concerning the flock ("My sheep," "My lambs") supplements and completes the story of His care for His own.

The reference to the "one," namely the individual, is often applicatory. Thus Christ's entry into Jerusalem may be described, namely His reception by the multitude, and then the question may be put about His entry into your heart and mine.

Allied to the "all and one" group is that of "the many and the few," as Jesus for instance says, "Many are called, but few are chosen," and illustrates this by by a parable in which many receive the invitation to the Great Supper, but only few put on the wedding garments and enter the banquet hall. Even of these few who enter one is found without the wedding garment.

A further example, Luke 12, 49-57.

**Three Against Two, and Two Against Three.**

*I. It has to be.*
*II. Thank God that it is.*
*III. Where do you stand?*

The theme states the general rule, and the first two parts elucidate this rule. But with a division like this among men, the question naturally arises for each one of our hearers just where he will be found.

8. *The Purpose and the Means Group.* — A purpose requires ways and means for its execution; and

means are meant to be used for a purpose. There is thus a relation between the two which may be used for theme cleavage.

Example, John 6, 37-40.

### The Way to a Blessed Resurrection.

I. *The way of Christ's redemption.*

II. *The way of His gracious Gospel call.*

II. *The way of the faith and life He makes ours.*

IV. *And thus the goal will be reached at last.*

In the first three parts we have the means in graduated order, and in part four the purpose as it will be achieved. — Example, John 7, 10-18.

### The Way to Real Spiritual Certainty.

I. *There are divine realities.*

II. *They must be brought to us.*

III. *We must come into living touch and actual experience with them.*

IV. *Then will we be certain indeed.*

In the theme the term "way" signifies the means, and "spiritual certainty" the purpose to be achieved. Parts one to three deal thus with the means, and part four presents the accomplished purpose.

Themes like the following find their proper cleavage in this fashion. "What shall I do to inherit eternal life?" The purpose (aim, goal) is "eternal life," and "what shall I do" asks about the means. — "How shall I obtain forgiveness of sins?" "Forgiveness" is the purpose to be achieved; "how" inquires about the means. Whenever "how" thus refers to ways and means, we have this type of cleavage. It is actually indicated in passages like John 3, 16. For us to have eternal life is God's purpose, and the giving of His Son and our faith in Him are the means (objective, and subjective). Also 1 Tim. 2, 4, "Who will have all men

to be saved (purpose), and come unto the knowledge of
the truth (means)."

9. *Time and Space Group.* — This group is of
wide application, and the examples under it are many.
Example, Luke 17, 20-30, in which space and time are
combined.

### Between the Two Great Advents.

> I.   *Behind us the cross.*
> II.  *About us the Kingdom.*
> III. *Before us the glory of the end.*

"Behind," "about," "before" are terms that refer to space,
yet here implying time.   On the same text the following.

### The Question, When the Kingdom of God Should Come.

> I.   *It has come.*
> II.  *It comes now.*
> III. *It shall come.*

The parts deal with the past, the present, and the future, thus
showing all that lies in the Kingdom's coming. — In the following, on Luke 10, 17-20, three parts deal with directions in
space, namely "deep," "lofty," "vast" (i. e. down, up, around),
and the last with the concept of time.   Thus time and space
may combine, for they are closely allied.

### There is No Joy Like That of Being a Child of God.

> I.   *There is none flowing from so deep a fountain.*
> II.  *There is none rising to such a lofty height.*
> III. *There is none taking in so vast a range.*
> IV.  *There is none enduring to such endless days.*

The following, on John 1, 43-51, uses parts of the day for
cleavage.

### The Epiphany Sun Rises in the First Disciples' Hearts.

> I.   *The dawn — Philip's word.*
> II.  *The first bright beams — Nathanael's word.*
> III. *The full noonday — Christ's own word.*

In this case the time concepts carried through in the parts are already indicated in the theme, which speaks of the sun's rising.

We may thus cleave themes by speaking 1) of how things look to-day, and 2) how they will look on judgment day; how the Church appeared 1) in the days of the apostles, and how it appears by comparison 2) in our own days; how Christ was received 1) by the Jews (centuries ago), and how he is received 2) by this generation (twenty centuries later).

Likewise we may go down, and then up. In John 3, 16 God's saving love reaches 1) down to the whole sinful world, in order to raise 2) up all that believe. — Or, on 1 Cor. 13, Paul's Praise of Christian Love, 1) Its depth; 2) Its breadth; 3) Its length; 4) Its height. — On Matth. 19, 16-26, we may show how far he has advanced, and yet how far he is behind, who claims that he has done all these things from his youth. — On Matth. 13, 31-35, The Progress of God's Kingdom, 1) Outwardly; 2) Inwardly. — On 1 Tim. 1, 17-17, The Chief Chapter in Paul's Biography: "I Have Obtained Mercy." 1) Before his conversion; 2) In his conversion; 3) After his conversion.

We must add that the time and the space idea underlie many types of division which use no words signifying time or space. This is the case with divisions like these: 1) origin; 2) manifestation; 3) consummation. Or, 1) the beginning; 2) the development; 3) the end. Take Matth. 28, 16-20,

**"The Glory of the Kingdom of God."**

I. *Its glorious Founder;*
II. *Its glorious expansion;*
III. *Its glorious consummation.*

The underlying idea is that of time, for the "Founder" takes us back to the beginning; the "expansion" covers the time between the beginning and the end; and the "consummation" is the end. These brief remarks show the wide applicability of this mode of cleavage, how richly it may be varied, and how beautifully it may be formulated. Of course all this takes mental effort, both in the way of penetrating thought and nimbleness of mind in using that thought. Yet that is what our minds are for.

10. *The Categories of Possibility, Actuality, and Necessity.* — This group might be termed ethical, because it generally deals with the will. For the same reason it has a psychological appearance. Yet we are not making the will, or anything ethical and psychological, the distinctive feature in this group. Its mark is that of modality. That means, that an act, or a course of action, an achievement, a goal, or a result, may be viewed in various ways. We may picture it as a possibility, show it as an actuality, describe it as a necessity. Or, to put it more simply, we operate with these ideas: I must — I ought — I can — I will — I am privileged — I rejoice.

Take the idea of bearing the cross. It means suffering, it is hard, hence I may well face it by saying: *I must* bear the cross. Yet it also means spiritual benefit, honor from the Lord, so that I may well add: *I will* bear the cross. Then the cross leads to the crown, so that I may rise still higher: *I rejoice* to bear the cross. And the theme may be, How the Christian Faces the Cross.

This type of cleavage underlies a number of divisions. Example, Luke 12, 49-57.

### The Discord Which Christ Brought on Earth.

I. *At first it perplexes us.*
II. *On second thought this is entirely as it should be.*
III. *Moreover, our only hope is in this discord.*

Part one deals with the possibility of this discord; part two with its actuality; and part three with its necessity. Part one asks, Can it be possible? Part two replies, It is actually as it should be! Part three adds to, and completes, the reply, It must be as it is! — Example, Acts 21, 8-14.

### "The Will of the Lord Be Done!"

I. *It may be very hard to say this.*
II. *Yet it is always good for us to say it.*
III. *And in the end we will rejoice in having said it.*

Part one deals with the possibility; part two with the actuality; part three with the necessity. In part one the soul asks, Can this really be the Lord's will? In part two the soul accepts the actuality that it is His will. And in part three the soul begins to rejoice in that will. — We add one more Example, Job 5, 17-26.

### "Happy is the Man Whom God Correcteth!"

I. *It may not seem possible.*
II. *Yet it is a fact none the less.*
III. *In the end we shall see that it had to be so.*

The cleavage according to the three features of modality is indicated in the parts, by the expressions, 1) possible; 2) fact; 3) had to be (possibility — actuality — necessity).

11. *The Question and the Answer Group.* — This has already been discussed in good part in chapter two, in connection with the logically important word in the theme, which please see. While there we considered only the logically important word which shows that the line of cleavage points to answers in the

parts, here the entire question is considered as demanding answers that are both pertinent and complete.
It is the nature of the question which thus determines
the kind and the character of the answers. The complete cleavage in the parts is thus determined, not by
the question as a mere question, but by the substance
of the question. This determines the individual quality
of the answers. In other words, each question has its
own natural and complete answer.

Thus Is. 2, 2-5.

**Why is the House of the Lord Set on a Mountain?**

   *I.   It is the one refuge of the nations.*
  *II.   It is the only light of the world.*
 *III.   It is the sole portal of heaven.*

These are not theoretical, notional, arbitrary answers,
but the concrete answers of the text, which fully and
completely satisfy the question. Nobody could pos-
sibyl furnish truer, more direct answers, or add anything essential not already covered by these answers.
Thus each question by its own substance indicates the
marks of cleavage for the answers or parts.

This is true of indirect questions as well as of
direct. It holds good also when the question is passed
on to the parts and the answers thrown into the elaboration. There are hundreds of good examples, so
that we need to add none here.

12. *The Metaphorical Group.* — This is one of
the largest and most attractive groups. Yet entirely
too little attention is paid to it both by writers on
Homiletics and by preachers. The author has often
marvelled at the students in his classes in Homiletics.
Given a text which is rich in figurative language, these

students will bring in outlines without a trace of figure, outlines built with abstract ideas which strip away every bit of the beauty in the text. It takes special effort to eradicate this tendency. The difficulty in weaning students away from abstractions in outlining is increased by the fact that homiletical works so often are full of the same fault, and much of the preaching of to-day knows little or nothing about metaphorical cleavage.

The Bible is full of figures. Some of the prophets stand unexcelled in the use of picture language. Our own language has been enriched by the influence of the Bible in this respect. In spite of ourselves we use Biblical figures and images in our preaching. Why then in outlining always let cold reason step in with logic, abstraction, and even generalization, when the text itself calls for the force, beauty, and warmth of a metaphor?

In every metaphor note the point of comparison most carefully. Technically it is called the *tertium comparationis*. With this point fully clear the imagery in the figure used will become distinct, so that its essential features will stand out and form marks of cleavage. As many figures as there are in our text so many cleavage patterns may be found for our metaphorical or figure themes

Example, John 6, 30-35.

#### The Feast of the Soul.

    I.   That feast is intended for *soul-hunger*.
   II.   That feast provides *soul-bread*.
 III.   That feast is intended for *soul-eating*.
 IV.   That feast nourishes *soul-life*.

The metaphor of the feast calls for the cleavage into hunger, bread, eating, and nourishment of life. — Example, John 4, 5-14.

### Jesus' Word to the Samaritan Woman.

    *I.   On thirst;*
   *II.   On water;*
  *III.   On drinking;*
  *IV.   On never thirsting again.*

Example on Ez. 33, 10-16.

### God's Antidote Against Death.

There is a sure antidote against death.

    *I.   It is God's grace.*
   *II.   It is taken by truly repenting.*
  *III.   It immediately works pardon.*
  *IV.   It is rapidly followed by amendment.*
   *V.   It infallibly kills death and creates life.*

Conclusion. — Get that antidote, it is dispensed without cost. And do not fail to take it.

Example, Jer. 8, 4-9.

### Is There Any Real Reason Why a Man Should Refuse to Repent?

Answer the question yourself, by looking at
    *I.   The man who falls down.*
   *II.   The man who takes the wrong road.*
  *III.   The birds who know their season.*
  *IV.   The horse that rushes into battle.*

All four illustrations occur in the text. The impenitent man is like one who falls down, and then like a fool lies there and refuses to get up again; or like the man who takes the wrong road, and when he finds out it is the wrong one refuses to return but just goes on. He is not like the birds which have sense enough to migrate when the time comes; but he is like the ignorant horse, prancing into battle with a proud mien, only to be ignominiously shot down.

Example, Prov. 9, 1-10.

### The Table of Divine Wisdom.

I. *It is set in the Church.*
II. *It dispenses the heavenly food of wisdom and life.*
III. *It is surrounded by needy sinners.*
IV. *It is barred against unbelievers and transgressors.*

The figure is plain: table — set — food — surrounded — barred. But in the four parts the realities are added to the figurative terms: set *in the Church* — food *of wisdom and life* — surrounded *by needy sinners* — barred *against unbelievers, etc.*

Example, Prov. 24, 14-20.

### The Story of the Two Candles.

I. *How they are lit.*
II. *How they burn.*
III. *What God will do with them.*

Any figure must be correctly carried out. Just as mixed metaphors are ludicrous, so mixing a metaphor in an outline, or even straining it, is, if not ludicrous, at least painful.

The figure must be carried through all the parts. It will not do to use it only part way, for one or two parts, and then to finish the other parts without the figure. It is like being invited to dine at a table covered with a beautiful table-cloth, but this cloth covers only half the table. Any figure that proves too short for all the parts must be laid aside.

Never build a sermon on a figure that is intended to disgust. Such figures are for incidental use, and are not to extend through an entire sermon. The wallowing sow, and the dog returning to his vomit should never appear in a theme or as a sermon part.

## III.  The Auxiliary Concept.

There is hardly anything as useful for building
themes with perfect marks of cleavage as the use of
auxiliary concepts.  For many a text this will be found
to be the way out.  One often finds the substance of
a theme, and even what he desires to say in the division, but effort after effort seems to fail when it comes
to forming an interesting and easily divided theme.

For the first anniversary of a church dedication
the author had selected Acts 20, 32 especially because
of the apostle's words, "I commend you to God and the
Word of his grace."  There was no difficulty about
the general idea and contents of the sermon as growing
from an earnest study of the text.  But how put the
matter into festive shape, for the occasion was rather
special?  At last the idea of erecting a memorial on
this anniversary day came to mind.  The search was
ended in a flash.

At this your first dedication anniversary raise

#### A Festive Memorial to God and the Word of His Grace.

Beneath the golden letters: "To God and the Word of
His Grace," there ought to be a line in the inscription to mark
that

*I.  You appreciate the gift of this Word and Grace.*
Then another line declaring that

*II.  You submit to the power of this Word and Grace.*
And the whole rounded out by a line telling how

*III.  You glory in the inheritance made yours by this
Word and Grace.*

The rest was very simple.  Now this idea of erecting a memorial,
one on which inscriptions could be carved, added to the great
thought about God's Word and Grace as furnished directly by
the text, is what we mean by an auxiliary concept.

An auxiliary concept is any suitable term oₓ expression by the addition of which the general theme thought drawn from the text may be advanced to form an actual theme showing a line of direction and marks of cleavage.

The definition may seem more difficult than the idea itself. Take Jer. 31, 31-34, with its general subject or theme thought, "The New Covenant." This cannot be split except arbitrarily, as it lacks both line of direction as well as marks of cleavage. But let us add the auxiliary concept "description," and at once we have a theme easy to divide, namely "Jeremiah's *Description* of the New Covenant." The text furnishes the features of this description, 1) It differs from the old; 2) as being wholly inward; 3) as furnishing knowledge to all; and 4) as resting on the Lord's forgiveness. As in this case, the text itself may suggest the auxiliary concept, although it may also be found outside of the text.

Again, taking the same text, we may see in it "The *Heart* of the New Covenant: I will be your God, and Ye shall be My People." We have added "heart" as the auxiliary concept. And the parts now will accord with this directive concept, 1) God makes us His own by forgiving our sins; 2) God leads us as His own by His gracious and holy Word. That is the very heart of the covenant in which we now live. — There are still other auxiliary concepts which may be used with the idea of the New Covenant in this text, as shown by the following themes:

> *The Glory* of the New Covenant.
> The Priceless *Treasures* of the New Covenant.
> For *the New Church Year* the New Covenant of *God's Grace.*

Why do we *Need* the New Covenant for *the New Church Year?*

The *Perennial* Newness of our Covenant with God.

Often a metaphor may be used as an auxiliary concept. If well chosen, it helps to make an excellent outline and sermon.

We append a few outlines constructed with auxiliary concepts. Matth. 3, 1-11.

**The Great Confessional Service Beside the Jordan's Banks.**
*I. The Sinners; II. The confessor; III. The repentance;*
*IV. The absolution.*

In the following, on John 12, 1-8, the idea of our sitting down to the supper at Bethany is the auxiliary concept, which, of course, also determines the parts.

**Let Us in Spirit Sit Down With the Guests to the Supper in Bethany.**

> *I.   How fine to be in the company of Jesus and His friends.*
> *II.  How stimulating to see Jesus loved and honored.*
> *III. How sad to see falseness and baseness in the very presence of Christ.*
> *IV.  How comforting to hear Christ's words of defense of His own.*

**The Royal Charter of Missions.**

> *I.   It was granted by divine majesty.*
> *II.  It conveys unlimited divine rights and privileges.*
> *III. It bears the unfading seal of the divine presence. —*
>     Matth. 28, 16-20.

**Christ, the Specialist For the Eyes of the Soul.**

> *I.   He treats the worst cases* (the man born blind).
> *II.  He uses the most effective remedies* (His grace in Word and deed).
> *III. He attains the most marvelous results.*
> *IV.  He fails only where His help and remedies are rejected. —* John 9, 24-41.

**Do You Know That You Are Writing the Epitaph for Your Tomb?**

Let your life spell out these three lines:

I. *He had forgiveness, for he knew the Father.*
II. *He overcame the evil one, for he loved not the world.*
III. *He abideth for ever, for he did the will of God.* — 1 John 2, 12-17.

**Why Doctor Eliphaz's Patient Grew Worse Instead of Better.**

I. *He diagnosed the case wrongly.*
II. *He applied the wrong medicine.*
III. *He only distressed the patient the more.*
IV. *It was God who cured him in the end.* — Job 14, 1-5.

The best metaphors are those suggested by the text itself, or naturally in accord with its substance and thought. The imagery in the figure ought to be clear, simple, striking if possible, and beautiful. Rule out anything that is trivial, forced, technical, far-fetched, abstruse. A touch of humor is possible only for those who possess the delicate gift of using it, and they are few. Jesus could speak of a man going out into a thistle patch to gather figs. Above all shun anything that smells nasty or has a tainted taste of suggestiveness. Vulgarity ill becomes the lips that should speak blessing. Rough, coarse, drastic figures may seem strong, but this strength reacts in the wrong direction. Noble, pure, inspiring figures never turn the hearer's thoughts downward. The figures you use reflect what lingers in your own heart and mind.

*Rubrics of Division.* — An effort has been made to compile all the possible modes of division. Works of this kind have a very limited value. They may draw the attention of the preacher to certain types of division which he has overlooked in his preaching.

That is about all. We readily get into certain ruts, and so overlook ways of dividing which we might easily and profitably use, if at the time we happened to think of them.

But it is useless to attempt to find in such a work some pattern of division that we may impose on the text we have in hand. Such attempts are altogether too mechanical, and result in too many misfits and forced outlines. The living Word of God is entitled to far higher consideration. Hunting for outline patterns for some text is a lifeless proceeding, and only shows that the preacher has not mastered the noble homiletical art.

## FOURTH CHAPTER

# THE FORMULATION OF THEME AND PARTS.

Putting the theme and the parts into final, finished form is called the formulation. While we speak of it here in a separate chapter, in practice the preacher will formulate at once when he determines on his theme and his division. He may touch up the formulation as he works out the sermon; but usually this will not be necessary.

If getting the substance of the outline is important, the formulation is equally so. Thoughts are conveyed only through words, so every word in the formulation is important. Thoughts are clearly, adequately, and instantaneously conveyed only by the proper words in proper combination; hence our themes and our parts must be worded with great exactitude. Incidentally it is a very fine training to continue this care in formulation throughout life. He who weighs every word and every combination of words in his outlines in order to convey his meaning to his hearers most effectively, will tend to do the same thing all through his sermon, which certainly will improve it.

Those who object to spending care and skill on the formulation are left with a poor alternative, namely an indifferent, loose, careless, perhaps quite inexact formulation of theme and parts. This, of course, means also weakness, lack of beauty and attractiveness, and possible misapprehension of meaning. While over-refinement and excessive polish are never good, there are few men in the pulpit guilty of this homiletical sin. The tendency is rather in the other direction. And thus naturally they who are guilty of carelessness and inexactness in formulation are prone to rise up and defend it, if only, like the old Pharisees, to justify themselves before men, Luke 16, 15. Let us put our efforts to better use.

Good preaching in general, and skill in outlining in particular, demand a thorough knowledge of language, especially the language of the Bible. This means versatility in the use of all the forms of language, grammar, and rhetoric; a sense of the beauty, the rhythm, and the music of language; an instantaneous perception of the connotations and implications in words and forms of speech. To acquire all this we must continue reading the best literature, and reading it with intelligence. There is no end to the progress even the best of us may make. Perfection always lies just beyond. But this fact is the very thing which makes the efforts we put forth so stimulating. There is no room for stagnation in preaching, which begins with outlining. Homiletics ever beckons onward and upward. Love her for this very thing.

## I. Formulations That Are Better.

*Brevity is always better.* — In formulating the outline cut away all the marble that is not statue. The man who put it in this way was right. The entire unity of the sermon should be expressed in one terse statement. This should be as *precise* as possible, just the exact words needed, and not one word more. Cut away any genitive, adjective, adverb, anything like a clause, that is not clearly necessary to express the thought of the theme, or of the parts. The long way of saying a thing is the weaker way. There is more power in a few words, if they be the right ones, than in many words, whether they be the right ones or not. It is said of the court preacher Koegel that he could rip up a popular error with the thrust of a single sentence, and sometimes he used less.

On the other hand, in striving for brevity do not become too *general*, or too *indefinite*. "The Love of Christ" is certainly brief enough, but think of all that such a theme would include!

Theme and parts are not intended to convey all that the preacher means to present in his sermon. Then they would have to be long and involved. All that we expect of the outline is that it be an outline, not a sermon *in parvo*. By striking the central thought the sermon ought to stir the hearer's mind, both by what the outline actually conveys and implies, as well as by what it fails to say and leaves to be added.

We have true brevity when we use only *the necessary words*. That may be only one word, or it may be ten or twelve words. In both cases we may have the virtue of brevity. "No Millennium?" is brief, but to the point and wholly sufficient, for it is a concentration of the longer question, "Does the Bible really teach that there will be No Millennium?" As a theme the concentrated question is better than the expanded one. But on Luke 13, 6-9, the theme, "There is a New Year's Message for us in what was done with the Barren Fig Tree" also has brevity although there are more words by far. There is thus no fixed number of words for brevity. Brevity is not mechanical. We have brevity when we have the necessary words and no more.

*Color is always better.* — Most preachers use too
little color in their outlines, in fact, some do not seem
to know what color really is. When they do happen to
get a little of it into theme or outline it is only a happy
accident. Yet color is both valuable and attractive.

Every text has its own color, and no two texts
show the same color, unless they be close parallel
passages. The color of a text is in its peculiar wording.
When the words are uttered, "God so loved the world,"
we are at once made to think of John 3, 16 and no other
passage. "In the night in which he was betrayed"
immediately connects us with the Institution of the
Lord's Supper. There is, of course, stronger and
fainter color, but every bit of it is good. We have
color in the outline when it is so worded that it at
once recalls the text for which it is intended. Sometimes a mere word is enough, if it be strongly distinctive of the text. Sometimes the entire theme may be
an expression found in the text, and even the parts
may be expressions quoted from the text. Between
these two limits there are endless variations and possibilities.

Examples. "God's children are all childlike,"
using the word "childlike," recalls Matth. 18, 1-5 where
Jesus tells His disciples, they must all become as little
children. The color is in the one word. — On the same
text the theme may be "The Little Child in Jesus'
Arms," and at once we perceive that the color is
stronger, for the entire theme recalls the text to our
minds. — "Three against Two, and Two against Three"
is a quotation, very strong in color, at once connecting
us with Luke 12, 49-57. Quoted themes always do
this. — "What the Parable of the Talents Teaches us
Concerning Good Works." The Lord's instruction

centers in three key words, namely 1) "Servants";
2) "Talents"; 3) "The joy of thy Lord." Here the
parts are quotations and thus colorful, while the theme
has color, not from quotation, but from the title of the
parable. — Only rarely does a text permit us to quote
both theme and parts from it. Here is one, Is. 35, 3-10.

> **"Strengthen Ye the Weak Hands,**
> **And Confirm the Feeble Knees!"**
>
> I.  *"Behold, your God will come!"*
> II. *"The eyes of the blind shall be opened!"*
> III. *"In the wilderness waters shall break out!"*
> IV. *"The ransomed of the Lord shall come to Zion!"*

The parts may be read either as reasons for the command of
the theme; or as specifying what is meant by "strengthen"
and "confirm." — Another on Matth. 23, 34-39.

> **"O Jerusalem, Jerusalem!"**
>
> I.  *"How often would I!"*
> II. *"But ye would not!"*

Perhaps John 3, 16 is as good an example as any.

> **"God So Loved the World,"**
>
> I.  *"That he gave his only begotten Son,"*
> II. *"That whosoever believeth in him,"*
> III. *"Should not perish,"*
> IV. *"But have everlasting life."*

A clash in color results when the theme is a
quotation drawn from some other passage, and not
from the text. The clash is only aggravated when the
parts are also quotations from outside the text. Invariably the impression is made that the preacher is
using that other passage, and not his text, as the basis
of his sermon. If the outside passage quoted in the
theme is one well known, this discord becomes positively annoying. Why homiletical helps and prominent

preachers use strong off-color in this way probably belongs to the chapter of homiletical mysteries. Make it a rule to get your color from the text, never from some other passage. On 2 Sam. 3, 22-32 a prominent exegetical-homiletical work offers a sermon sketch with this theme quoted from Heb. 12, 1, "Let Us Run with Patience the Race that is Set Before us!" The violent clash in color is even aggravated, for instead of keeping to the idea of a race this is turned into a battle, and the parts speak of 1) the strength, 2) the weapons, 3) the climax, 4) the outcome of the battle. And yet, neither race nor battle are in the text, and what is actually in it is serenely ignored. This kind of preaching turns the text into a side issue.

Texts rich in figurative language beyond question ought to transfer some of this color to theme and parts.

Color is derived only from the text, and from no other source. It is a mistake to seek color in the application to the hearers; none is there to seek.

Color in theme and parts always attracts, and is desirable for this reason alone. But it also individualizes, specifies, differentiates, makes decidedly concrete. This is the chief value of color. Without a touch of color many a theme would be too general or too abstract.

Yet color, genuine strong color, cannot always be attained — the more is the pity. We are at times compelled to state the theme in words all our own, instead of words reminiscent of the text. This is even more true of the parts. Yet this makes us appreciate color only the more when we are able to get it. So train your mind and your eye always to seek it, for it is lovely and valuable.

*Rhythm and beauty are always better.* — All rhetoric and language study corroborates this statement, so that we need to add but little in this connection. Beauty of phrase is always appreciated. In preaching this means far more than literary excellence. The subject matter with which we deal is spiritual truth, which in itself has the highest beauty, and like nothing else calls for the most beautiful language dress. Words that fall and rise smoothly; sentences that end strongly, with no weak trailer; compact statements that go straight home — these are the features we need in formulating outlines.

We have the finest language models in the Authorized Version. Many of its phrases and turns go back to the master translator of them all, Dr. Martin Luther. When the spirit of the King James' version animates the preacher he will rise above the common and commonplace, and all his outlines, as also his elaborations, will show something of the sweet nobility of language that is beauty in spiritual form.

Shun all affectation. Polish for the sake of polish is no polish at all. Glitter is only a delusion. Gaudy phrases are like gaudy dresses, conspicuous but inappropriate. Puffy phrases, high-flown expressions betray insincerity of thought. Some women paint themselves and imagine they are beautiful; but we who have to look at them see nothing to admire.

Avoid all poetry of your own. Only one out of thousands of preachers is a real poet by the grace of God. A thousand chances to one you are not the individual so favored. Keep your poetical proclivities like pets penned up in your back yard, and never exhibit any of them in the pulpit.

## II.  Source of the Formulation.

The substance of a sermon theme has but one source, namely the text. The form, however, into which the theme is put may be derived either from the text itself or from the use to which the text is put in the sermon.  This is due to the position and the function of the theme.  It really stands between the text and the sermon, and it acts as the hinge, making the sermon swing on the text.

*The Text as a Source.* — We have already shown how color may be secured for theme and parts in their formulation by drawing distinctive expressions or entire quotations from the text.  Here, however, we are not concerned with the individual feature of color, but with the general source from which the formulation may be derived.  The text is such a source as distinct from the appropriative or the applicatory use we may make of it.

In all analytical sermons the text is the source of the theme, for the very unity of the text is to constitute the unity of the sermon.  To obtain a theme for an analytical sermon the preacher must focus his mind on the text and must summarize its contents as exactly as possible.  The same thing is true of a homily in a slightly different way, for in a homily the theme is a descriptive unity of the parts of a text, which appear as the parts of a sermon.  All but the last form of synthesis follow the same general course.  In the simplest form we retain the unity of the text as the substance of the theme, and transpose only the parts. In intermediate synthesis one of these parts is elevated to the position of the theme, the remaining parts being used in the division. Thus the text remains as the source of the theme. In advanced synthesis new combinations of the various text thoughts are formed, and a theme is sought to cover their recombination. By way of this recombination the theme develops from the text.

In thus making the text the source of the theme various ways are open to the preacher.

A very short text may itself become theme and parts. John 3, 16 is an example (see the section on Color). Instances like this are few.

A quotation direct from the text may serve as a theme. Thus in Luke 10, 38-42, "One Thing is Needful." Luke 10, 23-37, "Who Is My Neighbor?" Luke 17, 11-19, "Where Are the Nine?" These cases are quite numerous.

The preacher may use his own words in the formulation, inserting, however, some distinctive expression from the text. This may be no more than an allusion, as on Matth. 18, 1-5, "God's Children are all Childlike." It may also be an expression taken directly from the text, as on Jer. 7, 1-11, "When Solomon's Glorious Temple Became a Den of Robbers." "Den of robbers" occurs in verse 11.

The formulation intended to convey what has been drawn from the text may be wholly in the preacher's own words, but in the parts he may utilize expressions from the text.

Example, Ps. 85, 8-13.

**The Jewels of Your Heavenly Necklace.**

I.   *The clasp:* "The fear of the Lord."
II.  *The four jewels:* "mercy and truth — righteousness and peace."
III. *The golden pendant:* "salvation."

Finally, theme as well as parts may be the preacher's own words. Example, Job 5, 17-26.

### Eliphaz and Job:
### The Riddle of Godly Suffering.

I. *Eliphaz understood only the first part of the solution* (and imagined that to be the whole).

II. *Job was wrestling with the second part of the solution* (was not helped by Eliphaz; God finally helped him).

III. *Neither Eliphaz nor Job knew the final part of the solution* (which has the greatest comfort of all).

In all these ways of formulating the text remains the source, in one or the other way controlling the formulation arrived at.

*The Special Use of the Text as a Source.* — Instead of the text as such, the special use to which the text is put in the sermon may dominate the formulation of theme and parts. This special use will be appropriative or applicatory, or both. Homiletical appropriation = the Christ *for* us, made ours (appropriated) by faith. Homiletical application = the Christ *in* us, his example, as well as the example of Christlike men, applied to our lives and works.

By allowing the special use to which the text is put to dominate the formulation of the outline we are by no means forsaking the text or turning our backs upon it. Remember that the theme of the sermon faces in two directions, back to the text, and forward to the sermon. Accordingly it may receive its formulation from either side. In fact the text as such, combined with the special use to which it is put, may together affect the formulation of theme and parts.

This is clearly the case both in superimposed analysis and in the highest form of synthesis (both of which see above). Superimposed analysis is added to the text, and thus comes from without, although it harmonizes perfectly with the text. For instance, what the text tells us may be used 1) for our instruction; 2) for our warning; 3) for our admonition; and 4) for our comfort. We thus look at the text from four different angles. Yet the text itself does not speak of instruction, warning, etc. But the formulation of the outline is guided by these four ideas which are brought to bear upon the text.

This is also true of the highest form of synthesis. In this case the text is viewed from the standpoint of some need of our hearers. This need therefore governs the formulation of the synthetical theme and parts.

In the examples given above, as illustrating superimposed analysis, the themes are drawn from the texts themselves, only the parts are formulated according to the special use to which the texts are put. In the following examples both themes and parts are wholly influenced and shaped by the use to which the text is put.

Example, Acts 17, 10-14.

### Personal Experience With the Bible.

I.  *Do you go to the Bible?*
II.  *Do you rely on the Bible?*
III.  *Do you abide by the Bible?*

Another on the same text.

### Use the Bible Aright!

I.  *Search it* — with readiness of mind.
II.  *Believe it* — with honesty of heart.
III.  *Cling to it* — against all opposition.

Another on Acts 21, 8-14.

### "Commit Thy Way Confiding
### When Trials Here Arise!"

    I. *Trials must come — the Lord sends them.*
    II. *Trials are necessary — the Lord has His purposes in them.*
    III. *All trials require confident submission — the Lord is ready to work this in us.*

Example for the highest form of synthesis as showing a formulation derived from the use to which the text is put, John 3, 31-36.

### Let the Greatness of Jesus Show You Why Faith and Unbelief Are So Decisive.

    I. *Faith honors Jesus the Son of God, unbelief spurns Him.*
    II. *Faith accepts the Son's Word, unbelief denies it.*
    III. *Faith bows to the Son's rule, unbelief rebels against it.*
    IV. *Faith takes the Son's gift, unbelief casts it away.*
    V. *Faith joins to His followers, unbelief joins to His foes.*

The need is set forth in the introduction. So many people cannot understand why faith should be so decisive, especially why "good "people should be damned just because they do not believe in Christ. — Similarly the tragic text Is. 63, 7-16. The introduction sketches the extreme need. Even grace has its limits. Hence the tragedy of being

### Too Late!

    I. *For agonizing appeal.*
      Once it would have been swiftly heard — no longer now.
    II. *For abject confession.*
      Once it would have brought instant pardon — no longer now.
    III. *For poignant longing.*
      Once it would have induced a rich response — but now only judgment waits.

The text and the main outline as well are negative. But the first half of the elaboration of each part is strongly positive, thus balancing the sermon between negation and corresponding affirmation.

### III. Objective and Subjective Formulation.

The great saving acts, facts, powers, and gifts of salvation are objective. They are unalterable realities. They remain such, no matter what men may think or say about them, or what attitude they may assume towards them. Now the sermon that deals with any of these objective realities must present them in an objective way. This cannot be done too effectively, for men always incline to the delusion, that these objective realities are like rubber and can be made what their thinking and their desiring would like to have them be.

All the examples in the Scriptures, from Christ's own on down to that of His humblest followers, including the negative examples of any and all opposition to Christ, plus the sins, weaknesses, and faults of His own followers, are likewise objective. They stand forth in the Scriptures as realities — good in the sight of God, or bad in His sight.

The same is true of all the doctrinal part of the Scriptures. All of it is in the highest degree objective. In other words, all Biblical doctrines present realities. For doctrine, which is teaching, simply tells us what the great acts, facts, powers, gifts, etc., really are, what they mean, and what they effect. Likewise, doctrine tells us what the examples are, what they mean, and what they are intended to effect. All of this is evidently objective, i. e. wholly unaffected by any thinking, desires, or actions of ours.

Now in formulating an outline we may abide by the objective form. In theme, as well as parts, the realities which we treat may be spoken of simply as realities.

Objective formulation has its special uses. Sermons for the great Christian festivals, for instance, ought to be objective to a large degree. At other times it will also be advisable to make the realities stand out simply as realities.

On the other hand, all the great saving acts, facts, powers, and gifts of salvation are intended for our appropriation, which takes place by means of faith. All appropriation is subjective. The moment our sermon shows how the saving realities are made our own, for us to have, to obtain their benefits, to use for ourselves, and to enjoy in time and in eternity, we are dealing with them subjectively.

The same is true of all the objective examples in the Scriptures. They are all intended for our use and benefit, either to copy in our own lives, or to avoid copying. This is called application, and all application is subjective. Any sermon which treats an example so as to produce an effect in our hearts and our lives deals with that example subjectively.

This is also true of doctrine, whether it deals with the saving realities or with the ethical examples. The moment the sermon presents any of these objective doctrines so that we are moved to believe or to copy and obey, that moment the treatment adds the subjective side to the objective.

Now the formulation of an outline may consist in a subjective presentation. In other words, appropriation and application may appear in the form which theme and parts assume.

Just as objective formulation has its special uses, so also has subjective formulation. Any second sermon connected with the great Christian festivals may well be appropriative, subjective in this way. Applicatory formulations are highly desirable at almost any time.

No sermon as a sermon should be wholly objective or wholly subjective. We can never dispense with the realities, for unless we have something to appropriate or apply we can do neither. A sermon that lacks the realities would cease to be a sermon. The only question that may arise is this: To what extent may subjective treatment be permitted? There may be more of it in the elaboration, or less of it — there should always be some. But the subjective presentation may appear already in the outline, in both theme and parts, or in either of them.

Even in building objective outlines the preacher's thinking should be strongly subjective. Too much objectivity tends to put the great realities too far away from the hearers. The sermon thus may become cold. A noble example, like Stephen's, may be pictured in such a high and distant way that the hearers may merely admire it, while silently they feel that certainly no one can reasonably expect them too to rise to such heights. This is overdoing the objective. — On the other hand, fervent appeals to our hearers, prolonged and intense urgings often defeat their own purpose because the decisive realities, with their own convincing power, are not sufficiently set forth. Too much pulling at the hearers by subjective exhortation is a psychological mistake, since it causes an adverse reaction. The over-eager salesman loses too many customers.

The use of the second person is a mark of subjective treatment. This becomes the first person plural when the preacher includes himself. In some of St. Paul's Epistles we note how he alternates "you" and "we." The objective treatment is marked by the third person "he" and "they." Yet one may present some reality in a way that goes right to the heart of a hearer though using the third person. Show me just what I lack, or diagnose my case exactly, and I will understand you, without you telling me, *"Thou* art the man!" This mode of procedure is highly advisable in some cases. At a funeral, perhaps, we may have unchurchly and worldly hearers who would simply resent any direct call to repentance. But an objective presentation, picturing the wretched state and fate of the impenitent man, and on the other hand the penitent man with his priceless pardon, his comforting assurance, and his happy end (all done in the third person), may touch the hearts of these sinners and produce surprising results.

Two examples, both on Prov. 2, 1-8, the first objective, the second subjective. In the former the appropriation goes into the elaboration, while in the latter it appears already in the outline.

### Wisdom's Son:
### The Man With the Golden Necklace.

   I.   *How he acquired it,* v. 1-4.
  II.   *The gold it is made of,* v. 5-6.
 III.   *The pendant attached to it,* v. 7-8.

### Are You a True Son of Wisdom?

   I.   *Have you been trained in her school?*
  II.   *Are you crowned by her gift?*
 III.   *Do you walk in her way?*

Two examples on Acts 18, 24-28, the first objective, leaving the application to the elaboration; the second subjective, bringing the application into the outline.

### The Humble Tent-Maker's Christian School.

*I. The teachers. — II. The pupil. — III. The instruction. — IV. The graduation* (v. 27-28).

### Learn From Aquila and Priscilla the Value of Christian Knowledge.

*I. The value of you also having such knowledge.*

*II. The value of you also employing such knowledge.*

We add two examples on doctrine, one objectively presented, the other subjectively, both on Luke 15, 11 etc.

### The Prodigal an Illustration of the Doctrine of Divine Forgiveness.

*I. Of the contrition that precedes forgiveness.*

*II. Of the absolution that constitutes forgiveness.*

*III. Of the new life that springs from forgiveness.*

### Your Justification and Mine Described in the Parable of the Prodigal Son.

Here is pictured

*I. Our sin-laden and guilty hearts.*

*II. Our contrition and confession.*

*III. Our faith and pardon.*

*IV. Our new life and joy.*

## IV.   Structure in Formulation.

Every true theme is a *judgment,* fully expressed, or implied.   Anything less than a judgment may be a mere subject; it is not a theme.

Grammatically, as well as logically, every theme consists of at least *a subject and a predicate.*   There may be more, there is never less.

On this basis rests all that follows.

1. Little needs to be said on themes in which subject and predicate appear side by side: "Jesus Lives!" "One Thing is Needful," and many others. Of course, adjective, adverbial modifiers, and appositions may be added, for which we hardly need examples. But there are other possibilities.

2. There may be two subjects, with the predicate implied, for instance, "Christianity and Liberty." The theme here really is, "What is the relation between Christianity and liberty?"

3. There may be two clauses, or the equivalent of two clauses. On John 6, 60-69, "Shall We Go, or Shall We Stay with Jesus?" Rom. 6, 12-23, "Slavery or Liberty?" = Shall we submit to slavery, or attain liberty? Besides coordinate clauses we may have a main clause and a subordinate one. John 11, 20-27, "Christ Bids Us Look upon Him, Who is the Resurrection and the Life" (relative clause). Matth. 9, 9-13, "O the Blessedness of Christ's Kingdom: Sinners are Called Into It!" (appositional). On the same text, "Blessed He Who can Believe, Jesus Sinners doth Receive!" (object clause). Matth. 10, 24-33, "What Will Happen, When We make a Fearless Confession of Christ?" (adverbial clause).

What is true of the structure of the theme, is equally true of the structure of the parts, for which we will hardly need examples. The theme, as well as the parts, may use declaration, interrogation, or exclamation. This, too, needs no examples.

4. Theme and parts may be in the form of just one extended sentence. This is a little difficult, for the parts may not stand out distinctly enough, yet occasionally this structure is used. Acts 9, 36-43.

**The Humble Dressmaker Dorcas Was Raised from the Dead,**
  I.   *In order that her lowly example of fruitful faith*
  II.  *Might stand out by God's own act for the Church of all ages*
  III. *As an example to stimulate·us to like fruitful faith.*

Example, Jer. 7, 1-11.

**When Solomon's Glorious Temple Became a Den of Robbers:**
  I.   *Then they who were robbing the Lord,*
  II.  *And thought they could do so with impunity,*
  III. *Were told they were robbing themselves,*
  IV.  *And discovered their awful loss too late.*

Example, Is. 2, 2-5.

**Our Epiphany in the Light of the Lord's Word.**
  I.   *It illumines the nations*
  II.  *So that they see the Lord's ways,*
  III. *Are corrected by the Lord's judgments,*
  IV.  *And brought to the house of eternal peace.*

There are a number of interesting and attractive *structural arrangements* for themes, with which the preacher ought to be acquainted.  We list the following.

1) *Opposites and their Solution,* also described as the juxtaposition of thesis, antithesis, and synthesis. 2 Chron. 1, 7-12.

**Let Wise Solomon Show Us What Money is Worth.**
  I.   *Mighty little.*
  II.  *A great deal.*
  III. *According to the heart that handles it.*

The thesis and antithesis are like a paradox, which the synthesis then solves. — Ez. 33, 10-16 has the paradox all in the first part, and the solution in the second.

**"Why Will Ye Die?"**
  I.   *Let us die before we die!*
  II.  *That we may not die, when we die!*

2) *Contradiction in Terms*, also called *contra-dictio in adjecto*. Both sides of the contradictory statement are true in the divine economy of God's Kingdom. Acts 26, 22-30.

### St. Paul—A Victor in Chains.
I. *Though chained he preaches a victorious Lord.*
II. *Though chained he proclaims a victorious Gospel.*
III. *Though chained he confesses a victorious faith.*
IV. *Though chained he displays a victorious love.*

"A victor in chains" is really a contradiction, yet there are such victors in the Kingdom. So also we may actually live by dying. We may possess a rich poverty. Our weakness may be our strength. The more helpless we are the greater help we have.

3. *Syllogism.* Jesus used syllogism in a most effective way. Take John 8, 47, with its negative conclusion.

### A Test for Divine Childhood.
I. *He that is of God heareth God's Words* (major premise).
II. *Ye therefore hear them not* (minor premise).
III. *Therefore ye are not of God* (conclusion).

The same reasoning is used on the spurious claim of descent from Abraham, John 8, 39-40. 1) Abraham's children do Abraham's works. 2) Ye seek to kill me, which Abraham did not. 3) Ergo, ye are not his children. — Example, 1 Cor. 3, 16-17.

### The Sacredness of God's Living Temple.
I. *Him who defiles God's temple God shall destroy.*
II. *But now ye are God's Temple.*
III. *Therefore sanctify your hearts and lives.*

While actual syllogistic divisions are scarce, logical deduction is oftener used as a basis. Thus Prov. 24, 14-20.

**Your Expectation: Will It be Realized?**

I.   *It will surely not be if you just think it will.*

II.  *It surely will if God has told you that it will.*

III. *It surely will make a great difference, whether it will, or will not, when the time comes.*

IV.  *It surely ought to be of great concern to you right now, whether it will, or will not.*

Example Ps. 90.

**Moses Teaches Us the True Wisdom at the Beginning of a New Year.**

We are wise if to-day we

I.  *Face the actual facts.*

II. *Draw the true conclusion.*

4. *Chiasm*, also called inversion. This is confined to two parts.

Example, Luke 23, 39-46.

**Christ and the Repentant Malefactor.**

I.  *The Savior brought to the sinner.*

II. *The sinner accepted by the Savior.*

Also John 8, 31-36.

**"The Truth Shall Make You Free."**

I.  *The truth which produces liberty.*

II. *The liberty produced by truth.*

Likewise Mark 10, 13-16.

**The Children and the Kingdom.**

I.  *The Kingdom is for children.*

II. *The children are for the Kingdom.*

5. *The Chain.* This needs at least three parts. Each part has two members. The last member of the first part is made the first member of the second part, and so on through the parts. More rare is the use of the first member of the first part as the second

member of the second part, and thus on through the parts. Illustration:

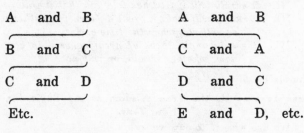

Example, Ez. 33, 10-16.

### "Why Will Ye Die, O House of Israel?"

I. *There is a way of escape through repentance.*
II. *Because repentance assures justification.*
III. *And justification assures life.*

Example, 2 Kgs. 5, 1-19.

### The Story of Naaman's Faith.

I. *How he is compelled to seek the prophet.*
II. *How the prophet gives him nothing but the Word.*
III. *How the Word finally brings him to faith.*
IV. *How faith proves his highest blessing.*

Example, Dan. 9, 15-18.

### The Godly Life is Always Marked by the Genuine Confession of Sin.

I. *It could not be godly without getting rid of sin.*
II. *It could not get rid of sin without confession.*
III. *It could not confess without dropping all self-righteousness.*
IV. *It could not drop all self-righteousness without casting itself on God's mercy.*

Example of the reverse order, using the last outline, would make the parts read as follows.

I. *Without getting rid of sin it could not be godly.*
II. *Without confession it could not get rid of sin.*

III. *Without dropping all self-righteousness it could not confess.*

IV. *Without casting itself on God's mercy it could not drop all self-righteousness.*

An extended and beautiful chain is found in 2 Pet. 1, 5-7. Further examples in the *New Gospel Selections* by the author, p. 397 and 521.

*The Wording.* — In all good writing much depends on the way our thoughts are worded. To think that any wording that may come to mind will do is to fall into the vice of slovenliness, which soon incapacitates the mind from ever rising to a higher level. Themes and parts worded exactly right, are not only better, but far better, than themes and parts indifferently molded.

We have already discussed *rythm*, smoothness, and balance in wording. We may add that natural alliteration is acceptable, but not the artificial kind. Example on Matth. 16, 15-20.

**The Savior's Word to St. Peter on the Christian Church**
*On I) its foundation, II) its function, and III) its foes.*

The *heterogeneous* wording of the parts shows only that no care was used in the work. Unless you desire to make that impression, use something better. The wording is heterogeneous when there is no apparent correspondence between the parts as worded. An example would be

1. A complete sentence.
2. A mere noun.
3. An adverbial phrase.
4. An exclamation.

The taste that is satisfied with a thing like this is just naturally poor taste.  Yet one might have 1) a noun, 2) an adjective, 3) a verb, 4) an adverb, or an object, provided these are arranged as part of a sentence; in other words, these parts would show a natural relation or correspondence.

We all admire *symmetry*, and parts symmetrically arranged are always pleasing.  We might even speak of a law of symmetry in this connection.  There are any number of symmetrical arrangements in wording which the preacher may use to great advantage.  All we need to do here is to indicate a few.  They are nearly always easy to construct.  Little more is needed than the general appreciation that symmetry in wording is the better way.

Here is an example on John 6, 30-35 using one term parts, each part a compound.

### The Feast of the Soul.

   *I.   Soul-hunger.*
  *II.   Soul-bread.*
 *III.   Soul-eating.*
 *IV.   Soul-life.*

Here is one on John 3, 31-36 with three terms in each part, a possessive pronoun, an adjective, a noun.

### Christ the King of Salvation.

   *I.   His royal descent.*
  *II.   His royal rule.*
 *III.   His royal gifts.*
 *IV.   His royal servants.*

On the same text three symmetrical sentences.

### The Eternal Supremacy of Jesus.

   *I.   His revelation is supreme.*
  *II.   His salvation is supreme.*
 *III.   His dominion is supreme.*

In these three examples another feature of symmetry appears. In the first example the first half of the compound is identical in all four parts, namely the word "soul," and only the second half of the compound changes, namely "hunger," "bread," "eating," "life." — In the other two examples likewise only one word changes, "descent," "rule," "gifts," "servants"; "revelation," "salvation," "dominion." All the other words remain identical for the respective parts.

But it may be equally well to change two words down the line of the parts, three words or terms, or still more. All the parallel terms in the parts may change, or only some, or only one.

Here is an example on Matth. 21, 33-44, with two members in the parts, an adjective and a phrase, and both changing down the line.

**The Story of the Wicked Husbandmen:**
**The Way Which Led Jesus to the Cross.**

It is a way
  I. *Dark with sin.*
  II. *Beautiful with grace.*
  III. *Straight with purpose.*
  IV. *Glorious with power.*

Compare this with another arrangement on the same text. Here the prepositions change, also the final verbs. But the first noun runs through unchanged, as well as the subject of the relative clauses "his death."

**The Wicked Husbandmen and the Passion of Christ.**
Behold here:

| | | | | |
|---|---|---|---|---|
| I. | The sin | for which | his death | *was rendered.* |
| II. | "   " | by which | "   " | *was brought about.* |
| III. | "   " | over which | "   " | *triumphs.* |

We add one more on Matth. 12, 38-42, in which all the corresponding expressions change.

### The Significant Deliverance of Jonah From the Belly of the Great Fish.

Jonah's deliverance

|      |                 |                             |                  |
| ---- | --------------- | --------------------------- | ---------------- |
| I.   | Prefigured      | *the passion and resurrection* | *of Christ.*  |
| II.  | Foretold        | *the coming*                | *of the Gospel.* |
| III. | Bids us prepare. | *for the judgment*         | *of the last day.* |

Of course, there may also be clauses in the parts. All forms of language may be used.

While the symmetry may be *close*, as in the examples used, it may also *vary* to some extent. There is some variation in the last example, for we have two verbs in the last part, with only one in the first two parts. There is more variation between the second members in each part, and a little even in the last members of the three parts. As long as the symmetrical effect is not destroyed, such variation may pass.

Example of symmetry with variation, Luke 19, 1-10.

#### Zaccheus:
#### God's Hour of Grace.

I. *It may come unexpected —*
   *yet God prepares it.*
II. *It always brings salvation —*
    *Christ's help and pardon.*
III. *It invariably leaves a great change —*
     *repentance and thanksgiving.*

Each part has two members, which constitutes the symmetry. There is further symmetry in the first three members. Yet we have variation all throughout. Symmetry thus is a combination of law with freedom.

When the parts are direct quotations from the text, as also when they are quotations from hymns, there can, of course, be no symmetry in word arrangement. Yet structures like this cannot be classed as asymmetrical. The symmetry consists in the juxtaposition of the pithy and weighty statements that are used. For quotations from hymns see below.

For quotations from the text we offer on Luke 19, 1-10,

### The Blessed Story of Jesus and Zaccheus.

We may read it in three chapters, marked by three words in our text.

    I. *"He sought to see Jesus, who he was"* — need.
    II. *"To-day I must abide at thy house"* — salvation.
    III. *"The Son of man is come to seek and to save that which is lost"* — redemption (love and purpose).

The symmetry is expressed in the idea of chapters, each of which has a caption quoted from the text. — Example on Luke 7, 36-50.

### The Heart of the Gospel in the Words Which Christ Spoke to the Woman in Simon's House.

    I. *"Thy sins are forgiven."*
    II. *"Thy faith hath saved thee."*
    III. *"Go in peace."*

In symmetrical wording there is a natural tendency to use greater length for the last part. Example, Luke 24, 1-12.

### The Great Easter Gospel on Our Lord's Resurrection From the Dead.

We read it in

    I. *The useless spices.*
    II. *The empty tomb.*
    III. *The shining angels.*
    IV. *The startled women.*
    V. *The doubting disciples.*
    VI. *Hearts filled with Easter joy and faith.*

Also on Acts 1, 6-11.

### The Miracle of Christ's Ascension to Heaven.

*I. A miracle of divine power.*
*II. A miracle of divine blessing.*
*III. A miracle the power and blessing of which fill us*
*with joy and hope.*

Occasionally the wording may consist of *quotations from hymns*. Well known hymns and hymn lines are best. Example, Col. 3, 1-4.

### "Heavenward Doth Our Journey Tend."

*I. Here we roam a pilgrim band."*
*II. "Yonder is our native land."*

Example on Heb. 12, 1-6.

### "Sure, I Must Fight, If I Would Reign!"

*I.* Hence I pray: *"Increase my courage, Lord!"*
*II.* Hence I vow: *"I'll bear the toil, endure the pain!"*
*III.* Hence I trust: *"Supported by thy Word."*

Example, 1 Cor. 1, 21-31.

### Let Him That Glorieth Glory in the Lord!

*I.* In *the cross* of Christ I glory,
Towering o'er the wrecks of time."
*II.* "In *the gifts* of Christ I glory,
Crowning me with grace divine."
*III.* "In *the friends* of Christ I glory,
Gathering round his throne sublime."

Other examples in *The Eisenach Epistle Selections* by the author, II, 203; and *The Eisenach Gospel Selections*, II, 175.

PART FOUR

# THE ELABORATION

## FIRST CHAPTER

# THE MATERIAL ELABORATION.

The preacher has his theme and his outline. The question now is, how he shall complete his sermon. In particular, what material shall he use? Also, where shall he obtain it?

In other words, how shall the basic thoughts contained in the bare outline be expanded to form a complete discourse? Or, how shall each part unfold in a natural way, like a seed that grows to a mature plant, so that when all the parts are developed, there shall be a rounded and well-balanced sermon, complete in all its details?

It is well to remember that the theme is to be developed, not the text. To be sure, the text is to be used in the sermon, but it is not the text in general, or any part of it in particular, that is to be expanded into a sermon, but the theme based on the text, with its natural branches called the parts.

The process, which is usually called the elaboration, is very similar to the one employed in obtaining the theme with its parts from the text. Now, however, the operation is more advanced. As we started with the text and by concentrated effort of thought formed an outline to fit it, so we go on, and by concentrating upon each part in order make it expand, until the sermon is complete.

The process is neither mechanical nor theoretical. There are no rules or devices. All we can say is that it is *thinking* — but it is straight and true thinking. It never relinquishes the text. Nor does it for one moment deviate from the outline. It constantly visualizes the hearer individually as well as the congregation collectively, to provide exactly what in this case they need. And this thinking draws on all the mental and spiritual resources of the preacher, sounding them to their depths, reaching out to their farthest extent, and yet proceeding selectively, taking only what in each case serves as the best for the great purpose in hand.

And this purpose is the sermon, namely the type of sacred discourse understood by this term. Whatever is serviceable in building such a structure is sought, and at once shaped and molded in line with this purpose. Working out a practical commentary, a devotional meditation, or a theological essay is a different thing. Both the material as such and the handling of it are different. An essay merely elucidates its subject in one or more freely chosen directions. A devotional meditation is a series of reflections on one central thought, possibly on two, or on several, also freely chosen. A practical commentary attaches interpretative and applicatory ideas to one Scriptural statement after another, and thus treats chapter after chapter. But a sermon is intended for oratorical delivery, is limited to a certain length, is a unit resting on a unit text, and aims at a unified effect upon those who come to hear it. Hence the selection and the treatment of the material are governed by this conception, and by this alone.

There is a certain amount of *material in the text itself*.

There are a number of major and minor concepts, all of them quite rich in content, some of them of vital importance. There are statements or thoughts in the text, often of the greatest weight, and, according to the length of the text, more or less in number. Furthermore there are implications, connotations, presuppositions, etc., sometimes in single words, then also in single statements, as well as in the connection of statements. Sound exegesis brings all this text content to view, spreads it all out on the preacher's work-bench.

He has already mastered it in working out his outline. But all of it, as he now proceeds, is material of the highest value also for his work of elaboration. The sermon that passes by this most precious material in the text itself condemns itself. The first thing to get hold of in expanding an outline is the very material from which the outline itself grew in the preacher's mind.

The text material is really to form the heart of the elaboration. There is nothing else that could be substituted for it. Whatever else is used must crystallize around this essential substance of thought. Yet the text material is not enough by far to constitute the elaboration. We see that at once when we compare a well elaborated sermon with a text whose native material we have laid out before us.

There is sermon material in *homiletical text exposition*.

**Explanation.** — This term is used in a technical sense. Explanation deals with all those ancient objects, situations, features, and also ways of saying things that now are foreign to our people and therefore ought to be explained so that they will not be misunderstood.

Homiletical explanation differs from scientific explanation. The latter goes into all foreign matters as completely as possible. It deals with them exhaustively. It gathers every bit of information from all available sources. Homiletical explanation limits itself. It explains for the practical purpose that the hearer may grasp what the text says on the point, and may not misunderstand and draw false conclusions.

The preacher should, of course, be versed scientifically in all archaic matters in the Bible. He will be equipped with works on Biblical archeology, with the best Bible dictionaries, and with scientific commentaries. Yet for the sermon he will use only what is necessary on any one point for his hearer, and while he knows a great deal more on each subject he withholds this completer information.

In Luke 7, 41 it is not vital for the sermon to figure out with exactness just what the 500 and the 50 pence amount to in our money to-day, or what the present purchasing power of these amounts is. In John 2, 6 the sermon does not need to go into all the details of Jewish modes of purification, though the amount of liquid these water-pots held should be stated briefly. In Matth. 20, 2 etc., the hearer should know that the "penny" is not an American cent, but the ancient day's wage for a common laborer. In Luke 15, 16 the explanation is vital that the "husks" are not corn-husks, but the pods of the ancient carob-tree, used as feed for hogs, and sometimes eaten by very poor people.

So hundreds of things need explanation — the high priest, the lamb, Pilate, the Sanhedrim, the scourging, the myrrh, the hyssop, the tomb. Likewise the Jewish mode of betrothal, burying treasure, some of the Levitical rites, the way the Jews prepared bodies for burial, etc.

In using this material the preacher must remember that the human heart is the same in all ages, no matter what the outward things and ways of doing things among which it moves. Explanation must never be pedantic. It must be combined with a true knowledge of life. Often it will need only a word or two, a sentence or two, very seldom more than that. It is sermon material, quite necessary, but small in quantity. It is usually merely inserted when the subject is touched.

Example, Matth. 11, 16-24. "We know how children like to copy their elders. But do we know, too, how many times they illustrate the very spirit of their elders? That is what Jesus saw when he watched them playing in the cities where he wrought his greatest miracles. Many a time some of them were determined to play wedding, and when the rest would not follow and skip in dancing to their whistling, they complained. Again, some determined to play funeral. They started to wail like the old Jewish mourning women, hired for the purpose. They demanded that all the children should beat their breasts like the Jewish mourners used to do. When these others would not, those who started the game complained again. It was exactly the way their elders acted when God sent them the Law and the Gospel," etc.

Example, John 6, 16-21, on the four "watches." "The storm never abated, and so they labored on through the three hours of the first watch, through the three of the second to midnight, then on through the next watch, another three weary, long drawn hours. Would the day never come? the storm never cease? They were all exhausted when the fourth watch came, with no relief in sight." — In this description the "watches" are explained as lasting each three hours, the first two before midnight, the last two after midnight.

**Interpretation.** — This deals with the thought, and thus differs from Explanation. It deals with the thought objectively, and thus differs from Appropriation and Application which turn to the subjective.

Interpretation unfolds the thoughts of a text so that they will be fully understood. Every text requires this treatment in a sermon. Interpretation varies with the nature of the text and the subject-matter it contains. We list a few of the forms which Interpretation assumes.

1. The thought is restated in the simplest form so that it may be quickly apprehended. It is fully restated so that all of its features are made clear.

2. Its setting is given, either the connection in the text itself, or the connection with what precedes or what follows the text, i. e. the context. This often sheds much light on the thought.

3. In long texts the run of the thought (sometimes of the argument) is set forth so that it will be clear; also the chief point is lifted out and held up to view.

4. In historical texts the situation is described, the event or the events pictured. This should always be interesting.

5. In parables and all figurative language the point of comparison, the so-called *tertium comparationis*, is brought out, together with the significance of any details that are vital.

6. In doctrinal texts the doctrine stated, or involved, must be brought to view. The vital points must be pointed out in their relation to the whole and to each other.

7.   In general, any one thought must be illumined by showing its connection with other related and pertinent thoughts.

8.   Difficulties demand clearing up.   Apparent contradictions or disharmonies must be stated and their true solution given.

9.   In prophecies already fulfilled the fulfillment should be added.

Interpretation most frequently takes the form of teaching, and its general object is instruction.   It will thus use definition, induction and deduction, the syllogism, description, division and enumeration, elucidation, etc.   But in the sermon all this must be done in the oratorical, never in the schoolroom manner.

The superficial purpose of Interpretation is that the hearers may enter into the thought of the text fully and grasp its entire contents mentally.   But the deeper purpose is that the truth with all its saving power may be brought to the apprehension of the hearer so that it may reach his heart.   The preacher's business is to clear away every obstruction, to remove any darkness, to open up the inwardness of the truth fully, and to bring out all its power.

**Appropriation.** — Appropriation deals with the great saving acts of God, as these acts are recorded historically in the Scriptures, and also as they are set forth and explained doctrinally.   Our salvation rests on the Incarnation, the Passion, the Death, the Resurrection, the Ascension of Christ, and on the Mission of the Holy Ghost.   The histories setting forth these acts are therefore called histories of the first **rank**.   The doctrine that sets forth their significance is of the same rank. None of these acts could have been omitted, or could have been other than they were, without making void our salvation. These acts, and the doctrine involved in them, underlie all else in the Scriptures, for all else would be spiritually value-less without this foundation. Involved in the central saving acts of God are a number of other realities and acts, such as the existence of God, Creation and Provi-dence, the Law, Judgment, etc. All else recorded in the Scriptures is ranked homiletically as secondary, because all other recorded acts might have been indi-vidually omitted, or might have been individually otherwise than they were, without voiding our sal-vation. The miracles of the Exodus, the changing of water into wine at Cana, and a hundred other incidents, might not have occurred, or might have been entirely different, and yet our salvation would stand intact.

Only the histories and the doctrines of the first rank admit of Appropriation. This consists in dis-playing the value of the great saving acts for your soul and for mine, so that by faith we can make them ours. The preacher shows what God (Christ) has done *for us*, thereby kindling and increasing faith (trust, con-fidence) in our hearts.

There is a collative and efficacious power in these supreme parts of the Gospel. The collative power extends a gift (forgiveness, life, and salvation). The efficacious power works (normally) the acceptance of this gift (faith). Both powers always operate to-gether. For by the divine offer the human heart is drawn, moved, and enabled to accept.

The Church has raised the great saving acts of God into due prominence by means of the great festivals in the church year, Christmas, Good Friday, Easter, etc. These festivals demand Appropriation above all other things. Yet any text that at any time refers to the central saving acts of God cannot be adequately treated in a sermon without Appropriation. Too many preachers have failed to note this fact.

Appropriation thus deals with saving faith, both its production and its increase. In the same way it deals with regeneration and spiritual life.

In Appropriation the preacher directs his words in the strongest manner to the heart and conscience of his hearers. While his message should always come from the heart and go to the heart, this touch of heart to heart should reach its climax in Appropriation — the whole heart should go out to the whole heart.

This demands that the preacher should himself fully appreciate the grace and salvation he is offering. The faith and the life he would awaken in others must throb in his own bosom. Nothing is worse in the pulpit than a hypocrite, especially when it comes to Appropriation.

Interpretation leads up to Appropriation, and easily merges into it. So also the two are usually interwoven. The objective presentation of Interpretation is combined with the subjective appeal of Appropriation. The latter makes extended use of the second person "thou" and "you," plus the first person "we," sometimes individualized in "I."

**Application.** — This deals with the histories of the second rank. They cannot be treated by means of Appropriation. Christ died *for me*, and I appropriate His death and its benefits; but Peter did not confess Christ for me, and I cannot appropriate any benefits from his act. In Application a third element enters in, which is not the case in Appropriation.

In Application we 1) take a minor incident of Scripture, 2) show the characteristic feature involved in it, and then 3) apply this to ourselves to-day. Thus 1) the story of Peter's confession as it actually occurred; 2) the general idea of confessing Christ as the Savior; 3) then the application, how we should confess Christ in the same way, and how perhaps we have failed to confess him.

Application embraces all *the examples* in the Bible, both good and bad. It extends from the accounts of individual actions, what this man did or failed in, to general conditions, as people were or acted generally in those days, etc.

Application runs in two channels, positive and negative. *As then — so now:* what this man did thou shouldst do now; what occurred then also occurs now; what was true for those people, is equally true for us all to-day.

1 John 4, 17, "As he is, even so are we in the world" — as he lived, labored, suffered, etc. This includes the good as well as the evil. The faith, love, good works of the Bible characters have their counterparts now. The evil deeds of a Pilate, a Herod, the Pharisees, etc., have their counterparts in the same way. The field of comparison is exceedingly wide.

Then there is the negative. *As then — so not now;* or the reverse: *as not then — so now.* Circumstances, opinions, customs may now be different. What this person did we should not do; what he did we should not do now. We to-day may have more knowledge, may be under a better government, may not suffer persecution, etc. Our obligation may be greater, our responsibility likewise. What God or Christ did then, They may do the more — or the less now. What was necessary then may be even more so — or less so, now. Others may have had greater virtues, severer trials, etc., than we have now; or they may have had fewer benefits, less wealth, etc., than we have now.

Back of all such comparisons lies the great principle, that the Word of God is identical for all people and all times. There is an infinite richness in the Word, it is inexhaustible for Application. All the preachers in all the world will not be able to make all the possible applications.

Application embraces all the ethical precepts of the Word. Whether there is an actual case of charity, purity, temperance or not in the text makes no difference. The text may name directly the virtue or the vice, saving us the trouble of drawing it out from the act of a specific person or of specific persons, it is Application when we refer such virtue or such vice to ourselves.

Application is so easy to make, and there is so much Bible material for it as well as so much territory for it in our present lives, that preachers are inclined to overdo in using this material in their sermons, the while they overlook or omit Appropriation. One may therefore safely follow the rule: Use Appropriation wherever the text permits, and Application will take care of itself.

In every case of Application the comparison must be true. Never force the "then" and the "now" to make them correspond. We must adhere to the true sense of the Biblical narrative or statement on the one hand; and on the other hand, the present day parallel must match exactly. A thing like this will not do: "They have taken my Lord away," i. e. the body of Jesus from the sepulcher; which somebody referred to unbelievers who are without the Lord to-day. All fanciful applications are to be avoided.

**Application Approaching Appropriation.** — Between straight Appropriation and straight Application lies a territory that deserves special attention. There are many texts in which it is less the human person or act that ought to be considered, than the divine person and act. There are texts that present to us, in connection indeed with human actors, the power, love, mercy, compassion, etc. of Christ Himself. Other texts contain some word of Christ Himself. In all cases of this kind it would be a mistake to allow the sermon to give the greatest prominence to the human personages, to permit them to overshadow Christ, the supreme person. This is a common fault among preachers, and one not recognized by them as such. Let our rule be to place Christ (God) at the head of the sermonic table, in the chief place, whenever the text announces His presence. When this is done we will rise above ordinary Application and approach more nearly to Appropriation. In other words, the Gospel contents of the sermon will be increased to a marked degree.

Examples. — Take the raising of Lazarus. Ordinary Application puts Lazarus in the forefront, and gets this result: as Lazarus was raised from the dead, so shall we be raised at the last day. But when Christ is put into the forefront, when we approach Appropriation in our treatment, the sermon will proclaim Christ as the Master of Death, and bid us all believe on Him.

Take the storm at sea. Ordinary Application: So we, too, pass through severe storms, so our strength and skill comes to an end, so we must cry out to the Lord — thus putting the disciples forward in the picture. It is a higher type of preaching which uses Application akin to Appropriation: Christ stands revealed as the divine Ruler over all the forces of nature — believe in Him.

Look at the sinful woman in Simon's house. Ordinary Application: so we, too, are great sinners; so we, too, must repent, etc. But the higher type of Application puts Christ forward, instead of the woman: Christ in His pardoning grace.

In thus putting the divine into greatest prominence nothing is lost as far as the human is concerned. In fact, all the ordinary applications can be worked into the sermon just as well, moreover they will now be enhanced and fortified because the divine is back of them. All the miracles should be treated in this way. Ordinary Application cannot do justice to them. For instance, Jesus heals a blind man in the text. Can we say, that now He also heals blind men? He certainly does not. Because true Application fails, many preachers resort to what is called Allegory. They allegorize physical into spiritual blindness. They tell their people: so Jesus now opens men's eyes spiritually. But the text in hand says nothing at all about this spiritual work of Christ. It is imported into the text. The preacher does this sort of thing because true Application fails him. Let him focus attention on Christ, on His power, mercy, compassion; then there will be no need of Allegory, and the sermon will rise to its proper height, by approaching Appropriation.

In preaching on the Passion History during Lent (and otherwise) let us stop using Judas, Peter,

Caiaphas, Pilate, Herod, etc., as the chief figures in our sermons, overshadowing Christ. Let us make all men see Christ first of all. Always strike a note as near to Appropriation as possible.

But all the material contained in the text, and all that is obtained by homiletical Interpretation, Appropriation, Application, etc., is still insufficient to constitute a complete sermon. Elaboration of the outline must proceed much farther. It must advance to what has been aptly called Homiletical *Inventio*. The term is used in a technical sense. Homiletical Invention is the art of combining with all that the text itself furnishes such material from other sources as naturally amalgamates with what lies in the text and is indicated in the outline. It is called "invention" for two reasons. First, because this material must be found by the preacher, which requires a certain kind of training and skill. Secondly, because this material must pass through an intelligent selective process which uses only what is truly serviceable for the purpose of the sermon and shapes this material accordingly.

There is nothing arbitrary about Homiletical Invention. The preacher does not grope around in his mind; there is no guess-work, no haphazard trial of this thought or that. Nor is there anything like uncertainty, as if he could have used something else just as well. The material finally selected and woven together with what the text offers and the outline maps out, is all exactly what it should be to complete the message of the text to the hearer. If in any given case there is material which bears a foreign stamp, which digresses from the true purpose of the sermon, which is only loosely attached, this is evidence that the preacher's *inventio* has gone astray in this case, perhaps that he has not learned this highly necessary art of his profession.

Homiletical Invention always follows three established courses. The material it seeks for amalgamation with the text thoughts as mapped out by the outline is found by analysis, and by a double type of synthesis, the one narrow, the other wide in scope. Yet not all that is thus secured is actually used in the sermon. A selective process chooses from the rich and varied material thus secured. And that which is selected is carefully adapted to the purpose for which it is found fit.

**Elaborative Analysis.** — Analysis unfolds. It is like opening a box and showing its contents. It lays out each piece in order, or rather holds each piece up to view, turning it now one way, now another. It proceeds thus till we actually see in detail all that lies in a concept, all that a great thought contains, all that an action involves, all that an account or an argument means to convey.

Elaborative analysis is used extensively with Interpretation, in fact, Interpretation consists of this analysis. But it is used also with Appropriation and Application.

It demands a keen and penetrating mind on the part of the preacher. He must be able to see all that is in a thing. Mentally he must turn this thing over and over, until it has yielded up to him all that it stands for, all that lies in it. Especially must he find out what is distinctive of the thing, peculiar and new perhaps, unlike what similar things contain. Analysis is thus the opposite of generalization, which merely puts one thing together with other like things. Generalization requires little keenness of mind. It often tends to padding in sermonizing. So much of it is superficial.

Viewed from the standpoint of the hearer analysis is highly interesting and instructive. Everybody likes to see just what is in a thing, especially if what a thing contains is vital, valuable, perhaps surprising. Of course, if the analysis is merely superficial, or if the contents are only commonplace, few will care to listen. But elaborative analysis should never descend that low.

In this analysis the preacher starts with what in a way the hearer already understands. Jesus walked upon the sea — there is nothing difficult about that statement, we all know what it means. But when by simple analysis the preacher unfolds just what all that simple statement means and involves, the effect is tremendous. We now realize in a deep, true, real way just what it signifies that Jesus walked upon the sea. So with concepts. Take the word "grace." It is quite simple, and we all know what it means. But let the preacher bring out that it always connotes guilt, that it signifies favor wholly unmerited, that it is the opposite of justice and judgment, that it always gives, pardons, blesses — and the hearers will know much more about grace than they knew before. When synthesis adds to this product of analysis, the wealth of understanding will grow still more. This is what it means to elaborate.

In general, analysis will employ one of two ways, according as the subject to be treated by analysis is either abstract in its nature, or concrete.

The abstract is unfolded so that its contents appear. A concept, for instance, is thus unfolded so that we see just what lies in the term. A definition is unfolded so that we see just what it covers. A thought is unfolded so that we apprehend all that it intends to say. Synthesis may of course step in at any point and aid in the work by bringing in concrete examples, illustrations, etc. We shall treat of synthesis below.

Example from Luke 12, 4-9, "What is meant by *confessing Jesus before men?* Look at the name by which He designates Himself, and you will be able to tell. He is 'the Son of man.' That name He loved and used most often because it points both to what He is and what He has done for us. He, the eternal Son of God, became man for our sakes to be our Redeemer and Savior from sin. He who was more than man became man that He might die for our sins, by His blood remove our curse, and so make us children of God and heirs of salvation. And now you see what it means to confess Him before men. It means to recognize Him as the divine Savior, made man for our sakes, to accept the cleansing of His blood, to believe and trust Him as our Redeemer, and then to declare and show it openly by word and deed. The vital thing is the heart; that must cling to Him as our only hope and help against sin and damnation. But the heart governs the entire life. With your heart holding fast to Him, your lips will speak out, your words and acts will show that He is in your heart. And since you know Him only by His Word, by which He comes to you and gives you all His grace, your heart will cling to that, you will prize it, live in it, obey it, hope and trust in it. Your lips and life will show that you do. And that is what it means to confess Christ."

Example from John 15, 17-27, a single concept treated analytically. "What does Jesus mean by 'the world' in our text? It is easy to understand when He tells us what the world does. He tells us, the world hates Him. And that, too, after He has shown the world all that He came to do for it. The world, then, includes all men who have seen the saving power and grace of Jesus, and yet have turned wickedly against it all, preferring their own sin and all that is connected therewith."

Example from Luke 16, 10-17, on money, which Jesus calls "that which is another man's." "When we come to think of it the Lord is right, our money is really never our own. It never becomes part of us. We have it in our pockets, stored in some safe place like a bank, or invested in business or property; it is never really a part of us. And we are constantly paying it out — always handing it over to some other person. We own it only for a little while, sometimes the briefest space of time. And at the last we do not own it at all. We die, and that very instant every dollar we had legally belongs to somebody else. Even the richest millionaire in the world does not take one penny of his wealth over into the other world. Money — there is no money over there."

Analysis halts the hearer and makes him carefully weigh some point which otherwise might easily be passed over. — It is free to use the negative in elucidating the positive, or vice versa. In analyzing life use death; in showing what light is use darkness, etc. — Often a strange thought is analyzed by asking how it can be, and then furnishing a true answer.

Concrete objects, persons, actions, situations, etc., are fully described. This should always interest. The Bible so often draws only a few brief lines. This invites us to fill in and complete the picture. In doing so a subjective element enters in, whether we desire it or not. The preacher draws the picture as he conceives it. This will vary somewhat from the reality as it actually was. The variation, however, dare only be slight, in unessentials, never so as to disturb the hearer, and never so as to conflict with the text or its parallels. Leonardo da Vinci painted his famous picture of the Lord's Supper with the figures all seated on chairs about a table. The Christian world has accepted the painting with complete approval. Yet we know that Jesus and the disciples actually reclined on couches when they partook of the Passover. So there will be deviations from the strict realities.

It is a question hard to answer, just how far one may draw on his imagination in reproducing Bible figures and Bible scenes in the pulpit. All we can say is this — remain within safe limits. Do not romance like the novelist. Follow close and exact study. Remember that one jarring note will ruin the entire melody.

Example from Luke 12, 16-21, the Rich Fool, simple Interpretation. "He was a fine man, a substantial, prosperous farmer. He owned a stretch of fruitful fields, a well-built home, a good sum of money, and at the time he died his fields were heavy with grain, heavier than ever before, and he had just finished his plans to rebuild his barns in order to store the exceptional harvest. I am sure, his neighbors admired, and many envied him. He had a good name, his prosperity and his progressiveness were an asset to the community. If only he had lived, how fine his place with its new buildings would have looked, and how happy he would have been managing and making the most of it all. But now he was dead. The end came very suddenly, he himself had not expected it at all. When people heard of it they were startled. Many wondered whether he had made a will, and who would now get his fine property. That was the man."

Again, on the same text, fuller Interpretation. "It was the day before he died. He had just finished his plans about the new storehouses for his coming crops. When all was done as well as any man could have arranged it, he spoke to his own soul, and his soul listened to what he said, and was fully satisfied and happy. 'Soul,' he said, 'soul, thou hast much goods laid up for many years; take thine ease, eat, drink, and be merry.' — Consider what Jesus thus reveals concerning this man and his soul. He spoke of his earthly 'goods,' of these alone. They were great and rich indeed, yet they were

earthly goods only. They were, we may add, also God's gifts,
honestly, honorably obtained, but even so they were earthly
gifts only. Did his soul think of that? No; there is no indi-
cation; all we know is that his soul listened to this man's
voice speaking thus, was satisfied, and smiled. — He spoke of
his having enough for 'many years.' Do you understand? he
spoke only of earthly years. He thought of them stretching
far into the future, beautiful, lovely years; but even if they
had been granted him, they would have been nothing but earthly
years. Did his soul think of that? No; his soul added nothing,
it accepted the dream, and was happy in anticipation. — In what
he said the man did not mention God. Strange — a man so
experienced, so careful and wise in many ways, yet not one
word about God. Did his soul notice that and interpose? No;
his soul never objected at all; it seemed not to observe the
omission. — And the man said nothing about death. That,
too, seems strange. He was no longer young, and he had seen
many die. Did he not know that he, too, finally must die?
Of course, he knew that, but it really did not seem to impress
him; his thoughts always followed other channels. And so
now in this prosperous moment he did not think to mention
it to his soul. And his soul? It also was satisfied to leave
death unmentioned, left out of the reckoning. — He did not
speak either of salvation, the spiritual treasures of God's pardon for sin, of the hope of everlasting life. He omitted these.
No, he was not an infidel, a scoffer, or anything like that. He
went to church, but when the service was held he generally
thought about his fields, his work, his plans, and the like.
He was naturally a practical man, and these spiritual things
did not seem so real to him that he should mention them in
any special way to his soul. And his soul never missed what
he withheld; it had been well trained not to expect these things,
and so it was quite undisturbed and content without. That is
the way with poor souls when advantage is taken of them.
Even that last afternoon before he died, when he had his
last special conversation with his soul, even then his soul,
with only earthly things mentioned, was satisfied. And so
the man died!"

Example from John 19, 28-37, analytical description used
in Appropriation. "Our Savior dies, with the great work

for which He had come into the world triumphantly brought to an end. He had come to redeem us from our sins, to remove our guilt by the shedding of His blood, to open heaven and blessedness for us by His death that we might enter in. That glorious work was now finally done. Not one stroke more needed to be added, not a single further effort was required. The glorious goal set by God and clearly imaged in the prophecies of His Word was now attained. Jesus had redeemed the world — your salvation and mine was won. What a moment of triumph for the Savior's soul! The stains of His battle are still upon His body, but the victory, the eternal victory over our sin, guilt, and death are in His hands. It is this that fills His soul now and makes Him cry with all His might: 'It is finished!' Thus He died. — Let that word ring through our hearts," etc.

Example from Matth. 18, 1-5, analytical description used in Application akin to Appropriation. After describing in Interpretation the little child in Jesus' arms with its childlike trust and humility, the sermon continues: "Have you thought of your souls after the manner of this little child in Jesus' arms? Do you realize that your soul is wholly dependent just as a little child is? What could you do for your soul if left to yourself? As little as a tiny child could do for itself, if it were abandoned. It would perish, and so would you. And dependent means that one far greater, wiser, mightier than you must open His arms to you, stoop down to you, and with His mighty love embrace your soul and give it what it needs, just as Jesus pictured it in taking up the little child. You know what this love of His is. You see its outstretched arms on the cross, when Jesus died to wipe out your sins with His blood. You hear His loving voice in the Gospel, 'Come unto Me, all ye that labor and are heavy laden, and I will give you rest.' You feel its power when this love absolves you from all your sins, assures you that you are God's child, comforts you with the sweetest promises," etc.

Example from Acts 17, 10-14, analytical description in simple Application. "It is so easy to repeat the experience of the Bereans to-day, easier than ever since the New Testament has been added to the Old. A little knowledge is enough to find the very words of Christ Himself and take them into your heart; to discover all that Christ did for us, all that He would do now, and to fill our hearts with that. Why not take this Word, then, as the Bereans did? Why not put away all our own blind and foolish thoughts, and let Christ come to us as He really is, and God come to us and give us what He has for us in Christ? If your thoughts were wrong on any of these things, do you want to keep on in that wrong way? Do you want to be like a man who has taken the wrong road, and when one comes to set him right refuses to listen, and goes on farther and farther on the wrong track until it is too late? Or do you want to base your soul's faith and hope of salvation in eternity upon what some man says to you? What if he does mean well enough by you? It would be bad enough if you had no one else to guide and help you. But here is God Himself, God's own Son, your divine Helper, God's own Spirit of truth and light, and these come to you personally here in their Word, to tell you all that you need to know, yea must know, to be safe now and in all eternity. Away with every objection and plea! Do as the Bereans did — search the Scriptures daily, find Christ for yourselves, and all the treasures of salvation for your souls. This is what the Bereans did."

All elaborative analysis — and especially descriptive analysis — must go sufficiently deep. It goes deep enough when it penetrates beneath the outward features and brings to view the inner significance that touches the hearers personally. Literary beauty is an asset, but the chief thing is always the spiritual touch. Often in descriptive Interpretation the hearer will think of himself throughout, without any further effort (Appropriation, Application) on the part of the preacher. This is the thing for which to strive.

**Elaborative Synthesis (Narrow).** — Analysis elaborates by unfolding what is in the subject itself. Synthesis elaborates by casting light upon the subject from other sources. There are sources close to the subject, affording synthesis in the narrow sense of the term, and sources farther away, affording synthesis in the wider sense.

Elaborative synthesis in the narrow sense operates with the idea of *necessity*, or of *possibility*, or of *actuality* as connected with the subject in hand. In doing this it may elaborate on the *presuppositions* involved, on certain *conditions* that must be satisfied, and on other *pertinent facts* that are determining.

Examples from Acts 18, 24-28, on *necessity* elaborated by a number of pertinent *facts*. The example of Apollos "is exactly what we need to-day." Note the word "need." Now the facts follow. "Our country is full of great schools, colleges and universities. And only too often they who attend them and graduate from them are filled with a false pride of worldly learning. They imbibe the spirit of unbelief, and give up the humble Christian faith they have had. They either disdain the truths of Scripture, or begin to pervert them to make them agree with science as they have learned it, "science falsely so called" as the Scriptures term it. Think of them going like Apollos to a tent-maker's shop for the real wisdom! Their humble old church is too far behind the times for them. They have advanced — yes — in the wrong direction. . . . The very thing every one of us needs, and needs in a special way when he climbs the educational ladder, is the fullest and most thorough instruction in Christian knowledge. Without that, the more a man knows the farther will he go astray; but with the full knowledge of Christ and His Word, the more you know, the more will you be able, with your purified and sanctified knowledge, to glorify God."

Example from Acts 9, 36-43, on *possibility* elucidated by pointing to certain *conditions* that must be satisfied. "Is it possible for you to follow the example of Dorcas? It certainly is not, if you withdraw to yourself and live only to yourself. Dorcas might have done that, but she never thought of such a thing. It certainly is not, if you try to find excuses for yourself, and they are easy to find. Dorcas might have excused herself, for she had only one little talent. So you might say, I am able to do so little, so why try to do anything at all?

But such a thought never entered this woman's mind. — It certainly is possible for you to follow the example of Dorcas, if only you will think and act as Dorcas did. Look around you, as she did, and see the opportunities that beckon to you; drop all excuses, as she did; and put your talent to work, as she did, and find joy and satisfaction in the Lord's work."

Example from Luke 16, 10-17 on *actuality* resting on certain *presuppositions*. The elaboration runs as follows: Your money is an actual aid in your church membership (this is the actuality). But this presupposes 1) a right estimate of your money as "that which is least," as "the unrighteous mammon," and as "that which is another man's." It also presupposes 2) the right use of your money, in that you always remain master of it, and never let it master you, in that you never try to serve both God and mammon, and in that you spend your money for God in the opportunities He offers you. These two great presuppositions make money a great asset in your church membership. — Actualities resting on presuppositions can, of course, be turned into necessities resting on facts, or into possibilities resting on conditions to be met. It depends on how the preacher decides to treat a given subject.

Again a subject or thought, conceived either as a necessity, a possibility, or an actuality, may be elaborated by pointing to the *consequences or results* involved. And these may be theoretical, practical, or historical, as the case may require.

Example from Acts 18, 24-28, possessing knowledge such as Apollos gained from Aquila and Priscilla *(actuality)* elucidated by pointing to *the results* (practical and theoretical combined). "It has always been so, and it always will be so (as in Apollos' case) in the Christian Church. Close the gates of Christian knowledge, and you shut out thousands of Christian blessings, both for yourselves and for others. The tree that finds too little soil cannot grow and bring a harvest of fruit. But see what happens when God's blessed truth is sought, appropriated and used. Here are parents like Aquila and Priscilla filling the hearts of their children with imperishable wealth. In all their lives these children find blessing and bring blessing to others. Among them some may be like Apollos, who become teachers and pastors in the Church. Many a godly mother especially has thus left a priceless legacy to the Church, and eternity alone can show how far this legacy has spread. In the manifold relations of life, when friend speaks with friend, one workman with another, one Christian brother or Christian sister with another, what good may not be done when we fully know the grace of God, the preciousness of Christ's atoning blood, the wisdom of God's ways and judgments. See the good seed you can sow for eternity if you have the seed to sow. Think of the woeful ignorance in the world in spiritual things. Endless opportunities are yours, if equipped with Christian knowledge, to let your light shine and help others upward on the way to God."

Example from Acts 5, 1-11. "The devil likes to put hypocrites into the church *(actuality)* to harm the church as much as possible. (Now *the results.*) "When people suspect hypocrisy among the members, especially the more prominent ones, they often are quick to turn away from the church. That is a far greater pity for them than it is for the church. For while there are some hypocrites in the church, there are far more outside of it, where no Spirit of truth rules. And they who leave the church because of some hypocrite they think they have discovered, will in the end meet that very hypocrite, if he really is one, in another place, where all they who leave Christ openly and who leave Him secretly by hypocrisy will be compelled to stay in each other's society."

Example 1 Cor. 15, 12-19, the apostle's own words. "But if there be no resurrection *(possibility)*, then is Christ not risen *(consequence* of the assumption, and also the *further consequences* follow). And if Christ be not risen, then is our preaching vain, and your faith is also vain. Yea, and we are found false witnesses of God; because we have testified of God that He raised up Christ; whom He raised not up, if so be that the dead rise not. For if the dead rise not then is Christ not raised. And if Christ be not raised, your faith is vain; ye are yet in your sins. Then they also which are fallen asleep in Christ are perished. If in this life only we have hope in Christ, we are of all men most miserable." — He also adds the reverse:

"But now is Christ risen from the dead *(actuality)* and become the firstfruits of them that slept" *(consequence, which is then elaborated)*.

Certain subjects and thoughts need *supplementation* in order to be fully understood. Often the text presents only one side of a truth, and we must add the rest. Every Christian virtue grows from true faith. Hence when a text urges us to practice a virtue, without mentioning faith, we must add what is needed on faith.

Example, Luke 15, 1 etc., add the atonement for the Prodigal's sin. — "The Lord knoweth His own," add the marks by which He knows them. — 1 Cor. 4, 4, "Yet am I not hereby justified." But how am I justified? — Matth. 21, 28-32, the two unequal sons, add that there is a third way, namely saying yes to the Lord and then working in his vineyard. — There are many cases of this kind.

A word may be added on *doctrinal* and on *ethical* subjects and their elaboration by means of the narrow synthesis.

Doctrine and all doctrinal statements are elaborated analytically by unfolding the full meaning in any given case. The elaboration becomes synthetical when we add proof. Scripture proof stands supreme, and no doctrine can be received without it. But we may add evidential proof from Christian experience, which, of course, only they can grasp who have had such experience. Finally, there is proof due to inner necessity, proof from connection with other known truths, and proof from the connection with man's absolute needs. Descriptions of sin, for instance, may be both Scriptural and experimental, for we see sin around us in countless forms. The character of sin may also be shown by what of necessity lies in sin, and by the death it produces. Any description of forgiveness must meet the doctrine of sin — one truth here sheds light on another. Man's need under sin sheds light on God's provision for freeing man from sin. And thus all along the line with doctrinal statements. Read Rom. 1, 21-32 and see how St. Paul proves the doctrine of sin from human experience; yet in Rom. 3, 10-19 he uses Scripture proof to prove universal sinfulness. In Rom. 4, 1 etc. the apostle elaborates the doctrine of Justification by using the example of Abraham, and a quotation from David's Psalms. Any number of good examples are thus found in the apostolic writings.

Ethical statements are elaborated synthetically, first by showing the motives that lie back of all ethical actions; and secondly by showing actual examples of ethical actions. When, for instance, St. Peter confessed Christ, the motive was faith; and again, his confession as an example shows how we, too, can and should confess. We operate with ethical necessity when we deal with the motives and the roots of action; and with ethical actuality when we use ethical examples. Rom. 12 first lays down the ethical motive, which is an inner transformation in man's heart. Out of this flow all the virtues and good deeds enjoined upon us in the rest of the chapter. Heb. 11 contains a long line of examples of faith. The Bible is exceedingly rich in both positive and negative ethical examples. So these two lines of elaboration will be easy to follow, 1) that we ought, or ought not, to think, say, or do (necessity of obligation); 2) that we certainly can, and thus should think, say, or do, or avoid thinking, saying, doing (actuality), even as others have shown us.

**Elaborative Synthesis (Wider).** — This utilizes the association of ideas, which always runs in two channels, positive and negative, or, which is the same, similarity (identity) and contrast. The material thus provided naturally must be carefully sifted, and only that which is best and most useful will be retained. We list the following.

1. Scripture Passages. — For every thought in the text there are other Scriptural statements, supporting that thought in one way or another. Every doctrinal or ethical statement used in the sermon can be fortified with some passage or other. Sometimes a passage will come to mind which seems to contradict what the text or sermon offers. Here the solution may be brought in.

A copy of the Bible with central columns of references will be found a great aid, especially for beginners. Thorough Scriptural knowledge, especially genuine exegetical knowledge, is a necessity, for which there is no substitute.

The use of Scripture passages in the sermon is a spiritual art which cannot be too highly developed. It is a mannerism to read the passages used from the Bible itself, turning to the place where each is found. Such reading is far less effective than quotations from memory. It is useless to name the place where each passage is found, for no hearer can possibly retain the places.

Use only telling passages, such as are to the point and easily understood. Use none that themselves need further explanation.

Use only a few for any one point. One telling passage is better than several that are not to the point or decisively clear.

At times a passage, or several, may be quoted verbatim; again it will suffice if only the substance of a passage is used, or if only an expression from a passage is quoted exactly.

Example from Acts 17, 10-14 begins as follows, " 'Thy Word is a lamp unto my feet, and a light unto my path,' said the Psalmist.—'To the law and to the testimony,' cried the great prophet Isaiah to his people, 'if they speak not according to this Word, it is because there is no light in them.'—'We have also a more sure Word of prophecy,' adds the holy apostle St. Peter, 'whereunto ye do well to take heed, as unto a light that shineth in a dark place, until the day dawn, and the day star arise in your hearts.'—And on all these Jesus Christ Himself sets His seal when He bids us, 'Search the Scriptures: for in them ye think ye have external life: and they are they which testify of Me.'—One thing more we need in addition to these testimonies and admonitions from great men of God and from God's Son Himself, namely an example of what their words mean. We have it in our text today—**The Shining Example of the Men of Berea.**"

Example from Matth. 16, 15-20. "But are we not mistaken? Did not Christ say, 'I will give unto *thee*,' namely Peter, 'the keys of the Kingdom of Heaven'? Was not Peter thus made the head and pope of the Church to bind and to loose, to let in and bar out of the Kingdom of Heaven? This is the great error of Rome. . . . The keys and the power He laid not in the hands of Peter alone, or even of all the apostles alone, but into the hands of the whole Church on earth, of all His believers. 'Tell it unto *the church*,' Jesus said, when a man has sinned and will not repent; and He adds, 'Whatsoever ye shall bind on earth,' ye the church, 'shall be bound in heaven; and whatsoever ye shall loose on earth,' ye the church, 'shall be loosed in heaven.' " Etc.

Example from Acts 2, 37-40, passages not fully quoted. "It is absolutely true, as the Scriptures declare, that 'no man hath seen God at any time.' And again they say of God, the only Potentate, the King of kings, the Lord of lords, who only hath immortality, that 'He dwelleth in the light which no man can approach unto; whom no man hath seen or can see,' except by gracious revelation of Himself. Nor do the Scriptures leave us in doubt why sinful man cannot of himself see God, for they call Him 'a consuming fire.' " Etc.

2. Confessional Statements. — In the confessional writings there are many excellent passages that deserve to be used in sermons. Among them are illustrations, definitions, and choice ways of saying things.

Example from Matth. 16, 15-20. "Paul preached only one grand theme, not the theme Peter, but the theme Christ and Him crucified. John preached, not Peter, but the blood of Christ which cleanseth us from all sin. The Apostles' Creed confesses not, 'I believe in St. Peter,' but, 'I believe in Jesus Christ, His only Son, our Lord' — the same confession with which Peter rested his soul on Christ."

Example from Luke 3, 15-18. "What do we need in our day? This 'fiery angel St. John, the true preacher of repentance,' as one of our confessions calls him," etc.

Example on Rom. 3, 20-26. "Let me tell you exactly what St. Paul preached during his entire ministry, in fact, the chief thing in all his preaching. Our confessions sum it up in these words. 'That men cannot be justified before God by their own powers, merits, or works; but are justified freely for Christ's sake, when they believe that they are received into favor, and their sins forgiven for Christ's sake, who by His death hath satisfied for our sins.' This is the central doctrine of the entire Bible."

3. Quotations from the Church Fathers, especially also Hymn Writers. — Short sections are preferable, some of the gems from this rich treasure house. Yet the quotation from hymns should not

become a mannerism. Only in rare instances may Latin or other foreign languages be used in quotation. *"Ecce Homo"* or *"Jesus Christus, Rex Judaeorum,"* and a few others may pass.

Secular writers should not be quoted. It is decidedly a mistake to quote from modern newspapers, magazines, novels, and the like. None of them deserves the honor of pulpit mention, not even when their assertions are contradicted. There is too much first class spiritual material for quotation for any preacher to descend to the secular at any time.

Luther will always be a favorite, Augustine, Chrysostom, and a few others also.

Examples from Luther, "Faith is not a human notion and dream, which some think it to be. But faith is a divine work in us, that changes and regenerates us." — Luther says of Mary that she was probably the daughter of an ordinary poor citizen, altogether lowly in her station, so that lordly Annas' and Caiaphas' daughters would not have desired her for their maid. Yet she was chosen to be the mother of the Lord, not one of these haughty ones. — "If our Lord wore a crown of thorns, what right have we to demand a wreath of roses?" — "Let each his lesson learn with care, And all the household well shall fare." — And his remarkable word on faith and works: Faith does not wait until it is told what to do, but before ever it is told it goes and does everything all of its own accord.

Augustine, "Thou hast created us unto thee, and our heart is restless until it rests in thee." — "The Word comes to the element, and it becomes a sacrament." — "In essential things unity, in doubtful things liberty, in all things charity." — Chrysostom, "As the rose is contained in the undeveloped bud, so the future glory and blessedness of the child of God is contained in his faith."

4. Historical Incidents. — Bible references are the best, and the preacher should master their use. St. Paul is an example. In Rome 9 he uses the history of Isaac, then of Jacob and Esau, then of Pharaoh, exactly as one might do in a sermon. Compare his use of the history of Hagar and Ishmael in Gal. 4, 21 etc.

Example from John 12, 20-26, the grain of wheat dying in the earth and thus bearing fruit, "Ignatius was cast before the lions to die for his Christian faith. When he heard the hungry roars, he bade affectionate farewell to his friends and said, 'I am God's grain of wheat; to be turned into God's shew-bread I must be ground up by these wild animals.' Thus he died in time to live eternally."

Luke 11, 5-13, on prayer, "Luther wrote *Vivit — Vivit!* all around on the walls of his room, He lives! and cast his bag of cares out of the door, for God could not but hear him."

Matth. 9, 9-13, the Kingdom for sinners, "King Louis XII. of France had many enemies before he became king. After his elevation to the throne he made a list of these men and placed a black cross in front of each name. When his enemies heard it they promptly fled. But the king said, 'Be easy in your minds, my friends! The reason I placed a cross before the name of each one of you is that I may constantly be reminded of the cross of Christ and of the word which He spoke on the cross, Father, forgive them, for they know not what they do!' Thus, though we have been enemies of the Savior, He Himself would mark our names and hearts with the cross which signifies forgiveness."

Mark 4, 26-29, the seed growing in secret, "When the Eastern emperors were crowned at Constantinople, it is said, they each chose one of a number of marble slabs for a tombstone. It was well for them to remember their funerals at their coronation. What shall be engraved on your tombstone? Let it be a sheaf of wheat, the symbol of a life spent under the power of the Word, ripening unto a blessed harvest."

"Justin Martyr vainly sought God among the ancient philosophers. Finally he withdrew into solitude at the seaside. Here he met a venerable saint who directed him to the prophets and apostles with the admonition to pray that Christ might open his eyes. 'Then I felt,' he tells us, 'a divine fire kindling in my soul.' It was the same fire that warmed the hearts of the Emmaus disciples."

5. Conditions and Happenings in Every Day Life. — The preacher must have a keen eye and a keen ear for all that meets him day by day. He will discover a wealth of material for his sermons, in fact, so much of it that he will be unable to use it all, selecting only what is most telling for his spiritual purpose. He will see about him many things that tally with the good or the bad mentioned in his texts, and again many things that can be put in contrast with what is in his texts. There is no need to invent where the actual realities are so abundant.

Example from 1 John 4, 7-14. "Yes, we believe, God is love. That is an easy thing to say, as long as we are in health, have plenty of money, and live in the sunshine of good fortune. Then, like a lark rising aloft over verdant fields our Jubilate will warble and sing, 'God is love!' But ask the men in prison cells, whether they believe God is love. They will reply, that there is no God at all, and if there is, that He is cruel and a God of hate. They will say that they are no worse than thousands of others, and yet are deprived of liberty and joy. How can the God of love permit a world-order like that? Ask the laborer who toils and sweats at his daily tasks and grumbles at his wrongs, that he must lead a life of hardship while others enjoy ease and plenty. Ask him whether he believes that God is love, and he may give you the same kind of answer. Shall we inquire also of the grief-stricken beside the freshly turned grave, or of the sufferers on their beds of pain, whether God is love? He who is uniformly fortunate, with abundance of earthly treasure and enjoyments, lightly speaks of the love of God — but is that all the word means?"

Example from John 7, 10-18, "The world around us is full of utterly false certainty, of complete uncertainty, and of all shades and degrees of doubt concerning things religious. One does not need to go far to find men firmly believing the most outrageous and preposterous things in religion, and staking their souls on what they believe — when it is perfectly plain that what they believe is wholly imaginary and without reality. Besides these with a false certainty there is a host completely uncertain. Ask them, and they are not sure, and many of them think nobody really can be sure. They have come to the conviction that religion is a mere matter of opinion, and one opinion is about as good as another, especially if it tends to make people kind and brotherly toward one another. A third class includes many church members — they say and confess indeed with the church that they believe in Jesus Christ, but they are not really sure about their faith, they have all kinds of doubts, and are easily disturbed and upset. Many of them, when put to the test, fail utterly and fall away from the faith."

Example from John 3, 31-36, "There are many people who have trouble to see why the Bible promises so much to faith and threatens so severely against unbelief. It seems to them as if salvation and damnation ought not to be decided in this fashion. Secretly they feel as if there is a sort of injustice in this decision. Here is a miserable sinner, a criminal perhaps, like the malefactor on the cross, or the prostitute in the house of Simon the Pharisee, and these people believe, and lo, heaven's door swings open before them. While here are men of standing, respected and honored in their communities, like the Pharisees of old, with great men like Gamaliel among them, governors, princes, kings, perhaps, whose names adorn history, some of whom men call great, and yet just because they did not believe in Jesus they are to be damned for ever. No, we hear some say openly, 'We believe no such doctrine. Either God is going to be kind to all and allow them all to enter heaven at last, or He will surely take all who have tried to do right, and banish only those who are utterly vicious.' This is the doctrine that appeals to people, not this old Bible doctrine which makes everything turn on faith."

Sometimes the things from every day life are only briefly referred to. Examples: "What a blessing are strict parents and teachers! We remember them gratefully years after they are in their graves. And those that were lax, like Eli of old, we feel that they cared little for us, and if they did not harm us too much, we are ready to forget." — "How we like to pick and choose among the commandments of the law! We boast of having done this and done that, while we say nothing of what we have left undone. To select your own commandments is to make yourself your own law-giver, and to provide convenient room for sin." — A certain preacher castigates the sins of impurity by pointing to young girls hurrying into marriage to escape greater shame, to the birth of fatherless children, and to the indifference of the congregation toward these transgressions in its midst, thus actually helping to promote them.

6. Illustrations of All Kinds. — These are highly desirable in every sermon, and the world is full of them. The Bible is a masterpiece in the art of using illustration. The preacher must produce his own illustrations. Only occasionally will he be able to pick one up elsewhere suitable for his purpose. A few standard illustrations allow repeated use. Never be fooled into buying books that pretend to furnish sermon illustrations. All such books are a delusion. Here are a few illustrations the author has used.

A chain of pearls that is torn at any one point spills all the pearls. Destroy faith and love at one point, and you will look vainly for it at another. — Deeds are recorded, and once the record is properly entered upon the court files our possession is established. So our names are written in heaven; so our property there is made surely ours. A man may own many acres and yet not actually live upon them; they are his nevertheless. So, though we have not yet entered upon our heavenly estates, they are ours none the less. — Lydia, like the chalice of the lily turning to the sun for light. — Luther, "A man bears a hundredweight, a child only the weight of a pound. Yet a man is not angry because he bears a hundred-weight, and not, like a child, a pound." — When a fruit-tree is shaken the fruit does not always fall at the first effort. We then shake again and again, we brace our feet and use all our strength, till the fruit falls. So do in praying. — The Gospel is no rubbish that you may sweep hither or thither at pleasure. The human heart is no sponge to suck up the Word, and to have it squeezed out again as often as you may wish. — Cabbage has a far larger seed than the mustard tree, yet never grows to the size of the latter; so human works and systems often have an imposing start, yet soon disappear again, while the Kingdom still endures. — The Kingdom is a hospital, with a Great Physician in charge, and many assistants and nurses. You will find many patients there. But you must not expect to find unchecked contagion and infection. — An old illustration that has become classic: Eternity — if a bird would fly once in a thousand years to an adamant mountain and there whet its bill just once, when the mountain finally would be thus whetted away completely, one minute of eternity would not yet have passed.

7. Individualization, Specialization. — Instead of generalizing or discussing in abstract terms, paint concrete, individual, distinct pictures. Instead of speaking at length on the general topic of brotherly love, describe actual cases of one Christian showing love to another, or of neglecting to show it. Instead of piling up sentences on worldliness or godliness, picture an actual worldly man, an actual godly man, how each thinks and acts. Do not merely define faith, but rather show us a man who trusts the Lord or His promises in actual life. This is sometimes done in the first person, even as David said of himself, that he would rather be a doorkeeper in God's house than dwell in the tents of wickedness. Sometimes it is done in the second person singular, as when you ask the hearer, whether his conscience ever reproves or worries him, whether he

really knows what peace with God is, how he will meet the Lord on judgment day, etc. Jesus expounded all the Scriptures to the two disciples on the way to Emmaus. In preaching on this take up a few of the chief passages and show how they point to Christ's suffering and resurrection.

Example from John 6, 16-21, description of languid faith by specializing, "It does not run to Christ in prayer in every need, generally going to other helpers first. It does not worship Him in proper humility and trust, with holy ardor and zeal. It does not walk with lively hope, as if heaven were really open before us, and every step taking us nearer to its glory. It will not confess Him before men as it should, nor fight the good fight of faith, putting on the whole armor of God, and laying hold with both hands on eternal life. It does not rejoice to run the way of His commandments, strong in love of Him, putting on the new man, as indeed created in Christ Jesus unto good works."

Example from John 3, 31-36, "Unbelief rises up, proud and haughty, and says: What do I care for the Son's Word? I deny that Word! So unbelief casts it aside, and will not even look at it except to raise objections against it. (Unbelief individualized). What would you do, if you had given your word, at such a price to yourself, with such love and mercy, to miserable sinners who deserve not one syllable of it? (Individualization by means of second person)."

Another from the same text, "Men like to receive gifts. Our children are happy at Christmas time because of the gifts they receive, and older people are just as happy to receive them. Give a man a costly gift, one that fills some great need of his, and see how he will act. Give a poor pauper clothes, food, a fine home, and a bag of money — what will he say? Give some poor prisoner liberty and honor again — what will he do? Lift some sufferer from his bed of pain, out from the shadow of death, to life, health, and happiness — what response will you get? But one of the incomprehensible things among sinful men is that the moment the Lord Jesus comes to lift them out of the beggary, bondage, and deadly malady of their sin **many** of them thrust His gracious hand aside and scorn the gift," etc.

Example from Matth. 22, 23-33, using the first person singular, "But no, they shall not rob me thus. This hope of Christ that reaches up to heaven, to the angels of God, to the blessed presence of God Himself, I will press to my bosom, hold in my heart, make my support in life and in death. Others may want their heaven for a day and a year in this life; I want a heaven like that of the angels that lasts for ever. Others may want a heaven of flesh and fleshly joys, sin-stained, curse-laden; mine shall be the heaven of the white purity of the angels, and of the inexpressible joys that radiate from God. As earthly days fade, and the shadows grow longer before the night of death, this hope shall grow brighter and brighter within me, until God's own angels shall come to carry me away, those angels whom I shall be made like unto at last."

All collectives ought thus to be individualized.

All this material must be worked up in a living way. It is impossible to furnish rules or lay down methods. Human insight must combine with spiritual understanding. There will, of course, be logic, imagination, feeling, etc., but in the last analysis the preacher's own enriched and living personality must penetrate everything he uses in his sermon from first to last.

*Sub-parts.* — One question remains. Shall there be formal sub-parts? The answer is, There may be, but there must not be.

Much depends upon the character of the material that is used in developing each main sermon part. Where a sermon has only two or three main parts the material for their development can easily be arranged in formal sub-parts, marked 1), 2), etc., or a), b), c), etc. In this case the part thus divided ought to be split just as we split the theme into main parts, and all that was said on this subject applies to the division into sub-parts. The sub-parts must especially be coordinate, must truly divide the main part concerned, and must embody fully what that main part contains.

Example from John 5, 19-29.

**Learn to Look at Your Life in the Light of the Last Great Day.**

You will rejoice then

I. *If it was full of honor for the Son of God.*

a) Honor, in the way you regard Him: 1) As the Son equal with the Father; 2) As the Savior, working out our salvation; 3) As the Fount of blessing, giving life; 4) As the eternal Judge.

b) Honor, in your conduct toward Him: 1) In receiving by faith His grace, gifts, blessings, etc.; 2) In confessing His name by showing yourself as His followers; 3) In worshipping Him by prayer, praise, etc.

II. *If it was full of faith in the saving Gospel.*

a) So that you *know* that Gospel (hear, read, understand — perceive and realize that it is life and salvation).

b) So that you *own and have* the Gospel in your heart (with its quickening life, deliverance from death — with its peace and joy, because you shall not come into condemnation).

III. *If it was full of hope and eternal blessedness.*

a) In the resurrection of yourself and your dear ones departed in Christ.

b) In the judgment, which for you shall be an acquittal before the whole world, as now you are acquitted in justification.

c) In the blissful eternity to follow.

Example from 2 Tim. 4, 5-8.

**Look at the Crown of Righteousness at That Day!**

 I. *Let it keep you faithful to the end!*
  1) Like Timothy, with so much of his life and labor still before him.
   a) He had to watch and be sober in all things, because of so many false teachers and foolish hearers.
   b) He had to endure affliction, such as was incident to his position and work.
   c) He had to make full proof of his ministry and perform faithfully all the duties of his calling.
  2) Like Paul, with his course nearly finished.
   a) He had kept the faith (fought the good fight; finished his course).
   b) He was ready to depart (to be offered up).
  These are our examples. Let us follow them; so shall the crown be ours.

 II. *Let it fill you with joy in advance!*
  1) Joy amid every difficulty, trial, etc.
  2) Joy ever brighter as the end approaches.
  3) Joy unspeakably great when that day arrives at last.

Example from 1 Pet. 1, 17-25.

**Consider the Precious Price of Your Redemption.**

 I. *Its value in what it brings you — do not lose it!*
  1) It is more than silver and gold can buy.
  2) It is deliverance from the curse and bondage of your fathers.
  3) It is faith and hope in God as your Father.
  4) Therefore walk in fear, lest the Father who redeemed you through the Son must nevertheless condemn you.

 II. *Its value in what it makes of you — do not hinder it!*
  1) Children of God by redemption.
  2) Partakers of the incorruptible life through the incorruptible Word.

3) Obedient children of the truth.
4) Therefore walk in love, that the newness of your life may appear before God and men, and especially also your brethren.

The sermon can also be built, and be built well, without formal sub-parts. Where this is properly done each main part is developed by carefully and correctly analyzing the substance of its thought. The material so arranged forms, then, a true development or elaboration of each part. This requires as close and correct thinking as the arrangement with formal sub-parts, perhaps even closer. The fault to guard against is loose accumulation. Starting with a statement of a main part the preacher may easily allow his mind to wander off in the general direction of that main part. So, indeed, he will have no formal sub-parts, but also he will have no real development of the main part either — which latter he must have, if the sermon is to amount to anything really worth while.

Example from John 12, 1-8.

**Mary's Ointment of Spikenard:**
**An Illustration of What Women Can Do For the Lord Jesus.**

I. *When like Mary they first sit at Jesus' feet.*
Mary's deed had its root in her learning of Jesus, and so the highest and best forms of service always come from receiving fully the Master's teaching. Some try to serve and honor Him without knowledge, and fall into errors. Let us keep before us Mary's example.

II. *When like Mary they follow the holy impulses of their hearts.*
Mary let nothing deter her, and something did happen to cast blame on her act. How many good impulses we allow to perish, like buds blasted before bloom,

by letting our opportunities pass, by letting false
considerations deter us, by pausing until our enthusiasm fails. How much better to act as Mary did.

III.  *When like Mary they rely in simplicity on Jesus'
      commendation.*

Mary knew, she had that. There is nothing higher
for any of us. But be sure you have it.

> "Men heed thee, love thee, praise thee not;
>   The Master praises — what are men?"

Never ask, What will people say? but, What will
Jesus say?

---

Example from 2 Cor. 3, 12-18.

### What Do You See in the Scriptures?

I.  *If you use a veil.*
    A law — works — fables and myths — just history —
    just morality.

II.  *If you discard all veils.*
    Christ — liberty from works, i. e. salvation — a power
    that transforms us into the image of Christ — the
    way to spiritual glory here and heavenly glory
    hereafter.

---

Example from Prov. 16, 1-9.

### The Man Who Thinks He is Independent.

There is something woefully wrong with him.

I.  *With his heart.*
    A heart that is independent of the Lord's mercy and
    truth is held fast in unpurged guilt, and faces an
    evil day, v. 5 and 4; and when that day comes
    even this sham independence will be dispelled. —
    Add the counterpart.

II.  *With his brain.*
    Does he think, because he can make plans and cal-
    culations, that he can also control his steps and
    the outcome? Or that such pride will go unpunished?
    Verses 1, 9, 5. — Contrast with the dependent man,
    his good sense, and safe ways of thinking, v. 3, etc.

*III. With his life.*

He may have many friends, great revenues, seem clean in his own eyes, v. 7-8 and 2; but every life like this ends in disaster, v. 2b, 4b, and 6 turned negatively. — The dependent life, even the poorest as to earthly appearance, and what this life attains here and hereafter.

## SECOND CHAPTER

# THE ELABORATION ACCORDING TO PSYCHOLOGICAL NORMS.

The preacher aims at the heart of his hearer, which means at the very center of his being. Psychologically stated, the sermon is to reach the intellect, the emotions, and most especially, the will. The preacher will succeed in this only when he so shapes his material that it will agree with the norms according to which the will acts in things religious. He will fail, or be quite ineffective, if he ignores or violates these norms of the will.

Some preachers instinctively follow these norms. But it is well to know just what they are and how they may be used in shaping the presentation of divine truth in the sermon. We here appropriate some of the findings of E. Pfennigsdorf, *Der religioese Wille*, p. 125 etc., but we go beyond his presentation.

## I. The Three Norms of Analytical Preference.

These are called analytical because they deal with elements of the same kind. A choice takes place, by means of a volitional act, between two or more of these elements. In each case the choice made by the will in its act is the normal thing. Hence we speak of religious norms of the will. According to these norms the will acts. If the person concerned does not act, he feels, knows, and is inwardly convinced that he should have acted, and has done wrong in not acting. Only self-delusion can hide this guilt from his consciousness.

1. **The First Analytic Norm: That which is of religious value is always to be preferred to that which is not of religious value.**

It is the preacher's business to present the alternatives concerned in a clear and decisive manner. When this is done, the will normally chooses the former and wills that, and normally rejects the latter and turns from it.

This norm applies to a goodly number of religious alternatives. They are mostly positive and negative, or equivalent to a yea and nay.

To trust in God — this is of religious value. It is full of all kinds of religious benefit. Every promise of God, as well as His entire character, reveal that, and draw the human will to put forth that trust by a decisive volitional act. The alternative is, not to trust God, or to doubt Him, or any one of His promises. This alternative may be fortified in the mind by wrong conceptions of God, of His attributes, of His purpose and will, or false notions about any one or more of His words and promises. These may incline the will in the wrong direction, or rather hold it fast in its doubt or distrust, causing it to put forth distrustful volitions. If unchecked, or greatly intensified, these false conceptions may harden the will into a fixed and permanent state of distrust (unbelief), which may remain proof against all the truth about God and His promises.

In following the norm which here applies, the preacher must put into clear and clean-cut opposition the two alternatives confronting the hearer's will: to trust God — not to trust God, i. e. to doubt and distrust him. On the basis of this opposition he must clear away all that beclouds this alternative, all that hides the true value of trusting God and His Word, as well as all that hides the absence of value and all that pretends a false value in doubting and distrusting God. With the shams, deceptions, and delusions swept away the alternatives must be made, through the intellect, to impinge with all possible force upon the will — either — or! on the one hand the blessedness and benefactions of trust — on the other hand the emptiness, the wickedness, the deadliness of distrust. When rightly done, the effect will be tremendous.

It is like pushing at a wagon. One may push at it from the side ever so hard, and the wagon will not move an inch. The same exertion directly from behind, in the exact line of the wheels, at once makes it go forward. Most preachers of the Gospel push hard enough, but some of them do not push in line with the wheels. Hence so many sermons are ineffective. The norms of the will are the wheels of the will. In its volitions the will moves only in the track of these norms. Great freight cars are pushed forward on the steel rails when the proper leverage is applied with crowbars at the rear wheels. The same and even greater force applied in a different direction leaves the car motionless.

The same truth holds good in the case of other alternatives. Take the following: to have God's blessing, or to have His curse; to get rid of sin and guilt, or to go on under sin and guilt; to be a child and heir of

God, to be an enemy of God; to die with a Savior, to die without a Savior; etc.

Take the Prodigal and his volition, "I will arise and go to my father." There was, on the one hand, the truth about his father's house, "How many hired servants of my father have bread enough and to spare." There was, on the other hand, the fact of his utter want and wretchedness, "And I perish with hunger." When both stood clearly before his soul, the great value on the one side, over against the utter emptiness on the other side, his will obeyed the natural norm, he went home. For a little while his will may have hesitated, when he thought of the pride with which he left and the humiliation with which he must return. This may well have beclouded the issue, making it seem in a way preferable to stay where he was (false value). But the realities in the alternatives prevailed, and so he returned. It is the experience of thousands of sinners.

2. **The Second Analytical Norm: Greater religious value is always to be preferred to lesser religious value.**

This norm operates with three types of preference, *1) intensity, 2) quantity, 3) duration.* There may be an alternative as between greater and less in regard to any one of these three types.

The religious values involved in this norm are usually apparent and require but little effort to clarify. This is due to the nature of the preferences, namely, that the hearer already possesses more or less of one and the same thing. Only he who has at least a little can be urged to accept more. Hence this norm is quite frequently obeyed, even by preachers who pay no attention to the psychological side of their sermons.

Take trust in God again. To have perfect and complete trust in Him is always preferable to having imperfect, weak and wavering trust in Him. This belongs in the group of alternatives marked by *intensity*. — To aid many men is preferable to the aiding of only one, or only a few. Here the choice is between *quantities*, greater or less. — To secure lasting happiness is always to be preferred to securing only momentary or transient joy. Here the division is on the point of *duration*.

And yet, while the issues for the will and its volitions seem so natural and easy in this norm, the task of securing such volitions is by no means always an easy one. We may easily achieve intellectual assent, just because the cases are naturally clear. When it comes to earthly things the will acts quite readily. A position with small pay is quickly exchanged for one with big pay. Higher honors soon secure the necessary volition when placed alongside of minor honors. Why is this readiness so often missing in the corresponding religious alternatives? Because of the flesh, which so often makes the religious will languid. People are satisfied with a little faith, knowledge, love, etc., with few good works, with transient ease and pleasure.

The preacher's task in applying this norm has a difficulty of its own. He must, of course, present the alternatives involved in a clean-cut way. But this is not enough. He must also press the alternatives home. This is done by showing, for one thing, how supremely desirable the greater is as compared with the less; and for another thing, how we may indeed, and by God's help easily, achieve the greater. The examples in the Bible are especially valuable in this regard. Dorcas, a woman with but one talent, achieved so much. Certainly we can do the same when we have more talents. In addition, the hindering and obstructing influences of the flesh can be exposed, together with the dangers involved. He who will not grow in grace is bound to decline in grace. He who will not strive for more begins to lose the little he already has. Thus this norm tallies with the law of spiritual progress and decline. When this is rightly apprehended and used, the sermon reaches the will by applying this norm.

3. **The Third Analytic Norm: That which is real in religious value is always preferred to that which is not real.**

Real money is always preferable to imaginary money. This is the case even when the real money is a small amount and the unreal or dream money a very large amount. A $100 that I earn by my work now are far preferable to a $1,000,000 that I imagine I can earn sometime. It is exactly the same with religious values.

The religious will thus normally inclines to the real, and away from the unreal. Whatever ideas, imaginings, or pictures the mind may conceive yield at once to any actual value that comes into my possession. In cases where the will at first is undecided and wavers between possible alternatives, it will normally always incline to secure the value which now, in this hour, and by myself, I can actually secure, and will pass by any value which invites me in the distance as a mere possibility.

Jesus came into the world, not to fill our minds with new ideas, but to make God's Kingdom real, i. e.

to make men actually do God's will. So He constantly
stirs our wills into action. We are not to philosophize
whether His doctrine is of God, we are to do it —
then, in, by, and through the doing of it, i. e. by the
real value we thus secure, we will know that the doctrine is of God. "Go, and do thou likewise!" "Son,
go work to-day in my vineyard!" "Verily, I say unto
you, that the publicans and harlots go into the Kingdom
of God," they actually go. In the parable of the
laborers the husbandman orders, "Go ye also into the
vineyard!" And they actually went. "Watch, and
pray!" is Jesus' command. Hence the test, "By their
fruits ye shall know them." The proof of God's love
is that He actually "laid down His life for us," 1 John
3, 16; and the proof of our love is the same. "He
that doeth righteousness is righteous, even as he is
righteous," 1 John 3, 7. "My little children, let us
not love in word, neither in tongue," by mere ideas,
distant plans, or any other unrealities; "but in deed
and truth," i. e. by genuine reality. 1 John 3, 18.
"Follow Me!" by actual volition and deed.

Thus this norm of the religious will is constantly
employed in the Bible. The appeal that wins, and alone
is expected to win, is that of reality in real volition and
deed, as over against mere ideas that remain unreal
and are never turned into action. This is the truth in
the old saying, "The road to hell is paved with good
resolutions," that are never carried out. This is the
mistake of the son who said, "I go, sir!" but went not,
Matth. 21. 30. In the last judgment not those who
said, "Lord, Lord!" shall enter into the Kingdom,
"but he that doeth the will of My Father which is in
heaven, Matth. 7, 21.

The application of this norm in preaching will mightily disturb the wills of the languid Christians who mean well, but fail to act. It will either vitalize them into action, or leave them more guilty for still continuing in non-action. This norm will get past the barrier of the intellectual Christian, who readily assents to the Gospel, but does not bring forth fruits meet for rightousness. Either the fruits will begin to come forth, or the guilt will increase the more. This norm will penetrate the emotional Christian, who delights to have his feelings touched, even to tears, but stops with that. Either the will gets into action, or the guilt of non-action will result.

All through his sermon on the Twentieth Sunday after Trinity Luther operated with this norm. Here is a passage, "Let not the thought deceive you, 'Oh, I shall attend to it in one, two, or three years!' For this is nothing but unreason and unwise thought of the careless, who let their own salvation, which they have at hand, slip by, before they are aware of it. They do not think what God's will really is, but put it off some place, until they have attended to their business and have waited too long. He now comes right to your door, that you may seek him, and He greets you, if only you will return His greeting. But if you let Him pass by, you need not imagine that you will find Him when He is gone, even though you ran through all the world. But while He is still there you may seek Him and find, as Isaiah 55, 6 says, 'Seek ye the Lord, while He may be found; call ye upon Him while He is near.' If you will not understand, and let Him go by, all seeking will be in vain."

## II.  The Three Norms of Synthetical Preference.

In analytic preferences the values (and non-values) lie on the same level. Thus trust is always to be preferred to doubt, more trust to less, and actual trust to the mere thought of trust. But there are also values which lie on different levels and yet compete for volitional decision. It is because they lie on different levels that we call them synthetical.

The first two of these synthetical norms deal with the competition of lower and higher religious values. The third with the competition of religious and non-religious values. We will explain them in this order.

There are three general values which pertain to man's entire mental life, including the religious life. *1. Pleasurable conditions. 2. Permanent personal improvement. 3. Great causes that lie above anything personal.* The first of these is the lowest value, and its appeal for volition is accordingly low. The second is much higher, and so is its appeal to the will. The third is much higher than the second, and its appeal to the will supreme. In the first of these values we desire *to enjoy*. In the second we desire *to possess*. In the last we desire *to create, help, and serve*.

We recognize and strive to secure conditions which afford us mental ease, satisfaction, in a word, pleasure and enjoyment. We enjoy pleasurable books, congenial friends, interesting travel, intellectual occupation that pleases us. Hence the condition which affords us such enjoyment is a value. But only of condition, only of pleasure, only of the feelings.

Again, we recognize and strive to secure as permanent possessions education, knowledge, wisdom, beauty, riches, honor, and other good things. These are values that are rated very high. They enrich our personal life; in fact, they become part of our person or are intimately connected with it. They have permanency, they are more than transient feeling, they raise our person to a higher level.

But there are still greater values, represented in great causes. We strive, not for anything even for our own person, but for grander and loftier objects. One lives for his art, another for science. One becomes a patriot and seeks the good of his country, another labors for his church and its spiritual interests. There are many great causes calling for our volitions.

Now again and again these three values are thrown into competition with each other. The will must decide which in a given situation it will choose. Then we meet the first two synthetic norms,

1) **Condition must yield to person;**
2) **Person must yield to a great cause.**

These norms apply in all that pertains to our mental life as distinguished from our physical life. They thus apply also in religion. And here we are concerned with these norms only as they affect our religious volitions.

1. **The First Synthetic Norm.**
   **Positive statement:** To give up excellence of condition for excellence of person is always to be commended.
   **Negative statement:** To give up excellence of person for excellence of condition is always to be reprehended.

This norm, of course, can be applied only where religious values are recognized as values. But where they are recognized, there is an inner urge, inherent in the very will itself, in its very constitution we may say, which impels us to choose the higher value in preference to the lower. In case the will chooses the lower nevertheless, it can do so only by means of self-deception, or only in the face of a feeling of guilt, i. e. deep down in his heart the person feels he should have chosen otherwise.

This norm applies in the entire field of suffering for Christ's sake. "Blessed are ye, when men shall revile you, and persecute you, and shall say all manner of evil against you falsely, for My sake. Rejoice, and be exceedingly glad: for great is your reward in heaven: for so persecuted they the prophets which were before you." Matth. 5, 11-12. By keeping quiet the apostles could have enjoyed their faith in Christ privately and undisturbed. Instead they braved the indignation and anger of the Jewish Sanhedrim, accepted imprisonment and scourging, "rejoicing that they were counted worthy to suffer shame for His name," Acts 5, 41, "and daily in the Temple, and in every house, they ceased not to teach and preach Jesus Christ." All the Christian martyrs are shining illustrations of this norm. They gave up life itself rather than their faith. — Following them are a host of saints who were not called to give up that much, but who suffered in mind, in the loss of earthly possessions, and in many other ways, but held fast to faith, loyalty, confession, and all that makes us children of God. Paul has recorded it, "By honor and dishonor, by evil report and good report: as deceivers, and yet true; as unknown, and yet well known; as dying, and behold we live; as chastened, and not killed; as sorrowful, yet always rejoicing; as poor, yet making many rich, as having nothing, and yet possessing all things." 2 Cor. 6, 8-10.

They all gave up excellence of condition for excellence of person, and we still commend them to this day. Some chose the wrong alternative. To gain safety, quiet, and peace they compromised, they did not openly confess. Their example is not used to-day except in warning. "Behold, we count them happy which endure." James 5, 11. Also Matth. 10, 22-26. Our greatest example is Christ Himself, 1 Pet. 2, 21; Heb. 2, 10, made "perfect through sufferings."

This norm applies in the entire domain of works. Many of them are unpleasant, connected with self-sacrifice, hard labor, little or no thanks. Yet there is Christian nobility for those that give up their ease and lay hand to these works. There is the example of the Good Samaritan, and Christ's word, Go thou and do likewise! Mary of Bethany anointed Jesus, and received small thanks from Judas and some of the rest. Certain of the women endured the hardship of following Jesus in order to minister unto Him, Luke 8, 1-3. To go into heathen lands and live in heathen surroundings is not nearly as pleasant as to live at home and enjoy our church membership, but missionaries still follow the call, "Go!" Thus every Christian work that is cheerfully done at cost of time, labor, and money, comes under this norm, as well as every Christian work of this kind that is left undone.

In using this norm to shape our material in preaching, the preacher himself must obey it in his own life. His own experience will then teach him how to draw a true comparison between the two alternative values.

While he will admit the relative value of mere religious joys and feelings of satisfaction, he will rip away
the deceptions which cause so many to rest content
with these. He will reveal fully the higher value of
personal excellencies in working and in suffering for
the Lord.

When thus we yield the lower value for the higher,
the joy and pleasure is not lost to us. It still comes to
us in rich measure, but at the same time on a higher
plane. Note how Jesus says, "Rejoice, and be exceed-
ing glad!" in connection with suffering, Matth. 5, 12;
and how the apostles who had just been scourged came
away "rejoicing," Acts 5, 41.

### 2. The Second Synthetical Norm.

**Positive Statement:** To give up excellencies of person
for some great religious cause is always to be commended.

**Negative Statement:** To give up some great religious
cause for excellencies of person is always to be reprehended.

This norm, too, presupposes a knowledge of the
values concerned, and thus deals with cases where the
alternatives that are possible compete for volition.
And again, in every competition or clash of this kind,
the will, not because of the strength of some motive,
but because of its own nature and constitution, normally inclines to the higher value. Only by means
of self-deception, which beclouds the issue between
the values, and makes the less appear the greater,
and vice versa, can the will be brought to a wrong
decision. Or the wrong decision is made in the face
of the truth about the values concerned, and thus with
a weight of guilt upon the conscience.

The supreme example for this norm is Christ,
who came not to be ministered unto, but to minister

unto others and to give His life as a ransom for many;
who like a grain of wheat was buried that He might
bring wonderful fruit; who sought not His own honor,
but only the honor of God; who did not His own will,
but only the will of His Great Sender; whose sole
devotion was the establishment of the Kingdom of
God; who came, not to judge, but to seek and to save
the lost; to whom thrice the voice spoke from the
heavens, assuring Him that God was well pleased in
Him.

The next supreme examples are Moses and Paul.
The former prayed, "Yet now, if Thou wilt forgive
their sin —; and if not, blot me, I pray Thee, out of
Thy book which Thou hast written." Ex. 32, 32.
The latter wrote, "For I could wish that myself were
accursed from Christ for my brethren, my kinsmen
according to the flesh." Rom. 9, 3. While both cases
are highly exceptional, and deal with hypothetical
possibilities, yet they exhibit the climax under this
norm. Both men were ready to accept damnation for
their own persons, if by so doing it were possible to
save their recreant nation. The giving up of personal
value for one still higher can go no farther.

But there are thousands of lesser cases where
these two values meet the will and demand a choice.
For even in the Christian religion, and in the field
of the personal excellencies which it is intended to
bestow, a kind of personal selfishness is possible, which
prompts a man to think only of his own soul, his own
salvation, his own faith and confession, his own round
of virtues and their exercise, his own opportunity to
have and hear the Gospel, etc. When then the call
comes to save others, to consider the entire congre-

gation or church body and its spiritual welfare, to contend for the faith and confession of the whole church, etc., this narrow selfishness refuses to act. Old people are often intent on divine services for themselves, and concern themselves not at all, or very little, for the children and younger people. Here this second synthetical norm applies, to show how reprehensible all such narrowness really is. The preacher must pluck away the shams and deceptions behind which such personal selfishness hides. He must display the higher value in all its greatness, and thus reach the will, either to win it, or to send it away guilty.

In the light of this norm we get the full force of Christ's word, "Whosoever shall seek to save his life shall lose it; and whosoever shall lose his life shall preserve it." Luke 17, 33. Or the rendering of Mark 8, 35, "Whosoever will save his life shall lose it; but whosoever shall lose his life for My sake and the Gospel's, the same shall save it." Also John 12, 25.

To find God (Christ); to lay everything at His feet; to bow to His Word only in everything; to defend His truth and any part of it at every cost; to heed God's will and obey it unquestioningly; to devote oneself to His saving will and work among men — in a word, to make God (Christ) and His Kingdom the one thing needful, is to achieve the highest of all religious values. Wherever the Bible touches any of these greatest subjects the norm finds application.

The usual self-deception is that one's personal religious advantage is identical with that of the Kingdom. But this is not true in many cases, as when I seem keen to cultivate my own faith unconcerned about thousands who never get an opportunity to obtain faith; or as when I earnestly read my Bible unconcerned about my own children, who perhaps read no Bible. So in applying this norm its negative statement must be used constantly in warning and in exposing self-deceptions.

Moreover, in honestly meeting this norm the real personal religious values are by no means lost, but are found in a higher and more genuine way, even as Jesus tells us. To lose religious selfishness in true religious unselfishness everlastingly enriches the religious life. Paul and Luther are immortal in our memories for this very reason. Thousands bless their names for the blessings these men were instrumental in handing down to future generations. So every higher devotion has its own supreme rewards. To use this norm aright in preaching the preacher must have obeyed it in his own religious life.

### 3. The Third Synthetical Norm.

**Positive Statement: To prefer religious values to non-religious values is always to be commended.**

**Negative Statement: To prefer non-religious values to religious values is always to be reprehended.**

This norm, of course, applies only when the two values, lying as they do on different planes, come into competition with each other in given cases. There are many of these cases, and they occur with great frequency. At times the decision made under this norm is decisive for a man's entire life.

This norm takes in all religious values of whatever kind, and on the other hand all possible non-religious values, however great they may be. The non-religious values with which the religious may clash are *1) material values; 2) intellectual values; 3) esthetic values; and 4) moral values*.  The norm may thus be restated by inserting the designations for these values.

1. **The willing of religious value is to be preferred to the willing of every material value.**
2. **The willing of religious value is to be preferred to the willing of every intellectual value.**
3. **The willing of religious value is to be preferred to the willing of every esthetic value.**
4. **The willing of religious value is to be preferred to the willing of every moral value.**

All four may also be put into negative form, and for warning are frequently used in this form.

1.   Christ Himself used this norm as the basis of some of His parables, notably Matth. 22, 1 etc.   One man preferred his farm, another his merchandise. In Luke's version, 14, 18 etc., one prefers his ground, another his oxen, another his wife — so they cannot accept the invitation to the Great Supper.   We feel at once how wrong their decisions were.   What makes it worse is that by their own volitions they make these material values clash with the spiritual.   For in itself there need be no clash between a piece of ground, oxen, a wife on the one hand, and the Great Supper on the other hand.   Our material values can often be sanctified by the Gospel, and will be the better for that.   But, alas, often they are used as excuses, not only for dismissing religious duties, but also for rejecting spiritual blessings, even the entire Gospel.

In Mark 4, 19 Christ shows the sad condition of those who allow "cares of this world, and the deceitfulness of riches, and the lust of other things entering in," to "choke the Word," so that it cannot bear fruit.

In Matth. 26, 41 the conflict in the will is described as a temptation, the spirit willing, but the flesh weak. In Luke 12, 37 and Matth. 25, 1 etc., He shows how we must watch, lest we take our ease, sleep, etc., and be caught without faith, the great spiritual value. In Matth. 19, 29 and Luke 14, 26 even father and mother and life itself are not to be preferred above the one great spiritual value of union with Christ. This is vividly illustrated in Christ's own case, when he asked, "Who is my mother? and who are my brethren?" Matth. 12, 46 etc.

There are many other illustrations under this norm. Compare Matth. 19, 28 etc.; 6, 24-34; especially also Matth. 16, 26, "What is a man profited, if he shall gain the whole world, and lose his own soul? or what shall a man give in exchange for his soul?" Luke 9, 57-62; 12, 16-21, the Rich Fool; etc.

So also the epistles, Phil. 4, 11-13; 1 Tim. 6, 6-12; 2 Tim. 4, 10, the case of Demas; Heb. 11, 32 etc. For our materialistic age this norm will have to be applied constantly. May the preacher himself never fall under its condemnation.

2. Where intellectual values are appreciated in education in general and in science and philosophy in particular, this norm again applies.

Christianity demands intellectual power and development. The Bible itself is a stupendous product, viewed merely from an intellectual standpoint. It never puts a premium on ignorance, but always rebukes it. The freethinkers called Sadducees, who philosophized away the resurrection, were told by Christ, "Ye do err, not knowing the Scriptures, nor the power of God," Matth. 22, 29. So in every instance, Christ exposed the ignorance of His supposedly learned opponents. In John 8, 37 etc. He crushes them with one negative syllogism after another, tearing their false conclusion to shreds. Jesus *knows;* His disciples must *know;* His opponents do *not know,* even when they crucify Him, Luke 23, 34. Paul's constant prayer is that his readers may know, Eph. 1, 17. Knowledge belongs to the restored image of God, Col. 3, 10. Yet conflicts are possible between the intellect and the tenets of the Christian religion. First, when the intellect is misled by some hypothesis of science or false philosophy; secondly, when the intellect presumes to penetrate beyond its bounds.

A false philosophy assailed the Corinthians when they began to doubt the resurrection from the dead, 1 Cor. 15, 12 etc., and we see how Paul met this intellectual error. He met it likewise among the scoffing philosophers in Athens when he addressed them on Mars' Hill, Acts 17, 32. Jesus confronted the same error among the Sadducees, Matth. 22, 29. Hence the general warning against "oppositions of science falsely so-called," 1 Tim. 6, 20.

The world has always been full of this false science. It constantly shifts its positions, often with great rapidity, thus literally by every new "advance" refuting its past positions. But the latest pronouncements of this false science and philosophy always rise up with great arrogance and self-assurance. Christian people, especially those who are educated, thus get into conflicts.

Back of this clash often appears the general presumption of the intellect which attempts to probe everything and to reduce even the mysteries of religion and of life to rational propositions. Thus the intellect runs foul of the miracles, of the Holy Trinity, of the person of Christ, and of doctrines such as justification, regeneration, providence, angels, etc. By means of the intellect men attempt what no intellect of man can possibly achieve. Thus conflicts are precipitated. The Christian must decide whether he will hold to what the Word teaches, or whether he will hold to what his intellect at the time tells him.

Here is where our final synthetical norm finds its application. The giving up of any supposed intellectual values for the everlasting religious values is always to be commended, and the reverse course reprehended. "Casting down imaginations, and every high thing that exalteth itself against the knowledge of God, and bringing into captivity every thought to the obedience of Christ." 2 Cor. 10, 5. Paul thus voices the norm in his own way. Again, 1 Cor. 2, 2 etc., "I determined not to know any thing among you, save Jesus Christ, and Him crucified. . . . And my speech and my preaching was not with enticing words of man's wisdom (philosophy, hypothesis, etc.), but in demonstration of the Spirit and of power; that your faith should not stand in the wisdom of men, but in the power of God." So the entire section on human wisdom as over against man's wisdom, 1 Cor. 1, 18—2, 16. Philosophies and hypotheses have come and gone, but "the Word of God liveth and abideth for ever," 1 Pet. 1, 23; and again, "the Word of the Lord endureth for ever; and this is the Word which by the Gospel is preached unto you," v. 25. "Heaven and earth shall pass away, but My words shall not pass away." Matth. 24, 35; also Matth. 5, 18.

All evasions of the norm here to be applied have long ago proven futile. It is impossible to lead a double life, the head and intellect skeptical, the heart believing the Gospel. One or the other is false. Or, to divide the Scriptures, one part dealing with science which may be denied, the other with spiritual truth which must be accepted. It is and will remain true, the Spirit who could not be faithful in that which is least (matters of nature) cannot be trusted in that which is greatest (spiritual matters), Luke 16, 10. Or, to accommodate exegesis to claims of modern science. Such juggling and compromises condemn themselves.

The truth of Scripture asks no illegitimate intellectual sacrifice. For Scripture truth has always been and always will be in perfect harmony with all genuine truth discovered in nature. There are clashes only with unsound theories, hypotheses, philosophies, and the supposed facts of nature, which in the end are always exposed as guesses. In applying this norm the deceptions rife in every age must be exposed, the issue must be clearly drawn, and then the regenerate heart will arrive joyfully at the true volition. Some intellectual tangles we may never solve in our lives — what of it? Even nature retains its many mysteries, concerning which one has well said, *"Ignoramus, ignorabimus!"* In the great crises of life intellectualism breaks down pitifully, or ends in blind tragedy; while faith rises to its greatest triumph.

3. Also where esthetic values are appreciated and sought our final norm applies. Genuine religious values always outrank even the highest esthetic or art values. Like the material and intellectual, the esthetic are

real values, which should always be granted. But art emancipated from the life in God may readily come into conflict with this lfe.

This is done in the esthetic canon, "Art for art's sake." Such devotees of art make the stage their church, and music, drama, painting, etc., their worship. Their moral canon becomes an art canon, "Whatever is beautiful is good." And with the veil of supposed beauty even sin and vice are draped. Only what is common and coarse is crime. Yet all of it falls under the condemnation of our norm.

In all the world there is no beauty like that of Jesus, the Son of God and man. In all the world there is no beauty like that of divine love and its supreme sacrifice. In all the world there is no beauty like that of the life restored by grace to the image of Christ. All secular art and its products appear cheap and tawdry beside this heavenly and spiritual beauty, though we meet it in a divine service held in a barn.

True art need never clash with true religion. Religion is the higher value and always will be. If either must yield, art must yield, not religion. It always must yield when it shows the trail of the serpent. In all other cases, no matter what the form of art, whether secular or religious, true religion will help to purify, ennoble, elevate true art, and so harmonize with the norm.

4. Moral value as such, apart from religion, is higher than esthetic, intellectual, and material value. It approaches religion closely, and thus has been placed in competition and conflict with religion.

How? A so-called "moral" life is frequently considered superior to a religious life. Usually, however, the religious life meant is one of empty outward forms. Certain deeds of humanitarian and philanthropic charity are put into contrast with forms of religious worship. This is a species of begging the question. — Again, the whole aim of religion is reduced to morality, namely doing good to others, helping, rescuing, etc. Moral "reforms" often take this course. Fellowship with the true God through Christ and the Gospel is lost. The truth of the life in God disappears. Thus one religion is counted about as good as another, especially the varying Christian types, as long as they make men kind and helpful. But all such efforts at elevating mere human morality above religion are exposed as false and spurious by our norm.

Mere morality, the old doctrine of works and the Law, is the greatest religious error of the ages. It produced the Pharisees in Christ's times. It produced monks and nuns in medieval times, down to the present. It produces to-day, in the churches and outside of them, those who expect to enter heaven by means of their own efforts.

Christ followed our norm when he described the last judgment in Matth. 25, 41 etc. Paul was tireless in exposing law-works as the destruction of justification by faith alone. Read Rom. 3, 20-5, 1; Gal. 1, 16; 2, 8 etc.; and many other passages. These supreme religious values substantiate the norm, that no moral values can ever exceed the true religious values. What God gives to us always exceeds what we can give to Him — infinitely what we can produce ourselves and offer to Him, and vastly what by His help we can produce and offer to Him.

Doubly this norm holds when we perceive the truth that only a good tree produces good fruit; to suppose the opposite is folly, Matth. 7, 17. Our righteousness must exceed that of the scribes and Pharisees, Matth. 5, 20. Only a regenerate heart can meet the spiritual requirements of the Law, Matth. 5, 22-28. Who can love his enemies except he have first tasted of the love of God, v. 44? Can anything be plainer than the parable of the Unforgiving Servant, Matth. 18, 21 etc.? Add to this Paul's word in 1 Cor. 13, to speak with tongues of men and angels, to prophesy and know all mysteries, to have miracle-working faith, to give all our goods to the poor and our body to be burned in martyrdom — without charity, i. e. the love born of faith (true religion), is altogether vain. So, in the last judgment, the righteous will appear with many works, but all born from faith and evidence of that faith, "Ye have done it unto Me," Matth. 25, 31-40. All other works of mere morality will be rejected, "Ye did it not to Me," v. 45.

We sorely need this norm. And that means that all delusions beclouding it must be fully exposed and swept away. The truth about Christ and morality is all found in one brief word of Christ, "Without Me ye can do nothing." John 15, 5; also the entire parable.

Unless the preacher moves the will his preaching is only as sounding brass or a tinkling cymbal. The will is not moved aright unless its psychological norms are obeyed in preaching. But when they are obeyed genuine results follow. If this kind of preaching fails, it fails just as Christ and His apostles failed. Some remain obdurate. The will of man has the terrible power to say no even unto God, and to take the consequences. But where the norms of the will are met, the preacher is guiltless, even as was Christ and the apostles.

We have studied the norms on the basis of the Scriptures only, because they are the purest source. There are, of course, also fine examples in sermon literature. The best of these, however, cannot excel what Christ and the apostles furnish us.

## THIRD CHAPTER

# THE INTRODUCTION AND THE ENDING

MOTTO:   Well begun — half done.

Writers on Homiletics dispute whether the introduction should be written immediately after the outline has been produced, or whether the preacher should first write the entire body of the sermon, and then add the introduction last of all.  Let the preacher do what he deems best, either following one or the other alternative as a custom, or varying between the two, as the cases may warrant.

Can we dispense with an introduction altogether? We certainly can — with many actual introductions that are preached.  For in these cases the sermon would gain, and anything that brings gain is the better of two alternatives.   A forty-five minute sermon with a fifteen minute introduction would gain thirty-three per cent by lopping off the introduction altogether, so that the sermon would begin something like this: "Our text invites us to consider" — then stating the theme.

But the moment we study a sermon with the right kind of introduction, our verdict will never be, Lop it off!  For in this case the sermon would lose, lose so evidently, that we should see the mistake of cancelling such an introduction.   Like so many questions in Homiletics this one too is correctly answered, not by setting up some abstract theory or principle, but by induction, by drawing our conclusion from actual cases.

Though it may seem presumptuous to say it, yet it is a fact none the less — most of the instruction offered in homiletical works on the composition of introductions is valueless, in fact often worse, because it misleads. To point a poor traveller to a wrong road is worse than to point him to none. All introductions composed to satisfy *some theory* regarding introductions are by that very fact mistakes. Clear the ground in front of the sermon elaboration of all theories. On one thing the majority is agreed — the introduction ought to be short. But how many know why? Leaving the requirement for shortness in the shape of a mechanical rule has produced in practice quite a number of introductions that honored the rule in the breach thereof. Those that were kept short honored the rule in a better way indeed, but only as a mere rule. Once we become acquainted with genuine introductions we shall see that they, like certain plants, all grow short, and never could trail out like a vine, because they are not that kind of plant.

To write a genuine introduction we absolutely must have *the starting point*. In this respect the sermon has the advantage over most other forms of public address. It always has a definite starting point. The reading of the text, when properly done, stirs corresponding thoughts in the minds of the hearers. These thoughts are the *real* starting point. They ought at least to be thoughts of interest. They may be mingled with a question or two. They may stir some feeling. But *whatever the thought aroused in the hearer, that is the starting point for the sermon.*

So the preacher must in spirit sit in the pew in the hearer's place and let the text come from the pulpit to his ears and his heart. The more perfectly he is able to do this, the more truly will he gauge the effect of the reading of his text, and thus see the starting point for his sermon.

From this starting point the introduction should move straight on to the theme. Since the theme is either the sum of the text or drawn directly from it, the line of thought forming the introduction is bound to be short. It could not, in the nature of the case, be long. The distance between the true starting point and the theme is only a few steps in thought. Hence the definition of a sermon introduction is simply *a straight line of thought from the starting point to the theme*.

We at once rule out a few faults. First, all perfunctory reading of the text. Read it with a full realization of what you are doing — clearly, distinctly, impressively, as if you meant to implant it lastingly upon the hearer's mind. No matter if it is long. Most carefully, if it is short. And no matter if you have already read it at the altar or lectern. Probably the most important thing you will do during the half hour you are in the pulpit is this reading of a portion of the divinely inspired Word of God. — Secondly, do not dismiss the text on having read it. That means, do not take a mental leap to some point far away from the text. Let it cling to your mind as you would have it cling to that of your hearer. — Therefore, thirdly, interlard no long prayer between the reading of your text and the first words of your sermon. The old custom according to which the preacher follows the

reading with a prayer in which he unburdens his heart
*ad libitum* is a vast mistake. Either put that prayer
at the end of the sermon or put it before the altar;
better still, omit it entirely. — Fourthly, it is an equally
grave mistake to let the choir, or the congregation,
or both, sing after reading the text. Any break between text and sermon blurs the starting point for the
hearer, and perhaps also for the preacher.

Illustration of a good introduction from a sermon
on Acts 6, 8-15:

There are two ways of reading the shining examples of
faith, such as Stephen's heroic death, recorded for us in Holy
Writ. One way is to read them with our faith asleep. Then
these examples of true faith loom up before us like lofty mountain peaks. We admire them indeed, but the flesh still in us
whispers that such heights are surely beyond our reach. We
lean back idly, supinely, telling ourselves in a discouraging
way that there is no use for us to vie with these men of old.
Have you ever read the Bible story of heroic faith in this way?

There is another way. It is to read these glorious accounts
with the eyes of our own faith wide open. This clear mountain
air of God's Word braces us. The clear light of its lofty heights
makes us see things as they are. Our miserable flesh receives
a severe setback. The prayer rises to our lips, Would to God
that my faith were like that! We come away from such reading
with new vigor in our spiritual system. Have you ever read
the Bible story of heroic faith in this way?

Well, this is the way to read the story of Stephen, the
only way. We ought to find in

**Stephen a Tonic for Our Faith.**

Let us try it with the help of God.

An illustration, on Luke 13, 6-9, starting slightly
away from the real starting point, but quickly getting
back to it — a method that is also good:

Happy New Year! Happy New Year! is the universal greeting to-day, and blithely men start out on the new year. There is a serious side to the beginning of another year of our earthly life, and the common greeting, meant well enough in its way, must not make us forget that. Here in our text a beautiful vineyard appears. Two men with serious mien walk down the vine-bordered path. They go to inspect the big fig tree which proudly rears its mass of branches and foliage near the center of the garden. That tree has not been doing its duty, and it has stood long already. Shall it be cut down now, or shall it be left another season? Shall justice take charge, or shall patient grace still continue? Yes, it was not a mere happy, sunshiny day for that tree, it was a serious, decisive day. Let us go along with those two men, the owner of the vineyard and the caretaker, and think of ourselves as they look at that tree and decide what to do.

**There is a New Year's Message for Us in What Was Done With the Barren Fig Tree.**

A message of **Grace mingled with Justice** in what was said of its past; a message of **Justice tempered by Grace** in what was determined about its future.

We may start directly with the story part of a text in the introduction — it is a good way. But we may also start with the truth substance in the text, reserving the story as a story for the parts. Thus on John 2, 18-22.

Is the Gospel really true? Sometimes a kind of unbelief stirs even in the hearts of Christians and tries to raise that question. We know that men around us raise it openly, and we also know the scoffing answers they give. The Gospel is true. It bears its own unmistakable stamp of truth in every part of it. Every one of its gracious gifts and blessings proves it true. They know who have these blessings. Is honey sweet? Taste it, and you know it is. The Gospel says it is sweeter than honey and the honeycomb. They who have tasted it know and need no further proof. Is sunlight bright? They who go out and live in it know. The Gospel light says that it is brighter than the sun, as bright as God Himself in His grace. They who walk in that light know.

But there are men who are not satisfied with this proof, they demand something more decisive still; and they act as if they are going to be aggrieved if they do not get it. Well, they shall have even what they want —

### The Sign that Decides.

Wait until the audience is well seated after you have read the text. Face the audience squarely as a man that is ready to begin, and wait till the last rustle subsides. Wait still a little longer. All eyes will fix themselves on you — waiting; and like a magnetic current, which you can actually sense and feel, the attention of the audience will rise to meet you. This is the psychological moment to begin. Do *not* begin before. Hold back, even if it costs an effort. Begin in a level tone of voice, and speak the very first word so that all can easily understand. Make the very first sentence fully justify the attention you have aroused. Make the next sentence, and the next equally strong, or more than that. And so go on. With a properly arranged introduction this will give a one hundred per cent start. You can have it every time, if you really want it. It costs no more than a ten per cent start.

Hence, do not start too soon. Most men do. Do not fuss with the Bible, manuscript, spectacles, handkerchief, or anything else, as if you were not quite ready to speak. Do not turn the eyes from the people. Do not begin in too low a tone of voice. Do not speak hesitatingly as if you were trying to get up steam. When the conductor cries, "All aboard!" and waves his hand, the limited rolls out majestically. Your sermon is the limited. No long or involved sentences for the start. No weak or disappointing thought.

The attention of the hearers is more easily lost at the start than in any other part of the sermon. And once thus lost, it is harder to recover afterwards, frequently it is not recovered at all. While a student, the author listened regularly to one of his professors on Sunday mornings. Whenever the start of the sermon gripped his mind he had no trouble to follow the sermon to the end; but when the start failed to interest, the sermon was one long fight against sleep.

The preacher has four assets to begin with. 1) The hearer's *attention*, if the preacher starts right. It is a wrong theory which counsels us to use the introduction for arousing attention and interest. We have both without effort on our part. All we have to do is to justify both in every sentence we speak. — 2) The *benevolentia* of the hearer. He has come for the very purpose of hearing you, and with the very expectation that he will hear something good. Take that good-will, justify, and do not disappoint it. — 3) The *docilitas* of your hearer. He has come to be preached to, even to be rebuked, admonished, warned, in a word, to be told the truth. He is ready to accept it from your lips. Take that docility and honor it with divine truth. Only occasionally will there be an attitude of hostility or prejudice to disarm, or a false impression to remove, at the start. — 4) *The thought awakened by the text*, namely the true starting point. Take it, and go on.

In *casual sermons* there are three things to be connected: text — case — theme. But they all lie on the same plane, and thus connect naturally. Usually the case is in the mind of the hearer; the text, if rightly chosen, tallies with the case; the theme centers in the text and points to the main feature of the case. Where the case or the occasion needs some explanation this should be briefly offered. It will all be in the line from the text to the theme. This applies also to the special significance of certain Sundays and certain festivals in the Christian church year.

There are two natural ways of drawing the line between the text and the theme.

1. Begin with *the objective substance of the text*. This may be done in a great variety of ways. We list a few.

Describe the scene of the text, the situation, the person or the people, the truth stated, or the doctrine involved. Sketch the main thought you mean to unfold especially, and then state your theme. This is a most excellent way. Sometimes you will pick up two or three threads from the text, state what they are, then tie a knot, binding them together, which will be your theme.

Examples.—*The Scene*, Luke 5, 1-11. "It was a beautiful, bright morning on the Sea of Galilee when Jesus taught the people from a boat, anchored a little way from the shore. At this time Jesus intended to do more than merely preach. He intended to show His disciples, as future preachers, the actual power of his Word. So he turns to Peter," etc. This leads straight to the theme, **Jesus Shows the Fishers of Men the Actual Power of His Word.**—Take Matt. 3, 1, etc. "John Baptist appears in our text in the midst of his work, preaching the Kingdom and baptizing those ready to enter it. Let us join the multitude and watch what takes place." Describe a bit further, and you will easily arrive at the theme, **The Great Confessional in the Wilderness Beside the Jordan.**

Thus we may describe *the Situation*, John 10, 23-31. "Our text really describes a very dramatic situation. For once Jesus walked alone in Solomon's Porch in the Temple, and the Jewish leaders, with a crowd of their followers, suddenly surrounded him. They meant to have it out with him here, and, if possible, to stone and kill him on the spot." Describe how Jesus never hesitated, never compromised in one point, etc. This will lead to the theme, **The Invincible Shepherd of His Sheep.**

Often we may begin with *the Person* prominent in the text, as in Acts 9, 36-43. "The name Tabitha, or as her Greek speaking friends preferred to call her, Dorcas, has been lifted to special prominence on the pages of Holy Writ." Show her lowly position; refer to the miracle of her return to life; ask the reason for her being distinguished thus. And your theme is ready, **Why was the Humble Dressmaker Dorcas Raised from the Dead?** — This can be done equally well when there are more persons involved, for instance all the disciples, or the Pharisees, and others.

We may begin by sketching *the great Truth* in a text, as in Luke 23, 39. "The story of the malefactor on the cross at Christ's right side is a living illustration of how pardon admits to Paradise." Sketch the great sinner, the wondrous pardoning act, the promise of Paradise. Tie the three great threads together, and you reach the theme, **Pardon Alone Admits to Paradise.**

As with the truth, so with *the doctrine* that fills a text. Take Rom. 3, 28, and you may begin at once by stating: "Our text is St. Paul's own summary of the greatest doctrine in the Bible." Sketch its main features, sin, grace, atonement, faith, and the pardoning verdict. You may use these five as parts of the sermon, tying them together in the theme, **How St. Paul Preaches Justification by Faith.**

Sometimes there are presuppositions that invite treatment in an introduction. They may lie in the context, or may be of an historical, psychological, doctrinal, or other nature. Take the story of Stephen's martryrdom, Acts 7, 54; it can scarcely be treated properly in a sermon without mentioning the historical context, and this may well be done in the introduction. Any sermon on any of the Christian virtues calls for a statement on the root whence these virtues spring, namely faith in Christ. If nothing is said on this point the entire sermon may be badly misleading. It would be well to begin the sermon in some way like this.

"Fearlessness and true courage are characteristics of Christ's disciples. They are possible, however, only where true discipleship exists. Faith is the victory which overcometh the world. The stronger your faith is, the stronger your Christian courage will be," etc.

At times there are vital points regarding a text which must be cleared up and fully settled before the sermon can unfold the real contents of a text. An example is Matth. 12, 38-42. Here the preacher may well begin as follows.

"Of all miracles in the Bible that of Jonah has received the most abuse from skeptics and unbelievers. First of all they fell upon the word 'whale,' and mocked at that, because the whale, with all its great size, has a throat so small as to prevent it from swallowing a man," etc. This is cleared up by pointing to Jonah's own word, "a great fish," and Christ's, a "sea-monster." — "But the claim is made that it would be impossible for Jonah to live in the belly of the fish. Impossible? Who is able to state in every case just what is possible and what not?" So this vital point is set right also.—"But there is far more in the miracle of Jonah than the question of whether it occurred or not. The Savior speaks of it to point out its mighty significance regarding Himself and regarding all men down to the end of time," etc. And this leads up to the theme, **The Significant Deliverance of Jonah from the Belly of the Great Fish.**

2. Begin with *the subjective use made of the text* in the sermon itself. There are thus two directions

in which the introduction can face, either back to the text, or forward to the treatment of the text. In the latter case the appropriative or the applicatory thoughts with which the introduction begins should at once appear as pertinent to the text; there should be no gap. Either the obvious connection should be positive in character, or negative.

Thus on Acts 18, 24-28, with the theme, **In the Little School of Aquila and Priscilla,** the introduction may begin in an applicatory manner, "We need more Christian knowledge. In order to secure it we need more desire for Christian knowledge." After thus pointing to the trend the sermon will take in natural connection with the text, we may continue, "Look into our text, and see how all this is meant," ending up with, "Here is a school we must enter, for there are some very needful things which we may learn here." And we are on the theme stated above.

Sermons which intend to meet a certain need of our hearers are well introduced in this fashion.

Example, Jer. 31, 31-34, "Variable winds; treacherous currents. Religiously men are adrift; each steers by the compass of his own brain or the brain of someone else. Countless numbers are wrecked. Only one course is safe, that indicated by the chart which God has made for all time. **God's Chart for Your Soul-journey in the New Church Year.**"

We add an appropriative example on John 6, 16-21, "No man knows Jesus except he know adequately the power of Jesus. The moment we grasp and hold aright the fact, that He is indeed the almighty Son of God, that it is literally true that all power is given to him in heaven and in earth, we will read in a new sense every word, especially every promise of His. Our faith will become a different thing and more nearly what it ought to be. Our life will assume a new aspect, one of confidence, hope, and joy." This leads to the theme, Open your hearts then to **The Revelation of Jesus' Power When He Walked Upon the Sea.**"

*Faulty ways* of beginning an introduction. These are rather numerous, but we content ourselves with the following.

1.   Do not begin with Genesis, and the fall of man, or with the story of sin, and then work on through the plan of salvation to the point on which you desire to preach.   Leave this approach to the students in the seminary.

2.   Never start with a genus and work down to the species in funnel fashion, thus:

INTRODUCTION

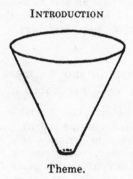

Theme.

Pour in at the top as many species of the genus as you like; finally, with a word or two mention the particular species you intend to treat.   This is a common fault.

Example, theme, The Blessings of Christianity in the Home Life.   Intro.: Christianity has brought us many blessings. Then follows a list and a running description of these blessings. Finally the introduction winds up with the special blessing named in the theme, perhaps in words like this: "Among these many blessings is the one mentioned in our text. Let us therefore consider The Blessing of Christianity in the Home Life."

This is the gentle art of *padding* resorted to not only in introductions but in the body of the sermon as well. The specific thing that is in the text is side-tracked for the time being, until all this long freight train of similar things rolls by, car after car. This certainly helps to consume some of the precious minutes allotted to the sermon. At last, when the thing in the text is reached, it is dismissed with a few brief words, generally just commonplace, whereas this specific thing in the text should itself have had all the time, and should itself have been specifically illuminated and set forth. These generalizations are an abomination in sermons.

3. The worst place to string things out in a sermon is in the introduction. Even if you do reach the theme at last you have trespassed on the good will of your hearers. Jacob strung his gifts out when he made a present to Esau — that was psychologically wise. But when you have no gifts, only common or trivial thoughts, it is psychologically foolish to pretend in a long-winded way that you are really offering something.

4. The common faults of introduction are the following, purposely put in a diagram in order to show how faulty they are, and how they should be avoided.

1.  The Correct Way.

I  |——————————————————————————————————|

True starting point ————————————> Theme

## 2. Digressing by the Way.

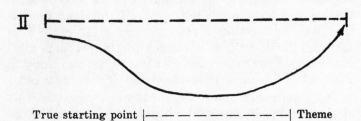

True starting point |— — — — — — — —| Theme

## 3. Starting Far Afield, Arriving at Last.

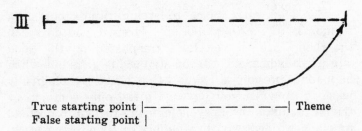

True starting point |— — — — — — — —| Theme
False starting point |

## 4. Starting Far Afield, Not Arriving at all.

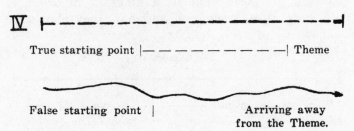

True starting point |— — — — — — — —| Theme

False starting point |                Arriving away
                                from the Theme.

In the latter case, after the time is consumed, the preacher usually makes a frantic leap in order somehow to land upon his theme.

5. Do not anticipate. It is a fatal mistake to use a stone for the threshold which you need afterwards in constructing the arch. This is liable to happen to him who is full of his subject.

6. Do not become ornate in the introduction. At times a "fine" introduction *must* be written out in order to get it out of the preacher's system. Write it, and then solemnly consign it to the waste basket. All introductions should be direct and simple.

7. Never overload an introduction. It is like rowing a boat with the heavy weight all piled in the prow. Keep the front end up.

8. Never start with something so dramatic or lofty that the body of your sermon is bound to drop below it and will seem tame by comparison. A start like this raises the expectation of the hearers to so high a pitch that you are unable to meet that expectation when you begin to unfold your theme.

9. It is a mistake to start with an illustration, to spin it out, and then to tell the people what it means. It is wrong psychologically. First get something to illustrate — then illustrate it. The mind does not naturally move in crab fashion. Some otherwise good preachers fall into this fault, which for all their adopting it remains a fault none the less.

Example, Gen. 3, 1-7, by a seminary student:

Many keys are necessary to open the different rooms of a large building. The individual who occupies one room has

a key which will open no other door but that of his own room.
The executive of all the rooms, however, has a master-key,
which will open all the rooms of the building regardless of
the differences in the locks.  Human history with its manifold
divisions also needs a master-key.  Let us examine

### The Mastey-Key to All Human History.

It would be far better to speak first of human history
and its many different manifestations, all of which can
be understood only by means of the revelation of God's
Word in regard to the fall of man.  Then bring in
this, or some other, illustration, as may be desired.

There are also certain *wrong theories* regarding
introductions to sermons.  Where these are taught,
they may help to weaken a man's entire preaching
career.

One of these wrong theories is that you must have
some special thought or subject for the introduction.
So the outline is duly constructed, and then the question
is asked, What shall I use for my introduction?  Finally
something is selected, or hit upon, and is "used" for
the introduction.  Often these introductions are special
Bible passages.  The result is an introduction quite
too long.  For when the preacher begins to elaborate
his special thought or subject for the introduction he
almost invariably gets going too strongly, and the
result is undue length.  This theory also results in
introductions that fail to arrive at the theme set in
the outline.  The introductory thought, when developed, has a tendency to become an independent thing
by itself.  It thus leads off in a direction of its own,
and will not bend enough to connect with the theme,
or the bending becomes unnatural forcing.  Often there

is a leap over the gap or gulf between the end of the introduction and the theme.

> Example, Matt. 20, 1-16. The introduction retells, in three sections, and at considerable length the story of the Prodigal and the Elder Brother, then tries to lead over to the theme of the sermon, by saying that God is ever ready to receive sinners, and then suddenly adds, "Let us now by the help of the Holy Spirit consider **The Laborers in the Lord's Vineyard.**" This sermon has been printed. Its introduction no more introduces this theme than it could introduce any other theme on this text. The man took as his special thought for the introduction the parable of the Prodigal — that was the trouble, namely special subjects for introductions, a false theory. There are many examples of this type, for the theory once was quite prevalent — is yet in fact.

A second wrong theory, one still advocated by homiletical writers, is that the introduction should "prepare the mind 1) to understand the truth which is to be presented, 2) to appreciate its importance, and 3) to accept its conclusions." The basic assumption in this theory is wrong. The hearers are altogether ready to receive the truth about to be presented, and merely suffer the preacher's labored efforts at "preparing the mind" toward that end. Instead of preparing them to understand the truth to be presented, proceed to present that truth, and then they will indeed understand it. Instead of talking first about the importance of this truth, tell them this truth, and then they will perceive of themselves whether it is important or not. And the same is true of any conclusions based on this truth — no hearer can accept them in advance, he must first be put in full possession of the truth involved. Besides all this, the business of preparing the mind by means of such an introduction always results in a little dissertation consuming entirely too much time.

Hence never begin, "In order properly to understand the truth contained in our text to-day, you ought to recall," etc., or "I must first remind you," etc., or any other words or thoughts to this effect. — Likewise, never begin, "We must realize the great importance of the word of Jesus (the apostle, or who it may be) when He said," etc., then dwelling on this importance, perhaps illustrating it, etc. — To combine both the "you-must-understand" idea with the "you-must-realize-the-importance" notion, doubles the fault, and to add as a third introductory point the idea "there-are-great-conclusions," simply swamps the introduction. The followers of the Herbart-Ziller philosophy of catechization attempt to build first a foundation upon which to rear what they wish to present, but all such philosophizing is spurious psychology. It labors to clear the road where the way is already open. It makes a difficult task out of one that is naturally easy. And its results are tiresome, instead of being delightful.

Suppose I have a wonderful new flower in my garden, and I want you to get acquainted with it. Do I stop you at the gate and tell you at length about its botany, or lecture on its rarity (importance), or dilate on what results you may get by growing it? Not unless I am pedantic. No; I take you right in, show you all its beauty, and then I tell you what I know of it. Of course, you are duly impressed. So in a sermon. Go right into the gate of the text, show the glory of what God has put there, and there will be no question about the effect.

**Ways of Stating the Theme.** — These are nearly as innumerable as are the introductions and the themes themselves. If the introduction is a real one it will merge naturally into the theme, yet always so that the theme is readily recognized. All formulas are therefore to be avoided, as well as all mannerisms. Seldom will two themes be introduced in the same way. When so many ways are ready to hand, why not use them freely?

So we will not wind up the introduction with the sentence, "Let us, by the help of the Holy Spirit, and on the basis of our text, consider," now stating the theme. This has done duty in the past so frequently that really we ought give it a long-needed rest. Some make it briefer, namely, "Therefore let us consider this morning," etc. It, too, is rather cold and formal. — Modern homileticians suggest that the introduction end with the words of the theme, and that the hearer then should be told, "Let this be the subject for our consideration," or equivalent words. The point, as far as we are concerned, is that such formulas, even if varied a bit, should not become stereotyped. For all stereotyped ways of launching themes are too stiff. Use variety and flexibility.

Examples. — After describing the two men walking down through the path of the vineyard to decide the fate of the fig tree (Luke 13, 6-9), the last sentence is followed by the theme without another word, thus,

"Let us go along with those two men, the owner of the vineyard and its caretaker, and think of ourselves as they look at that tree and decide what to do.

**There is a New Year's Message for Us in What Was Done With the Barren Fig Tree:**

A message of *Grace mingled with Justice* in what was said of its past; a message of *Justice tempered by Grace* in what was determined about its future."

On Matth. 11, 16-24 the theme is brought in as part of the last introductory sentence, "Christ wants us to ask our generation, as once He did of His:

**Whereunto Shall We Liken Our Generation?**

The answer is plain: Use first *the figure of the wayward children in the marketplace;* then add *the reality, the cities of the Jews and Gentiles of old.*"

Likewise, in a declarative way, Luke 10, 1-10, "May God touch our hearts to understand aright

**Christ's Gracious Purpose to Seek and to Save.**"

Also John 12, 27-33, "Look, then, with the eyes of faith on

**Christ's Vision of the Cross,**

a transcendent vision *of glory, of triumph, of salvation.*

On Acts 17, 10-14 the introduction starts with several Bible passages on reading the Word. Then it winds up, "One thing more we need in addition to these testimonies and admonitions from great men of God and from God's Son Himself, namely an example of what their words mean. We have it in our text to-day —

**The Shining Example of the Men of Berea.**"

Acts 18, 24-28, "Here is a school where we, too, must enter, for there are some very needful things which here we may learn. Let us take our place, then, beside Apollos

**In the Little School of Aquila and Priscilla.**"

John 12, 12-19, for Palm Sunday, brings in the theme by repeating the last words of the introduction, "As this text shows us once more the multitudes at Jerusalem honoring and praising Jesus as the Savior King, we in spirit and by every act of our worship join them to-day. And in this way, which we know is acceptable to Him, we offer Hosannas and palms for the King.

**Hosannas and Palms for the Savior King!"**

Emphatic repetition is a good way to mark a theme occasionally.

Luke 12, 16-21, the Rich Fool, "Do you know, he talked to his own soul a few hours before he died; and God also talked to his soul. Alas, his soul listened to the wrong voice.

**Soul, Soul, Whose Voice Are You Listening To?**

> *Your own voice of folly?* or
> *God's voice of wisdom?"*

Ushering in the theme dramatically is a good way occasionally.

Luke 13, 23-30, a case where the parts are mentioned before the theme is announced. After the first brief paragraph comes the second, "Here in our text He shows us the end and the judgment to come. He weaves into His words a parable, a simple and yet striking illustration, one intended to make us realize

> *The grace we have now,*

to bring home to us

> *The judgment coming at last,*

and thus to impress upon us

> *The warning contained in both.*

The center of this illustration, on which turns all that Christ here tells us in warning is

**The Door.**

The Kingdom of God is like a house to which entrance may be gained by one door alone, and that door is narrow. And the great judgment to come is like the moment when the master of the house rises, and shuts the door, not to open it again. On that door, then, we must fix our attention,

**The Door That Shall Be Shut."**

A good workman will put his theme across gracefully, effectively, quite simply, and yet distinctively. All will catch it for what it is, even if they have never heard a sermon with a theme before. He will not put it across awkwardly, pedantically, with a string of words in the effort, indistinctly so that one hardly recognizes it for the theme, and certainly not secretively as if he did not want to trust his hearers with the promise it contains.

## The Ending.

It has become generally customary to end the sermon, as we end our prayers, with Amen. The word has been taken over from the Hebrew and means truth, verity. At the end of the sermon it thus stands as a solemn assurance in the presence of God and His people that all the preacher has said is indeed divine truth. With this feeling, and as voicing that conviction, the word should be pronounced. Most preachers betray a great deal in the way they utter the amen. The last sentence of the sermon must be of such a character that it may be followed by the final amen.

A sermon needs no formal conclusion at all, yet it may have one. The last part of the sermon may be put in such fashion as to bring the sermon to its close. When this is the case it would be a mistake to attach something more, just because the preacher thinks it is homiletically necessary to have what is called a conclusion. If you are through when you have finished the final part, by all means say Amen, and depart in peace.

Yet a conclusion may be in order. It is natural, for instance, at the end of a sermon with several parts, to recapitulate. This should be brief, quite brief. Recapitulation should not descend to mere repetition. Many sermons that are preached would be improved if the repetitions at the end could be omitted. While certain pivotal terms that appear in the sermon must necessarily reappear in the recapitulation, these terms should be in crisp, telling sentences, making straight for a definite close.

Example from Matt. 16, 15-20, with the theme, **The Savior's Word to St. Peter on the Christian Church,** and the parts, 1) *On its foundation,* 2) *On its function,* 3) *On its foes.* This is the conclusion, "Let the words which Christ spoke to St. Peter concerning the Christian Church sink deeply into your hearts. Her foundation is everlasting, her function is divine, her foes are helpless. All this because with all her members she is the Church of Christ, the Son of the living God."

Example on Acts 17, 10-14. The last part closes with the prayer, "God help us to follow their shining example!" Then the recapitulation, "It is bright and shining indeed, what they did, how they did it, and what they gained by doing it. Shall we follow them? Let your whole life from this day forth be the answer."

Example on John 12, 27-33, **"Christ's Vision of the Cross,"** with three parts, closed with this single sentence, "Blessed are they who see the vision of the cross as Christ unveils it for them, and by its power are drawn unto him." Only the theme was thus used at the end.—Similarly, John 2, 18-22, **The Sign that Decides,"** the conclusion being, "Yes, there is a sign that decides! On the day of judgment all unbelief will cease. Blessed are they for whom grace and faith are enough!"

Example from Luke 17, 7-10, **"Look at the Question of Merit in the Light of the Unprofitable Servant."** Conclusion, *"Great merit? —* Why, there is *no merit at all! —* But thank God through Christ Jesus, there is an infinite measure of *unmerited grace!* That, and that alone, shall be our heart's joy and hope." The Italics recapitulate the main parts of the sermon.

The old style of reserving the appropriation or the application all for the end, and then presenting it in five sub-parts, is a mannerism. Yet the conclusion may naturally be some form of appropriative or applicatory address. The form may be threefold, 1) the preacher appealing to the congregation, making a final announcement to the congregation, or uttering a word of blessing upon the congregation; 2) the preacher combining himself with the congregation in admonition, announcement, or blessing (using the pronoun "we"; 3) the preacher speaking to God for the congregation, in vow, or in prayer, or in hope. All three types are good.

Examples from Acts 15, 6-12, **"Our Vital Relation to Our Sister Congregations,"** closes with the words, "Let us conserve strengthen, and abide in that fellowship (the preacher combining himself with the hearers). May the Lord keep it pure alway, and make it fruitful to the welfare of many souls and to the glory of His own blessed name! (a prayer)."

Example from Luke 13, 23-30, **"The Door That Will Be Shut,"** the preacher making solemn final announcement to the congregation, and adding a vow, "Remember the door that will be shut! Woe to those who are then without! Even if they sat long on the threshold they will be lost. Blessed are they who enter while its portal is open in grace! Behold, grace and judgment thus once more set before you. — Lord our God, we accept Thy grace and its deliverance from judgment!"

Examples from Matt. 5, 43-48,**"Love your enemies!"** "By the goodness of God, through the love of Christ, as the children of God — we will!" This is a vow.

There are many ways of closing a sermon which cannot be characterized especially.  An Easter sermon with a number of parts closed with the last verse of the hymn, the first stanza of which began the sermon,

> "Hallelujah! then I cry;
>     Christ, too, will from death restore me
> Take me to His throne on high,
>     Whither He has gone before me.
> Faith exults, Victoria!
> Jesus lives!  Hallelujah!"

A telling stanza from some hymn, perhaps sung by the congregation before the sermon, or to be sung after the sermon, at times makes an excellent conclusion, or the final part of the conclusion.

Example from John 11, 47-52, **"Caiaphas and the Doctrine of Substitution."**  This conclusion uses a statement of Luther, and weaves in two hymn stanzas.  "Luther in one place writes that our sins must lie either upon our own necks or upon Christ.  If they remain upon us we are lost for ever, but if they lie on Christ we are saved.  Take whichever you will, he says.  Can there be any question which we will take?  Let men pervert the doctrine of substitution as much as they will, let them misunderstand the whole Word of God and the greatest deed which it records for our good, we will cling to our great Substitute and pray in humble faith,

> 'All sin hast Thou borne for us,
> Else would despair reign o'er us:
> Have mercy on us, O Jesus!'

In face of our end, when we shall be called to meet the great Judge on that day, let us add this other prayer,

> 'Lord Jesus Christ!  Thy precious blood
>     Is to my soul the highest good:
> Of all my sins a perfect cure,
>     It quickens me and makes me pure.

    Thy blood, my spotless, glorious dress,
      Thy innocence my righteousness:
    Before my God I pardoned stand,
      And enter, crowned, the heavenly land.' "

Sometimes the thought of a sermon can be summed up in brief without recapitulation.

Example from John 12, 12-19 for Palm Sunday, "Down through the ages the echoes of that first Palm Sunday have come, reaching even to us this day. Those Hosannas and those palms of that far-off day stir our hearts now to offer like praise and adoration to our Savior King. As we joyfully answer this call, let us remember how the great procession of Hosannas and palms, of loyal hearts honoring Christ and proclaiming His praise among men, will move on down the coming years, until at last the great King of salvation steps forth from His throne to receive into eternal honor those who have thus honored Him. Will your Hosannas and your palms greet Him on that great coming day?" To end thus with a question is at times highly effective.

Let the sermon close in a quiet way, as a great liner moves into the quiet harbor. A skyrocket finish always leaves a peculiar effect, sometimes just a little ludicrous. If there is to be "a blaze of glory" put it elsewhere, not in the conclusion.

Faults. — Invent no conclusion theory of any kind. Theories are just as pernicious for the conclusion as they are for the introduction.

Never seek a subject for the conclusion, and then start to develop that subject. If anything is to be especially used for the conclusion, take only what fits perfectly the main thought of the sermon. If it does not amalgamate perfectly, reject it without mercy.

Above all make the conclusion short, and if you can, still shorter. Everybody groans when the preacher lacks terminal facilities. "He passed so many good stopping-places," said a young hearer of a long-winded sermon. When you are through, by all means stop.

There is a queer reason why some men have trouble in stopping. It is because they tend to keep their voices up at the end of each sentence. To keep the voice up in this way is a fault in delivery, to begin with. But keeping the voice up always means that something more is to follow. And so the speaker rambles on, sentence after sentence, each last one demanding another. Extempore speakers thus afflicted generally try hard enough to stop. Drop the voice! Then you can say Amen, but — say it with a falling inflection!

Thin and trivial thoughts in the conclusion make the sermon die out weakly. If you have no strong and pertinent statement with which to wind up, use nothing in the way of conclusion — there is no law against it.

Never end with law, with a threat, with severity. It is quite Scriptural, but will not do as the ending of a sermon, "He that believeth not shall be damned! Amen."

Prepare the final words carefully in advance, and do not depend on the inspiration of the moment. There is a psychological reason. A sermon well thought out in parts and sub-parts uses up the mental resources quite completely, so that when the last part is delivered the mind has poured out all its contents. There is then often little or nothing left for a happy inspiration. The result will be a weak ending. Extempore preachers may not close in the way they intended when preparing the sermon by intensive meditation, yet any advance preparation will prove helpful.

Do not try to recover anything in the conclusion that perchance slipped your mind in the body of the sermon. You may regret that you dropped some good point — it will happen even to the best of us. But let it go in peace. It is a mistake to paste it onto the sermon at the end. An hour or so after preaching you will feel better about the loss.

Let each sermon end in its own natural way. By all means avoid mannerism in winding up. Stereotyped conclusions are real faults, and it is so easy to avoid them. Like the first few sentences of a sermon so the last should be strong and effective. Then, after a little pause, say Amen in such a way that every one knows that you truly feel and know what the word means.

**Soli Deo Gloria.**